Contemporary Radio Programming Strategies

COMMUNICATION
TEXTBOOK SERIES
Jennings Bryant – Editor

Broadcasting
James Fletcher – Advisor

BEVILLE • Audience Ratings: Radio,
Television, Cable
(Revised Student Edition)

ADAMS • Social Survey
Methods for Mass Media
Research

NMUNGWUN • Video Recording
Technology: Its Impact
on Media and Home Entertainment

MacFARLAND • Contemporary
Radio Programming Strategies

Contemporary Radio Programming Strategies

David T. MacFarland
*A. Q. Miller School of Journalism
and Mass Communications
Kansas State University*

LEA LAWRENCE ERLBAUM ASSOCIATES, PUBLISHERS
1990   Hillsdale, New Jersey   Hove and London

Lawrence Erlbaum Associates, Inc., Publishers
365 Broadway
Hillsdale, New Jersey 07642

Library of Congress Cataloging-in-Publication Data

MacFarland, David T.
    Contemporary radio programming strategies / by David T.
MacFarland.
        p.   cm.
    Includes index.
    ISBN 0-8058-0664-4. – ISBN 0-8058-0665-2 (pbk.)
    1. Radio programs – Planning.   I. Title.
PN1991.55.M33   1990
384.54'42'0973 – dc20   89-16790
                                                        CIP

Printed in the United States of America
10 9 8 7 6 5 4 3 2 1

To Charlotte,
who always believed in this book
more than I did

Contents

Chapter 6
The Structure and Appeal of Acoustic Space   82

Chapter 7
**Air Personality: The Structure
of Spoken Gesture**   94

PART III
MUSIC PROGRAMMING

Chapter 8
The Appeals of Radio Music   115

Chapter 12

Factors in MEMO – Mood-Evoking Music Order

Chapter 13

Toward MERIT

Acknowledgments

This book would not have happened without the belief and encouragement of my dear wife Charlotte.

It was Gary Bond who first got me working on a (different) book in earnest; I am sorry that the focus of this one could not have included more of Gary's useful insights.

Without the late Top 40 pioneers Gordon McLendon, Todd Storz, and Bill Stewart, neither American radio's first revolution (nor my dissertation about it) would have happened the same way. Without Edd Routt, there would not have been as much access to that information. Without Larry Lichty, there would not have been the same way of approaching material, nor as much of an understanding of program structure and appeals. Without Chris Sterling's good humor, belief, and support that dissertation probably would not have been published.

Ray Carroll provided early encouragement and proved he meant it by offering to read the rough manuscript. Because he was working on his own book at the time, I let him off the hook on the basis of possible "conflict of interest." But Ray also put me in touch with Jennings Bryant, who encouraged me to submit the manuscript for possible publication by Lawrence Erlbaum Associates. I am grateful to Jennings for his warm follow-up, to Jim Fletcher and Alan Rubin for their fast but useful reviews of my proposal, and to Jack Burton at LEA for offering a contract. It was a delight and a relief to find such compatible people on my first attempt to locate a publisher. Everyone at Erlbaum has been cordial and helpful beyond any expectation. Senior Production Editor Robin Marks Weisberg has been the sort of helper you dream of working with: fixing the awkward constructions, following up the stray references, and figuring out the formatting, while leaving the ideas exactly as I intended them—or better.

Kate Anderson shared some material that introduced the important work of Manfred Clynes. Jack Carpenter pointed me to the literary criticism of Kenneth

Burke. Ron Roschke provided several pivotal and insightful brainstorming sessions, lent his books, and offered computer consultation. Marlena Adkison of KTPK-FM donated missing back issues of *Radio & Records* when I needed them the most. RCS donated instructional copies of their fine "Selector" and "Sampler" software programs to my academic department. Marcia Jensen assimilated and clarified my squiggly drawings and murky figures. Son Michael helped me to have a better understanding of major, minor, and blues scales, and son Jeff assisted with some additional informal music testing among his teenage friends, while they both put up with a cranky, preoccupied dad. My wife Charlotte read all the early drafts, offering valuable advice every time, Chris Sterling gave crucially important suggestions with gentle tact, and Brian Svikhart supplied helpful editing advice.

Members of the A. Q. Miller School of Journalism and Mass Communications at Kansas State University deserve special thanks for helping me to have a "lighter" semester during the time I was finishing the book. I appreciate the faith and protection provided by Department Heads Harry Marsh and Carol Oukrop. Bill Adams co-authored a grant proposal to the KSU Faculty Development Committee that funded research on announcer perception (as well as concurrent studies on music moods and oldies), and Bill was instrumental in the analysis of the data. Stephanie Harvey was indispensable in keeping tab of the funds and in setting up testing sessions, and Linda Davison helped track reprint permissions – there could not be two better secretaries in an academic department. Paul Parsons provided valuable consultation and advice about the publishing process. Rob Daly and Paul Prince both passed along useful articles, and Paul Prince and Bill Adams graciously succumbed to the dubious honor of reading and commenting on my first draft. Paul and Bill, along with RTV colleagues Lee Buller and Dave Deitch and graduate assistant Joe Montgomery, covered some classes and shielded me from the problems of our student radio station when this just had to get done. Lee helped get my clone computer running, and made the initial contact with RCS. Undergraduate students Laurie Anderson and Jodi Johnson both did literature searches on the subject of recurrents, and Jim Ridenour, Mark Kahler, Roger Burns, Ted Smith, Eileen Meyer, Jenny Jones, and Bruce Steinbrock all participated in original research that supports some of the book's premises. And students in several of my classes made comments on early versions of the manuscript that helped to refocus the book in new directions.

Rob Ogles, Steve Shields, and Frank Chorba of the Popular Culture Association's Radio Interest Group invited me to give a convention paper that constituted the first public presentation of my heretical theories of music selection and presentation. That positive experience on the academic side encouraged me to re-establish contact with Unistar executive Gary Taylor, who offered useful advice and insights over the part of the draft he was able to read before deadlines intervened.

When this book succeeds, it does so thanks to all the people just named. Its shortcomings are wholly mine.

David T. MacFarland

CHAPTER 1

An Overview of the Book

WHAT THE TITLE MEANS

It took 3 years to come up with the title of this book – not because it is such a catchy title, but because of the content decisions it reflects. *Contemporary Radio Programming Strategies* tries to be wholly descriptive of what this book is about. A brief explanation seems useful.

A previous working title for this book was *The Sovereign Listener.* That title succinctly described my belief that radio works best when the listener's needs are well served by the programming. Programming that attracts listeners is the dynamo that propels radio. But today, the proliferation of media choices has put the listener in the driver's seat. Today, it is not the station manager or the program director who is calling the shots at the successful station, it is the listener. The listener is the monarch.

Radio has always been my first love among the media. The volume that preceded this was *The Development of the Top 40 Radio Format,* a comprehensive look at how radio changed from a program medium to a station-format medium. It focused on the history of format-based radio in the 1950s and 1960s. *Contemporary Radio Programming Strategies* deals with radio as it is today, but in the light of the legacy of those format pioneers. The *Top 40* book drew its examples from the AM dial, because AM stations were dominant in the 1950s. This book draws its examples primarily from the FM band, because FM signals generally are today's dominant stations. The majority of the suggestions for new initiatives are likewise directed toward music FMs, because that is where the listeners are.

Prior to the advent of Top 40, many stations played what owners or announcers decided should be played, with little regard to what listeners actually wanted to hear. Top 40 pioneers changed that, by recognizing the primacy of the listener in determining music popularity. The original working title of this book, *The Sovereign Listener,* paid homage to the impulse that caused the original Top 40 radio managers to "let the people decide" about the music played, whereas the book itself challenges the assumption that merely airing the most popular music is still adequate today. Many of the "new" formats that have come along in the years since the advent of Top 40 have been largely imitative, not innovative. This book, by asking "What is it that listeners really want?" attempts to take the next step beyond Top 40-type formats where measures of music popularity predominate.

The term *programming* reflects the belief that the most important thing to manage in radio is the programming. It is also a belief absorbed from the people who pioneered Top 40. And the term *strategies* should be an easy one for a broadcaster to feel comfortable with, because radio has been a viable business for more than half a century. For much of that time, radio practitioners were so busy making radio that the basic question "What is it that we are trying to do here?" simply fell by the way. If, through this book, the reader can begin to answer that question, radio broadcasting may have a better chance of prospering into the 21st century. Although it is true that in modern times, when new media appear the older media adapt and manage to survive, today digital audio equipment for the home and the car is posing an ever greater threat to the analog technology of radio broadcasting. AM broadcasters have already learned how difficult it is to compete against the aurally superior FM band; perhaps someday soon, all of radio will find itself hard pressed to compete against digital playback technologies. Music radio is also highly vulnerable to further audience migration to MTV and other video music services. And increasing use of nonbroadcast music playback equipment threatens to decrease the time spent listening to radio. In any of these cases, simply continuing to pump out the hits, using a highly refined formula that still basically traces its roots back to Top 40, may fail to pull in big audiences. At that juncture, programming strategies beyond the ones derived from Top 40 may be called for. If that time comes, the companies that have taken the time to ask of themselves "What is it that we are really in business to do, and what means are we going to use to achieve that?" will be ahead of the game for having gone through the process. It is radio's very "dailiness" that keeps too many program directors and managers from getting around to the apparently postponable but actually vital business of defining the station's values.

WHAT THIS BOOK OFFERS

The theater has had Aristotle for over 2,300 years, and Stanislavsky for over four decades. Because the theater has these thinkers and others to point to, theater professionals are better able to express themselves. They can identify with one or another system of beliefs as they continue a search for a general understanding of values and reality. But there are few such rallying points in the radio business. There are people whose specific contributions to radio are admired and emulated, but those particular gifts are hard to fit into a gestalt of fully defensible, fundamental beliefs.

"Fundamental beliefs" is what the reader will be exploring here. Some people call it "the basics" and that's okay too, as long as they do not mean the mechanical aptitudes for cueing records and splicing tapes. For our purposes, the basics mean a common understanding of what the radio enterprise is—and should be—about: entertainment and information.[1] Although the term *information* has grown to encompass so many things that it is almost fruitless to argue about what is and is not information anymore, "entertainment" continues to be an elusive concept, one that appears to be heavily dependent on "the eyes of the beholder." A major thrust of this book is to arrive at a set of fundamental beliefs about the values and the realities of the radio business in regard to entertainment programming—a set of beliefs that may or may not be right, or true, or forever, but that might at least provide a basis for developing programming strategies.

Most other books on radio programming describe the formats and programming that already exist. This one starts with a clean sheet of paper and the question "What do listeners really want from radio?" Some of the answers to that question are derived from "uses-and-gratifications" research in the mass media. Instead of focusing on what mass media do to people, the uses-and-gratifications perspective seeks to discover what people do with mass media. The functionalist viewpoint of such research basically says that a medium is best defined by how people use it. That is also the approach of this book.[2] Having looked at some of the audience research that comes from sources other than the standard ratings companies, the book then goes on to demonstrate new ways for meeting audience needs and desires. Formats, production procedures, and announcing styles are all considered. Although the book concludes with several original methods for selecting and presenting airplay music based on the audience's moods, the book does not attempt to support a single formulaic approach for constructing or modifying a music format. Instead, it attempts to involve you, the reader, in thinking through the process of format development. Rather than merely observing a format element's obvious *form,* there is an attempt to make you a partner in appreciating the underlying *function* that that element should perform.

To borrow a concept from computer programming: This book is not intended to provide algorithms (a precise series of steps that lead to a precise outcome), but rather *heuristics.* Heuristics are exploratory, sometimes trial-and-error problem-solving tech

---

[1]A fine book for the serious student of broadcasting, which addresses some of the same issues in less detail (but with a helpful section on understanding ratings) is Shane, E. (1984). *Programming dynamics: Radio's management guide.* Overland Park, KS: Globecom. In addition, reading the manual accompanying recent versions of RCS's "Selector" music scheduling software is an excellent way to discover the myriad of options available today for selecting and presenting music for radio airplay.

[2]For a further description of uses-and-gratifications mass media research, see Rubin, A. M. (1986). Uses, gratifications, and media effects research. In J. Bryant & D. Zillmann (Eds.), *Perspectives on media effects.* Hillsdale, NJ: Lawrence Erlbaum Associates.

niques that deal with probable (not guaranteed) outcomes given a certain relation-ship. A book that takes a heuristic approach does not attempt to establish mathe-matical formulas, but rather seeks to explore likely relationships, including the inevitable exceptions. The practicing broadcaster, and the student about to enter the field—who are the dual audiences for this book—will not find all-purpose solutions here. Instead, you will find new ways of thinking about programming and its effects. Those new ways of thinking should then lead the thoughtful reader to develop his or her own strategies for a given station. Throughout the book, the assumption is made that the reader either already is—or intends to be—a radio professional. When a reference is made to "your station," an FM running some kind of a hit-based music format is the imaginary model.

ORGANIZATION OF THE BOOK

The first section of the book considers radio's arena, attributes, and audiences. Chapter 2 (Radio's Arena) looks at the competitive environment radio finds itself in today and the ways management and staff need to respond. Chapter 3 (Radio's Attributes) explores the several things radio does better than any other medium. Chapter 4 (What Radio Audiences Want) discusses the expectations radio listeners have, and lists needs and desires not usually considered in audience analyses.

The second section examines formats, soundscapes, and voices—the basic com-ponents of radio. Chapter 5 (Format Structure and Management) looks at the way all formats have evolved out of Top 40, and begins to show how some fall short of meeting the full menu of listener's needs. Chapter 6 (The Structure and Appeal of Acoustic Space) considers the parameters of sound and production elements, and argues that too much of radio happens without regard to an acoustic sense of place. Chapter 7 (Air Personality: The Structure of Spoken Gesture) explains the ways in which actors and announcers share technique.

Today, the majority of listeners turn to radio primarily for music. Thus, the final section, on music programming, offers a close examination of program content, beginning where the average listener begins: with music. Chapter 8 (The Appeals of Radio Music) explains the expectations and gratifications to be derived from music listening. Chapter 9 (Music Moods Research) gets deeply into the research that has been done on how music generates certain moods in listeners; it lays the ground-work for the consideration of the unique music selection and presentation systems in chapters 10, 11, and 12. Chapter 10 (The Components of a Mood-Evoking Music Progression) pulls together many of the elements introduced in the earlier chapters, to show how airplay music can be programmed on the basis of mood. Chapter 11 (Factors in "MOST"—Mood-Oriented Selection Testing) demonstrates several sys-tems for selecting or rejecting any given piece of music. And chapter 12 (Factors in "MEMO"—Mood-Evoking Music Order) explains and demonstrates use of the composite mood curve, a comprehensive system for presenting all of the elements in a music-oriented station's programming.

Finally, chapter 13 (Toward MERIT), offers a glimpse of a format that depends on–and in turn promises to generate–high audience involvement.

A list of major points follows each chapter in the book. These summarize the important arguments of the chapter but necessarily condense the discussion. Readers who would like an "executive overview" of the book can consult these pages, but should keep in mind that important detail will be missing.

The book builds many of its later cases and assumptions on material that is presented earlier. The logic, viewpoints, and arguments are intended to be cumulative. Therefore, the sections and chapters are best read in the given order.

MAJOR POINTS

1. Today, the proliferation of media choices means it is not the station manager or the program director who is calling the shots at the successful station, it is the listener.

2. *Contemporary Radio Programming Strategies* deals with radio as it is today, but in the light of the legacy of the people who pioneered the Top 40 format. This book draws its examples primarily from the FM band, because FM signals generally are today's dominant stations. The majority of the suggestions for new initiatives are likewise directed toward music FMs, because that is where the listeners are.

3. This book challenges the assumption that merely airing the most popular music is still adequate today. Many of the "new" formats that have come along in the years since the advent of Top 40 have been largely imitative, not innovative. This book, by asking "What is it that listeners really want?" attempts to take the next step beyond Top 40-type formats where measures of music popularity predominate.

4. If, through this book, the radio professional can begin to answer the question "What is it that we are trying to do here?" radio broadcasting may have a better chance of prospering into the 21st century. Today digital audio equipment for the home and the car is posing an ever greater threat to the analog technology of radio broadcasting. Music radio is also highly vulnerable to further audience migration to MTV and other video music services. If that time comes, the stations that have gone through this thought process will be ready to respond.

5. A major thrust of this book is to arrive at a set of fundamental beliefs about the values and the realities of the radio business especially in regard to entertainment programming–a set of beliefs that may or may not be right, or true, or forever, but that might at least provide a basis for developing programming strategies.

6. Most other books on radio programming describe the formats and programming that already exist. This one starts with a clean sheet of paper and the question "What do listeners really want from radio?" Some of the answers to that question are derived from uses-and-gratifications research in the mass media. Instead of focusing on what mass media do to people, the uses-and-gratifications perspective seeks to discover what people do with mass media. The functionalist viewpoint of

such research basically says that a medium is best defined by how people use it. That is also the approach of this book.

7. The book demonstrates new ways for meeting audience needs and desires – systems based largely around developing and sustaining moods rather than record popularity. It includes several novel methods for selecting and presenting airplay music based on the audience's needs, but it does not attempt to support a single formulaic approach for constructing or modifying a music format. Rather than merely observing a format element's obvious *form,* there is an attempt to make the reader a partner in appreciating the underlying *function* that that element should perform.

8. The practicing broadcaster, and the student about to enter the field – are the dual audiences for this book. Throughout it, the assumption is made that the reader either already is – or intends to be – a radio professional. When a reference is made to "your station," an FM running some kind of a hit-based music format is the imaginary model.

PART I

Radio's Arena, Attributes, and Audiences

The first section of the book considers radio's arena, attributes, and audiences. Chapter 2 (Radio's Arena) looks at the competitive environment radio finds itself in today, and the ways management and staff need to respond. Chapter 3 (Radio's Attributes) explores the several things radio does better than any other medium. Chapter 4 (What Radio Audiences Want) discusses the expectations radio listeners have, and lists needs and desires not usually considered in audience analyses.

CHAPTER 2

Radio's Arena

WHAT BUSINESS IS RADIO IN?

The answer to the question "What business is radio in?" is not as obvious as it seems. This is not a matter of images or public relations. Rather, it is a question of actualizing a positioning statement: of discovering the unique thing that radio does that other media do not do as well, if at all.

It is a cliche that a fish never realizes it is in an aquarium until it jumps out and dies in the air. When you are working in the radio business, it is very hard to see what it is that radio does best. It is easier to figure out what other businesses do well, even if they do not think of those attributes as strengths. As a way of understanding the problem of "examining your own navel," take the example of the daily newspaper.

The Local Daily Newspaper is in the Delivery Business

Today, many communities offer a wide choice of news sources. There are national newspapers like *USA Today,* and the traditional big city dailies. There are local radio and regional TV newscasts. There is often news on a cable system. With such heavy competition, it is much to the credit of local daily newspapers that their circulation remains as strong as it has. But all of those other sources of news lack one thing that the local daily has: a delivery organization that places a tangible product "in the hands" of a sizable chunk of the local citizenry every day. That is the one attribute that a successful local newspaper has going for it that no other information provider can claim: a force of people that can blanket the town with hand-carried delivery service. From my perspective as a person steeped in radio and television, it is curious that local newspapers do not do more to capitalize on the one thing that really sets them apart from every other information-providing medium. Instead of thinking of circulation as a necessary evil, why haven't local newspapers thought of circulation as a potential profit center? Why haven't they gotten rid of the term *circulation,* and replaced it with the much more all-purpose term *delivery?* Why haven't they started to think of ways to upgrade and professionalize the circulation department so that it is able to deliver a lot of other nonfirst-class-mail printed material that is now just hung on doorknobs or is sent via third-class mail? The newspaper's carriers pass virtually every house in the city anyway. Why shouldn't the newspaper get really good at the delivery business, and make money at it?

Local daily newspapers know they are not alone in supplying local news, but most have not asked themselves "What is it that we do which is *unique* to local daily newspapers?" The answer, "local delivery of printed material," usually does not occur to someone who thinks he or she is in the news business. And the same is true with radio. By the end of this section, a case is made that one of radio's "necessary evils" is actually its greatest strength. That is why it seems useful to spend time exploring the roles radio seems to play, and the attributes the listener-consumer ascribes to radio.

RADIO IS NOT IN THE "RADIO BUSINESS"

Radio people are not in the radio business so far as the audience is concerned. The way industry people tend to divide up the world (management, sales, engineering, programming, etc.) does not occur to the listener in the least. No, not even programming–as programming. As is argued later, listeners do not listen for formats, although they listen to them because that is what is offered. The radio listener tunes in for a certain set of gratifications that radio provides. But most of the time, radio is not unique in providing those gratifications or does not provide them consistently enough to suit some listeners.

In his 1960 essay about "the new languages" (nonbook media), Edmund Carpenter made the point that the newspaper, by juxtaposing various items that might interest the reader, puts him or her into the role of the producer instead of merely being a passive reader. Rather than a chronological or linear approach as would be found in a novel, the newspaper presents items simultaneously on the page, forcing the reader to choose.[1] In contrast to the effort the newspaper reader provides, is the dial-turning, button-pushing behavior of the radio listener searching for the particular content he or she is after. That person wishes he or she could be the producer. The only control available to such a radio listener is through "dial-hopping"–or plugging in tapes or CDs instead.

---

[1]See Carpenter, E. (1960). The new languages. In E. Carpenter & M. McLuhan (Eds.), *Explorations in communication, 1960* (pp. 162–174) (quoted in T. H. Ohlgren & L. M. Berk, eds., *The new languages.* Englewood Cliffs, NJ: Prentice-Hall, 1977, p. 5.)

CHOOSING RADIO

People today do not have to put up with listening to a radio station that is not exactly what they want. At home, cable TV and VCRs give them plenty of video ways to escape the lock grip of the network schedule. It is "demand access" consumerism: people getting what they want to hear when they want to hear it. If radio does not provide the program that accomplishes that, then cassettes or CDs can, and people will turn to them.

The in-dash cassette tape player and the cassette and CD player in the home are enormous threats to some radio formats, and specifically to the radio formats that lack human involvement, topicality, and so forth. A station can still afford to be a "music utility," but only if it hammers away at the "more music, less talk" theme in all of its promotion, and backs it up with actual percentages that the listener can understand as proof. Right now, four radio stations in my listening area are killing themselves playing "at least seven in a row," all of them promising "the most music." The listener knows they cannot all be right. The winner is either going to prove in clear comparison statements of minutes and seconds that they do have more music and do talk less, or they are going to win for some other reason.

A "What's-Your-Favorite-Medium?" Survey

Along with a wide choice of stations, many listeners today can elect to play tapes or CDs if the music on the radio is not what they are after. It is instructive to stand at an intersection where cars stop for a red light and do a survey of what people in that area are listening to. (Keep in mind that the location you choose may or may not get you a good cross-section of your city's population.) You may have to ask people to roll down their windows to be interviewed, which some will be reluctant to do. But with the windows down, you can hear what is playing in the car. You might ask them to name their favorite radio station, but what you would really like to know is, are they listening to *any* radio station, or are they programming their own media? Note what kind of artist they were listening to when interviewed. Note what time of day it is. Note their sex, and guess at their age. Did they have to turn down the music to talk, or was it already at a background level? After the interview, try to answer these questions: What function was the music serving? Was it foreground entertainment or background noise?

Now, correlate the answers to these questions with the way people use your radio station to see how "replaceable" you are by a tape or a CD. Also note if an ethnic, sexual, or age minority in your city becomes evident among tape/CD listeners. In my midwest town, a heavy percentage of Blacks listen to tapes because no radio station provides enough of the music they like at the times they are available to listen. And there are hundreds of blue grass fans in the town who cannot hear their music on any locally receivable station at any time. They are forced to buy and play tapes and CDs.

The LOP Theory

Stations that do not meet the special needs just listed are most likely programming a "mass-appeal" format instead. Too often, mass-appeal programming becomes very close to what former TV programmer Paul Klein called his LOP—Least Objectionable Program theory. LOP theory suggested that TV viewers did not tune in for the best show, but rather—because they were watching TV anyway—they would watch the least objectionable program. If true, then the way to satisfy such an audience is to supply the lowest common denominator of inoffensiveness. And the lowest common denominator of inoffensiveness goes hand in glove with the common radio management desire to achieve hassle-free consistency. It may not be exciting radio, but at least it will not offend anyone.

It is ironic that stations whose audiences may be largely comprised of LOP listeners may think that those same listeners are highly loyal to that station. The contest winner tells you yours is his favorite radio station because he just won something! But ask him which is his favorite pair of jeans, and you will usually get a greater level of emotional involvement.

The Least Objectionable Lunch

There are people who go to McDonald's for lunch not because it is the best food in town, but because when you only have a few moments, McDonald's provides a familiar product that is served up quickly and that is consistent over time. You know what to expect at any McDonald's, and that is its chief virtue. The same people might rather stay at a non-name but interesting-looking motel, but they end up at a Holiday Inn because they agree with their old slogan, "The best surprise is no surprises." Nobody can argue with the success of Holiday Inn and McDonald's for featuring consistency and standards. But what you eat and where you sleep are two basic, eternal needs in life (food, shelter). What you listen to (if anything) is a clear choice. It is not something people have to do every few hours or even every day. If what your radio station provides is not something people really want to have, then something is wrong. In other words, if they settle for your station because it offers the Least Objectionable Program served up in the most consistent way, then you will eventually come to be regarded as more a utility than an entertainment medium. And you may inherit the mixture of admiration and contempt in which people used to hold the telephone company (back when there was just *the* phone company). They admired the fact that it was always there, always ready to provide service. But they disliked the way the phone company seemed unable to adapt its policies to the diverse demands of modern consumers, policies that forced the user to conform to company procedure rather than the other way around. There is no alternative to the telephone if you want the capability to reach and be reached by hundreds of millions of people. But the alternatives to radio are many: other media, even silence.

What's New With You?

It is not that you want to run a radio station that is completely inconsistent. A basic program consistency can draw and hold a core of people who are searching for that LOP. But think of this: How many major new items were added to McDonald's menu in the 1970s and 1980s? When did they start serving breakfast? How many times have they remodeled their stores? How many dozen different commercial campaigns have they had? Now ask yourself: How many major new items has your station added to the programming in the last 10 years, especially if you air a syndicated service? Have you gone after and won over an audience that was out there all along but had never been served that way before (like McDonald's did with breakfast)? How many times has your listener sensed a remodeling and freshening of the total sound when he or she has tuned your station?

CONSISTENCY

Now we confront an oxymoron – that is, a pairing of two normally opposed words. The oxymoron is "consistent quality." Consistent quality is one of the selling points of radio automation systems, and one of the buzz phrases used to promote program services of all kinds, be they taped or sent by satellite. "Play our stuff," the flyers say, "and you'll enjoy consistent quality." But the two words do not belong together in radio. Quality radio programming must always include *in*consistency if it is going to work tomorrow as it does today. Not only is "a foolish consistency . . . the hobgoblin of little minds," it is also the hobgoblin of radio formats.

Positioning: Information, Format Structure, and Dependability

A 1981 dissertation by David E. Kennedy titled *Listener Perceptions as Dimensions of Radio Station Positioning: A Multivariate Analysis,* studied the ways radio listeners perceived competitive radio stations and "positioned" them in their minds with respect to each other. He found three factors common to the stations he studied: information, format structure, and dependability. Information characteristics that aided the stations' positioning related to being in touch with what was happening in the area, providing desired daily information, and having enjoyable announcers. Format structure characteristics included having games and contests that invited participation, and an acceptable number of commercials.[2] Dependability was defined by Kennedy as referring to

---

[2]Kennedy, D. E. (1981). *Listener perceptions as dimensions of radio station positioning: A multivariate analysis* (p. 92). Unpublished doctoral dissertation, Bowling Green. Bowling Green State University, Bowling Green, OH.

a sense of expected consistency; in other words, the listener knows what to expect on the station when s/he tunes to it, because the station has an overall consistent approach toward its programming. Consequently, the listener can "depend" on the station, and thus doesn't grow tired of it.[3]

I was with Kennedy up to the last sentence. There is not that much evidence of a positive link between a station a listener can depend on for consistency (as it is usually understood), and one that the listener will not grow tired of. In fact, the inverse may be the case.

The WMT Example: Expected Inconsistency

Consider these excerpts from a page-one article in *The Wall Street Journal* from October 6, 1982:

> CEDAR RAPIDS, IOWA – At 7:30 a.m., the day gets going at WMT-AM, 600 on your radio dial, with "ol' Cherokee," Jerry Carr, awakening a sleepy community with some rousing patriotic tunes interspersed with classical music and a little poetry.
>
> By all that is holy in the radio business, that kind of programming hodgepodge should guarantee WMT radio a spot near the bottom of the ratings. Where is the top-40 music for 18 to 25 year olds? Where is the country music for a legion of urban and suburban cowboys? Nowhere on WMT.
>
> Yet, according to Arbitron, the rating service, WMT last year had a 30% share of a 600,000-listener market, which ranked the station No. 1 in market share among the top 100 revenue-producing stations in the country, according to Television/Radio Age, an industry publication. For the past five years, WMT's market share has ranked in the top five of the nation's 2,700 radio stations, according to American Radio Report.[4]

What made WMT succeed with its admittedly 54 + audience? It has a strong signal, and it has been on the air since 1922. But here is the real answer:

> "We're just poking along trying to identify with the people," says WMT's station manager, Larry Edwards. Mr. Edwards believes that WMT's melange of programming is one of its greatest strengths. So Mama Cass records appear on the play list alongside Sousa marches; farm reports share time with reruns of the old comedy show "Fibber McGee and Molly." Says Mr. Edwards: "It's like going fishing. When you have 10 hooks in the water, your chances of catching a fish are a lot better than with just one."[5]

---

[3]Ibid., p. 93.

[4]Juffer, J. (1982, October 6). WMT has a recipe for successful radio that yields a stew. *The Wall Street Journal*, p. 1. (Reprinted by permission of *The Wall Street Journal*, © Dow Jones & Company, Inc. 1982. All rights reserved worldwide).

[5]Ibid., p. 1.

WMT was consistently *in*consistent. Of course, the station adhered to a program schedule, but within those programs, almost anything could go on the air. The only predictable thing about the content was that you probably would not hear much today that you heard yesterday.

Mass Appeal Need Not Mean Doing What the Other Guys Do

The handful of AMs like WMT that have succeeded fairly well at hanging on to their traditional audiences, become the beacons of hope for the many AMs whose audience declines have matched the decline in overall AM listening.[6] Like WMT, leading stations have rejected the notion that mass appeal must equate with playing the same music everybody else plays in the same way. When Gordon McLendon said in 1962 that "a radio station today should not serve the broadest need but rather the narrowest," he was making a statement from what was then the cutting edge of format specialization. Today, there are plenty of stations that play a mass-appeal format and yet have poorer ratings than stations that serve a narrower audience segment but do a better job of it. Many of those successful narrowly targeted stations have become leaders because they have asked themselves—and continue to ask— "What does the listener really want?"

THE CHALLENGE OF CHANGE

For the music-oriented radio station, there are two challenges that loom large at this writing. One is music videos. The other is digital audio. Music videos threaten to do to music on the radio what television did to drama on the radio: Take its audience away. And digital audio threatens to do to FM what FM has done to AM: Make it sound technically inferior, which also discourages audiences.

Music Videos

A study by Dr. Sharon Strover, titled "The Impact of Music Video on Radio" and funded in part by a 1986 NAB Research Grant, assessed just how radio was changing in that year as a result of MTV's presence in more than 30 million households. A survey of 250 program directors at Top 40 and "progressive" format stations turned up a list of both positive and negative impacts.

---

[6]A study conducted for the NAB titled "What America Thinks of AM Radio" found that AM stations must offer *both* good technical sound quality and good programming to attract the greatest number of listeners—either alone is not sufficient. Over three-quarters of the survey respondents said both were necessary. [Study shows benefit in news and information (1988, September/October). *KAB Transmitter*, p. 2.]

Accounting for their feelings that radio suffered little at the hands of music video, programmers said (in order of response frequency) that: (1) radio was a different medium with very different use characteristics (it is portable and people listen to it at different times and places than they would normally watch TV); (2) that music videos had some initial novelty that subsequently wore off; (3) that radio is simply immune to any effects from music videos; (4) that music videos' content qualities are different insofar as radio is more imaginative while the visual content in the videos destroys the listener's/viewer's creativity with the song; (5) that the age groups typically targeted by music videos are younger than those targeted by radio; and (6) that videos affect other leisure time activities more than they do radio.[7]

Strover's research seems sound, but not so the program directors' wishful thinking that it reports. Point 1: A Street Pulse Group telephone survey of music consumers found that 75% of their sample watched music video programming (MTV, VH-1, The Nashville Network, "Night Tracks," "Friday Night Videos," and so on.) Fifty-eight percent said that they usually *sit and watch* the program (rather than use it as a background music source). An even larger 66% of respondents under 18 said that was how they used the video services. Fully 88% of the sample watched for at least a quarter of an hour, and 66% watched at least a half hour per viewing session.[8] Point 2: There is not much proof that the novelty of music videos has worn off—only that the initial surge of interest has dropped back to a normal but habitual kind of viewing. Point 3: Radio—especially radio that leans heavily on current hit music for its appeal—is *vulnerable* to replacement by music videos, not "immune" to such effects. One 1983 study found that 43% of teenage MTV viewers watch MTV at times when they used to listen to radio, in spite of the fact that radio was thought to offer better songs and more musical variety. If forced to choose, two thirds of the teenagers in this study said they would choose MTV over radio.[9] Point 4: It is probably true that ". . . the visual content in videos destroys the listener's/viewer's creativity with the song," and research with college students seems to bear this out: those preferring radio over MTV as a music medium said that watching a music video channel limited their own interpretation of the song.[10] However, it should be pointed out that theatrical movies sometimes destroy the creativity that the reader brought to the book on which they are based, but for any given title, far more movie tickets than books are sold. It has sometimes been said that the mass audience generally opts for the medium that requires less "work." A better perspective is that the mass audience generally opts for more stimuli rather than fewer. Watching movies requires less work than reading books; however, watching music videos actually requires more work than listening to the radio. But both movies and music

---

[7]Strover, S. (1987, October). Research and planning: The impact of music video on radio. *Info-Pak*, p. 2. (copyright © by and published by The National Association of Broadcasters, Washington, DC).

[8]Shalett, M. (1988, May 20). Music videos: Heard but not seen? *Radio and Records*, p. 36.

[9]See J. Coleman, reported in Melton G. W. & Galician, M.L. (1987). A sociological approach to the pop music phenomenon: Radio and music video utilization for expectation, motivation and satisfaction. *Popular Music and Society, 11* (3), 36.

[10]Ibid., p. 39.

videos supply more stimuli than books or radio, with the additional stimulation a reward for the extra attention demanded. Also note that on MTV, the final round of the popular "Remote Control" game show requires its late-teen/early-20s contestants to name the artists who are performing the videos seen on nine TV screens. Winning contestants are able to identify the bands by sight, without ever really hearing the music. Radio airplay of the song is nearly irrelevant to these people. Their point of reference is the visual imagery. Point 5: Although it is true that many of MTV's viewers are teens and people in their early 20s, these are the very people who *used* to spend those years making a habit of radio listening. Point 6: A study by Gary Warren Melton and Mary-Lou Galician has shown that although both radio and video music helped their college student respondents to pass time, forget about problems, relax, and shift moods, music videos did a better job than radio in helping viewers to keep up with the latest fads and fashions, get in touch with feelings, and share an experience with friends.[11] In addition, these young people were more likely to find music videos helpful in escaping the real world, relieving tension, and getting in touch with feelings.[12]

Robert Pittman, former president of MTV Networks, Inc., spoke to the convention of the American Newspaper Publishers Association in 1986. One context in which the assembled editors and publishers heard him was from their concern about the loss of young people as readers. Pittman told the newspaper people:

> They have a much different way of dealing with information than the older generation. . . . They don't require a narrative line to take in information or entertainment. They readily respond to more elusive sense impressions communicated through feelings, mood, and emotion. . . . The visual media have moved away from the traditional linear mode. . . . In movies, images shift abruptly from one whole scene to another, and the transitions are left to the eye of the beholder. . . . If older viewers find this quick-edit communication motif disjointed or disorienting, the TV babies find it exciting and even stimulating.[13]

Researchers Gary Burns and Robert Thompson have said that

> the central myth of rock video, in our view, is the rejection of the "dominant" mode of consciousness – rational, scientific, unemotional – in favor of an alternative mode. The conventionalized form and motifs of rock video reflect this rejection. The alternative mode is irrational, expressive, playful, visually charged while tied to music, and self-conscious.[14]

Ronald W. Roschke, whose paper "Dream/Brain/Text" discusses in detail the relation of dreams to stories, made this comment about MTV during an interview:

---

[11]Ibid., p. 41.

[12]Ibid., pp. 43–44.

[13]Stein, M. L. (1986, May 10). The MTV generation. *Editor & Publisher*, p. 16.

[14]Burns, G., & Thompson, R. (1987). Music, television, and video: Historical and aesthetic considerations. *Popular Music and Society, 11* (3), 22.

MTV is daytime dreaming. It is bringing you a nighttime state in the daytime. MTV is an especially powerful storyteller because of the visual elements, but all of pop music succeeds best when it tells a story. Pop music does not lecture. The stories in popular music are very dense constellations of associations. Lectures are tight, self-contained intellectual units that are smooth on the outside and have all of their hooks pointing inward to connect internally. Stories are bristly and have many of their hooks on the outside so that it works like Velcro™ – you throw this Velcro ball at that Velcro board but it doesn't bounce – it sticks to all kinds of other associations that people have. MTV, and to a lesser extent, pop music as heard but not seen, is Velcro™ communication with all of these extended subliminal hooks. These kinds of Jungian and Freudian symbols are perhaps new as a TV music form, but they have historical roots stretching far beyond just popular music: apocalyptic literature worked the same way in the ancient world. Music that tells a story that we can relate to is music that has its hooks on the outside.[15]

In the quote just cited, Roschke said that "MTV is an especially powerful storyteller because of the visual elements." Perhaps this is because those visuals – maybe *especially* when they seem chaotic to the linear-oriented viewer – are providing the counterpoints and the surprise connections that are the hallmarks of dreaming. Roschke's ideas appear again in this book's final chapter about dreams, stories, and society as they relate to the development of an audience-responsive radio format – one answer to the impact of MTV.

As this is being written, most MTV viewers are still hearing the audio over their TVs, the majority of those sets being monaural. What that means is that millions of listeners have been attracted to the channel in spite of the generally poor sound reproduction ability of most television sets. But television receiver manufacturers are promoting stereo TV receivers heavily, and broadcast stations and cable channels that have converted to stereo typically have also upgraded other gear in the audio chain, with resulting improvements in fidelity. At some point in the future, when a majority of U.S. television sets have stereo capability, MTV will be even more of a threat to music on the radio intended for home consumption. FM stations may find FM receivers suffering the same *diaspora* that banished AM sets from the living room in the 1950s – and for the same reason: TV taking over. When that happens, automobile listening will again grow in importance as a target audience.

In the meantime, there have been some notable attempts to program a radio station so that it emulated at least the audio of MTV, right down to the use of anti-establishment liners. Westwood One Radio Group Vice President/ Programming Scott Shannon described the sound of Los Angeles station KQLZ as like "MTV on the radio." The format, known as "Pirate Radio," features hard rock and rock-flavored ballads.[16]

---

[15]From an interview with Ronald W. Roschke, Manhattan, KS., Jan 24, 1985.

[16]Pirate radio surprise attack clears deck for L.A. CHR war. (1989, March 24). *Radio & Records,* pp. 1 & 32.

Digital Audio

The other great challenge to the radio industry is from home and auto digital audio playback (CD) and record/playback (DAT) equipment. Digital's full frequency range and freedom from noise and distortion have been the qualities most touted by those radio stations that have converted over to playing digital media. Most stations make no mention of digital audio's awesome dynamic range – because they cannot begin to transmit it. The growing numbers of CD players in the home may do one of two things: (a) cause radio stations to update their audio processing so that it does less harm to digital dynamics, even though some fringe listeners may be lost, or (b) cause listeners to give up on the compressed audio much of music radio supplies now.

Methods may yet be developed to transmit over current broadcast bandwidths the staggering amount of data required of a true digital audio system. Meanwhile, present and future cable systems are gearing up to provide eight or more channels of full digital audio services to home subscribers.[17] But in the long run, FM may prove to be the perfect channel for the human voice (which is what some industry people have said – wishfully – about AM). The human voice has neither the dynamic range nor the frequency range problems of music. Voices on FM can sound very natural. There is little vocal material on CD or pre-recorded DAT with which to compare the fidelity of the voice broadcast over FM, so it is not so likely to suffer in contrast. And as veteran programming consultant Rick Sklar pointed out, high commercial loads are more compatible with talk than with music: compare up to 18 commercial *minutes* on a talk station with as few as 7 *units* on some FM music stations.[18] In the future, the nondigital-quality FM music station could try to compensate for its lack of musical fidelity compared to digital by surrounding the music it airs with the elements that radio has traditionally handled well: entertaining talk. Just as some AMs have succeeded by generating audience involvement through their air personalities rather than relying on the music, in the same way the analog FMs of the future could move farther from being "music utilities," and could instead re-commit themselves to "show business" as the only business to be in.

Technological solutions may eventually allow digital-quality audio either alongside or within present FM bandwidths. But during the near term, the safer industry position would be to de-emphasize dependence on the "high-fidelity" aspects of music broadcast on FM, and to concentrate on other features of the communications enterprise.

The Role of Radio in an Increasingly
Visual Electronic Society

Whatever its present or future shortcomings in technical production quality, there is no denying that just the *music* played each day on U.S. radio stations makes

---

[17]See N.Y. cable firm sets 8-channel digital service. (1989, February 4). *Billboard, 101* (5), 1.

[18]Sklar, R. (1988, August 26). Talk on FM: Mining the "new frontier." *Radio & Records*, p. 38.

hundreds of millions of impressions about lifestyles, mores, social problems, and so on, tieing in to our personal stories at a level of consciousness that is near dreaming. I believe that the agenda-setting function of the mass media is today carried out most pervasively not through journalism but through entertainment, especially the music aired on radio, and on MTV and its clones. (That is one reason why radio news operations are not covered in this book.) What our society believes, and what it aspires to, is today shaped as much by the songs on the nation's playlists as by newspapers and newsmagazines. For people under 21, and certainly for those under 18, one of the most powerful editorial voices in the United States is MTV – and the network never airs any "editorials" per se. Radio now often plays a supporting role to television in the generation of opinion among teenagers, but because of its sheer ubiquity, radio is still influential.

In his 1966 book *Language as Symbolic Action,* literary critic Kenneth Burke said "things are in effect the visible tangible material embodiments of the spirit that infuses them through the medium of words. And in this sense, things become the signs of the genius that resides in words."[19] In an increasingly visual age, this is less and less true. The first proof was the Vietnam War, playing on the evening TV news as ironic backdrop for Cleaver-family lookalikes sitting down to supper. Today, MTV has become the next generation's ritual drama entertainment. Someday, music videos without lyrics (instrumentals) will probably be as prevalent as those with words, because visuals will tell the story – because the visuals themselves are the "visible tangible material embodiments" of the actual objects. There need not be description. When watching video, we think we see the thing itself.

We began to understand how television was re-ordering society back in the 1960s. Marshall McLuhan sometimes went so far afield with his "probes," or worked so hard for a pun, that he was troublesome to follow. But McLuhan did break perceptual ice, and it is essential in an age dominated increasingly by electronic visuals to appreciate how things have changed for radio, and for society at large.

Video and Computers Are Changing the Commonality of Community

In the opening years of the 1990s, we are just beginning to understand how profound the effects of the proliferation of microcomputers may be. Their presence is perhaps most obvious in business, but they are increasingly available in schools and homes. In the home, computer hardware is changing the way we (especially the younger generation) perceive and manipulate visual presentations, and games software is changing the nature of narrative action and of fantasy. In the long term, the use of computers by a growing number of the general public promises a much greater sense of control by individuals over images, events, and environments. If in

---

[19]Burke, K. (1966). *Language as symbolic action* (p. 362). Berkeley & Los Angeles: University of California Press.

the 1960s television created a global village with itself as the communal fire, in the 1980s many villagers either stoked their own fires (the VCR available to timeshift or to play rental tapes), or retreated to huts where the hearth is a video monitor connected to a personal computer. In either case, the simultaneity of global video community made possible by the broadcast TV networks has begun to wane. We have not gone back to the monkdom of the written page, but the very proliferation of electronic media choices has modified the commonality of electronic community.

The change that the computer has made in what we can do with what we see has been most profound. Computers bring a new way of thinking about the physical world. No longer are curious children concerned with taking apart real physical objects. They can see them taken apart and put back together in exploded views on a screen. The manipulative skills that used to go into turning a screwdriver now are put into moving a joystick to produce changes in visual icons. And radio does not have an aural equivalent of the ideogram (a written symbol that represents an idea or object directly – as a computer icon does – rather than as a particular word or speech sound). The mouse-driven or touch-screen-selected icons that operate computer software today may be precursors of a time when we will do much of our communicating via ideograms, avoiding the written and spoken word altogether. But even if that day is far off, this point is supremely important in the future of radio: Today youngsters learn to use their hands to make changes in what they see. They press buttons on a TV tuner and the picture changes. Yes, they can adjust stereos and tune radios that way too, but only in this age has it become so easy for children to manipulate their visual environment so exactly. In the previous 40 years of TV, all you could do was change channels. Cable brought more channels, but still no interaction. VCRs brought more choices about content and when it was viewed, but still no interaction. Computers bring all of that, plus interaction. Today, working with a computer, you can create your own visual environment. Not just a picture, but an environment.

Music videos, digital audio, an increasingly visual society. This is the arena in which radio must compete for its share of the public's attention. And it is in this context that the rest of this book unfolds.

MAJOR POINTS

1. It is sometimes difficult to tell, when working within a mass medium, just what its special niche is. For example, the unique thing local daily newspapers do is door-to-door delivery.

2. Today's listener has many choices beside radio, so when he or she turns to radio, it is as a demand-access consumer – someone who is accustomed to getting what he or she wants to hear when he or she wants to hear it.

3. The station that is most vulnerable to replacement by cassettes and CDs programmed by the listener is the "music utility" – unless the station backs up the

usual claims of "most music" with clearly stated proof. A "What's your favorite medium?" survey can tell you how replaceable by cassettes and CDs your station is.

4. "Mass appeal" need not mean doing what the other guys do. Mass appeal stations do not have to settle for the lowest common denominator. Narrowly targeted stations can succeed if they continuously ask themselves "What does the listener really want?"

5. "Consistent quality" is a pair of words that do not belong together in radio. Quality radio programming must always include inconsistency if it is going to work as well tomorrow as it does today. Consistency eventually leads to boredom.

6. Music videos are one of the present and future challenges for managers of music-based stations. Program directors do not want to believe that music on TV is a threat, and that (especially for younger listeners) the power of visual imagery makes radio airplay seem weak by comparison. As TV increases its share of music listening time, radio audiences in cars will take on added importance.

7. The home consumer's adoption of digital audio stereo equipment will make the fidelity problems of analog FM transmission more apparent. The human speaking voice is reproduced well on FM, so FMs may eventually displace AMs in doing talk programming. Until music can be broadcast in digital form, less reliance on music as the staple "drawing card" will allow an FM station to hold its audience farther into the future.

8. What our society believes, and what it aspires to, is today shaped as much by the songs on the nation's playlists as by newscasts, newspapers, and magazines. For people under 18, the most powerful editorial voice in the United States is MTV – and they never air any editorials per se. Among teenagers, radio now plays a supporting role to television in the generation of opinion.

9. Words are becoming less important – even the lyrics in songs. We need lyrics on music videos less and less. We think we see the thing itself.

10. If television created a global village with itself as the communal fire in the 1960s, in the 1980s the villagers stoked their own fires with VCR tapes, or retreated to huts where the hearth was a video monitor hooked up to a personal computer. The commonality of the electronic community has waned somewhat.

11. Today, children learn to use their hands to make changes in what they see. Both with TV tuners, and with computer "mice" and lightpens, children can manipulate and even create their visual environment with great precision. This capability is unmatched by radio.

CHAPTER 3

Radio's Attributes

WHAT DOES RADIO DO?

Among the objective answers to the question "What Does Radio Do?" are these: It plays music. It tells the news. It predicts the weather and warns about traffic. It raises issues of public importance. It puts another voice in the room. As a result of those objective functions, the subjective perception is that it entertains (music), informs (news), empowers (weather and traffic), socializes (public issues), and befriends (companionship).

If we look at what audiences use radio for, one cluster of answers keeps occurring: entertainment, relaxation, enjoyment. Dolf Zillmann and Jennings Bryant suggested that *entertainment* may be "crudely defined" as "any activity designed to delight and, to a smaller degree, enlighten."[1] Over 20 years ago, two researchers published books that were among the first to acknowledge – and even celebrate the fact that mass media audiences are usually in it for the fun. Both of these two books are worth an extended look at this point in our discussion of the business radio is in.

MENDELSOHN: THE POSITIVE VALUES
OF MASS ENTERTAINMENT

Harold Mendelsohn published his landmark book *Mass Entertainment* in 1966. But its lessons are still largely unlearned even by the broadcasters who underwrote the research through a grant from the National Association of Broadcasters. In its 200

---

[1]Zillmann D., & Bryant, J. (1986). Exploring the entertainment experience. In J. Bryant & D. Zillmann (Eds.), *Perspectives on media effects* (p. 303). Hillsdale, NJ: Lawrence Erlbaum Associates.

well-written pages, Mendelsohn laid out every argument broadcasters would ever need to defend themselves from the charge that their programming was deleterious, wasteful, trash, and so on. But more than being a defense of the value of mass entertainment, Mendelsohn's book is an explanation of the positive values to be derived from entertainment delivered by mass media. Because the majority of the airtime of most radio stations is devoted to entertainment rather than hard information or high culture, it is important to have Mendelsohn's ideas in mind before proceding with the present discussion.

In his first chapter, Mendelsohn examined "The Attack on Entertainment" and made the case that the mass population of American society rejects the negative valuation put on entertainment by the more "responsible" sectors of society. Mendelsohn said that "It is from the gratifications that the mass population receives from entertainment that our knowledge about the phenomenon must spring – not from the assumptions of our guardians of social values."[2] Clearly, Mendelsohn's point of view is with the consumer of the mass media, just as it is in this book.

"Relaxation," Not "Escape"

In a second chapter that explores the sociological functions of mass entertainment, Mendelsohn said that "In sociological terms . . . in contemporary American society mass entertainment is equated with the 'good life'."[3] In refuting those sociologists and psychologists who think that those seeking entertainment are actually trying to escape negative factors in their daily living, Mendelsohn said "For the most part . . . the pursuit of entertainment in modern America can be seen more as a 'running toward' what Americans have defined for themselves as 'the good life' rather than as a 'running away' from an allegedly unrewarding social-economic life."[4] A later part of the chapter deals with *relaxation* – a term that is highly associated with radio listening by virtually all audiences.

> The word "relaxation" is not synonymous with "idleness" – either sociologically or psychologically. Rather, "relaxation" suggests a mere diminution of action – not an absence of it; it suggests a slackening rather than an abolition of work; an abatement of activity rather than a cessation of it. "Relaxation" . . . implies a sort of fruitful idleness that is not *completely* divorced from work and serious pursuits.[5]

Listening As Work Accompaniment

It is a given that a huge amount of radio listening is done as an accompaniment to actual work; the point to be added here is that the listener who identifies just radio listening as a "relaxing" activity may actually feel guilty that he or she is not paying

[2]Mendelsohn, H. (1966). *Mass entertainment* (p. 33). New Haven, CT: College and University Press.
[3]Ibid., p. 50.
[4]Ibid., p. 51.
[5]Ibid., p. 70.

attention to some job that needs doing. Although there is evidence that people (especially better educated people) feel more guilty about having "wasted" time with television than with radio, it is important to realize that radio listening is often thought of as "work accompaniment" rather than as entertainment in its own right.

Thinking of radio listening as work accompaniment—even if the listener is not actually working but believes he or she should be—is different from thinking of radio as a "background" audio service. Radio as work accompaniment can be very much a foreground service, with lots of talk and personality. This is true because much of the work that radio accompanies is performed by people working as individuals, and not even necessarily in the workplace, but in the car, in the home, or in an office cubicle. While TV viewing—especially in the evenings—often takes place with a surrounding group, most radio listening is never done in a group, but individually.

Solitary Versus Social Listening Experiences

The individuality of the experience of listening makes radio audiences more like readers of printed matter than like television viewers. The listening experience, like the reading experience, is almost always solitary. Yet, as Mendelsohn said of all media, "it is quite evident that mass entertainment allows the individual to share with others a wide variety of events of common interest and concern. The seeker of mass media-derived entertainment uses the entertainment experience to bind him with others who are similarly disposed."[6] The next day at the office, there is talk about what the guy said on the radio, what they wrote in the paper, what she did on TV. And yet, radio—because it is heard individually—lacks some of the impact of those media that are experienced with a social group, such as the movies. Mendelsohn said:

> All of us have experienced the sense of embarrassment that accompanies a loud outburst of laughter when we witness something funny while we are alone. This inhibition about the expression of elementary emotion is relieved by witnessing others doing the exact same thing. In an entertainment audience the cues for releasing emotional reaction are reciprocal, and consequently they enhance the enjoyment process. We need not feel embarrassed about a sudden surfacing of our deepest feelings in situations where we can see the same process occurring all about us.[7]

We have such group experiences at the movies and attending the theater, and to a lesser extent when watching television with others. But because we generally listen to radio alone, we probably feel more inhibited about reacting to some of what we hear. This needs to be qualified, however. Mendelsohn mentioned being embarrassed by laughing out loud when alone. At the same time, many of us would be glad to be alone if the emotion we are experiencing causes us to cry. The difference

[6]Ibid., p. 77.
[7]Ibid., p. 79.

is one of social norms: for example, in our society, laughter is usually a group experience, whereas tears are private. And although crying may not seem to be as pleasurable as laughter, the opportunity for the private release of such deep emotions may well be one of radio's assets. Both Mendelsohn and I have more to say later about radio reinforcing a listener's moods, but for now it is important to affirm that because radio is not usually listened to in a social group and if it hopes to have the emotional impact of media such as television and film, it probably needs to work harder at helping the individual to express otherwise repressed responses.

STEPHENSON: THE PLEASURES OF PLAY

In the first chapter of his 1967 book *The Play Theory of Mass Communication,* William Stephenson commented that he was puzzled when he began his research in 1958 that so few people were studying mass communications entertainment, rather than mass communication as an agent of persuasion.[8] Stephenson thus shares the same view as Mendelsohn: that mass entertainment is worthy of study. Information theory alone, according to Stephenson, can explain neither the "social control" that is manifested in the formation of public opinion, nor the "convergent selectivity" upon which advertising is based. Thus, the emergence of his play theory. Stephenson said, "Communication is not just the passing of information from a source to the public; it is better conceived as a re-creation of information ideas by the public, given a hint by way of a key symbol, slogan, or theme."[9] Stephenson asked, "What, indeed, does a person say to himself; what conversations does he carry on in his own mind? This is likely to be crucial in any consideration of the effects of mass communication upon him from whatever source."[10] Stephenson's concept that communication is "a re-creation of information ideas by the public, given a hint by way of key symbol, slogan or theme" is important. It underscores the subjectivity of the mass audience, while also stressing that there are common symbols and themes that may trigger common responses.

Socially Controlled Publics and Existential Mass Audiences

Later, in the chapter on Air Personalities, the late Arthur Godfrey is cited for his breakthrough idea that radio announcers should not try to address the mass audience the way a platform speaker talks to a crowd, but rather should talk to each individual individually. Stephenson made a distinction between the public (in the sense of a group that comes to a consensus opinion, under social control) and a mass audience,

---

[8]Stephenson, W. (1967). *The play theory of mass communication* (p. 2). Chicago: University of Chicago Press.

[9]Ibid., p. 8.

[10]Ibid., p. 9.

whose members are freer to think as they please than ever before in history.[11] The difference in announcing styles, pre- and post-Godfrey (discussed later in chapter 7), may be akin to the difference Stephenson drew between passing information to the public in order to form public opinion, as compared to letting the individual member of the mass audience, carrying on conversations in his or her own mind, bring his or her own set of notions and experiences to bear. He pointed out that in a mass-appeal periodical, as in all advertising, "ideologies are ignored and personalities and social character are reinforced."[12] Stephenson said, "It is my thesis that the daily withdrawal of people into the mass media in their after hours . . . is a step in the *existential* direction, that is, a matter of subjectivity which invites freedom where there had been little or none before."[13] Far from condemning the vehicles of mass media entertainment as having a "narcotizing" effect on the audience, Stephenson applauded the opportunity for the individual to exist for him or herself rather than for the public.

Definitions of "Play"

Stephenson also made an extended attempt at defining *play:*

> Playing is *pretending,* a stepping outside the world of duty and responsibility. Play is an *interlude* in the day. It is not ordinary or real. It is *voluntary* and not a task or moral duty. It is in some sense *disinterested,* providing a temporary satisfaction. Though attended to with seriousness, it is not really important. . . . Play is *secluded,* taking place in a particular place set off for the purpose in time or space: it has a beginning and an end. The child goes into a corner to play house. And play is a free activity; yet it absorbs the player completely. The player is unself-conscious if he plays with the proper enjoyment.
>
> Play has been explained by psychologists as abreactive, wish-fulfillment, instinctive, and much else. All that seems certain is that play is "fun.". . .[14]

It is worth examining these more closely for a moment before proceeding. Most people who listen to the radio do not think of themselves as "pretending" in the sense of stepping outside the world of duty and responsibility. This is because much radio listening is done precisely while performing some duty or attending to some responsibility. And that difference is important in the other factors Stephenson cited. Radio listening is not an interlude, because it is more likely to be an accompaniment. Like play, it is voluntary and disinterested. But it is not usually secluded—radio listening succeeds in part because it can be done almost anywhere. And it is not as absorbing as his description of play—at least not most of the time.

---

[11]Ibid., p. 35.
[12]Ibid., p. 39.
[13]Ibid., p. 45.
[14]Ibid., p. 46.

Pleasure

Stephenson also developed two meanings for the term *pleasure:*

> The one concerns our moods of elation, joy, sorrow, and the like; the other is retrospective, as when we say that we were so absorbed in an activity, so engrossed in it, that we "enjoyed" it. In the latter case the person may not have been experiencing any particular feelings – on the contrary he may have been so absorbed that he lost all sense of himself in the process. Thus, as I have said earlier, when people say they enjoy reading a newspaper, sheer absorption may be involved and not feelings at all.[15]

Listening to radio is likely to allow us a chance for the pleasure of play, the chance for some disinterested fun. But many of the items on the list just given can also be done by television, and a few can even be done by newspapers and magazines. So the question becomes, is there a factor – maybe even a problem area like circulation is to newspapers – that is really radio's forte? Yes.

WHAT RADIO DOES BEST

Radio encourages *in*attention. Radio's greatest asset, and the thing that most separates it from other media, is the fact that it is easiest of all to ignore. There are three components to radio's encouragement of inattention that help to explain why that is a virtue.

Radio Is Low Demand

You do not have to look at radio, and you do not have to hold it in your hands and turn the pages. It is just there. As concerns the listener's attention, radio is low demand.

Radio Is Encompassing

Second, although radio does not demand strong attention from the listener, it holds the stage in a way which no visual medium does – because human beings do not have earlids. We can close our eyes, but not our ears. Radio sound is either foreground or background in level – for the listener, there is no such thing as the audio equivalent of a "medium shot." And there is no corollary in sound to "tunnel vision" in sight – the sensation that all the peripheral visual detail is being blocked out and that we are concentrating just on the essential elements in the scene. A listener does not blot out most of the room and just see the screen as he or she does when watching TV, or just see the words on paper as when reading a newspaper or magazine. A radio listener is still able to utilize the full field of vision, which is why radios (unlike TVs) are legal in the front seats of cars. And, although the radio

---

[15]Ibid., p. 54.

listener can practice selective perception, and can decide just to hear rather than to listen actively, still, if anything is audible, the listener hears it all at once. To the listener, then, radio is encompassing.

Radio Is Open-Ended

A third element (which radio shares with the printed page so long as it is without pictures) is a lack of closure. Stan Freberg made the case for radio's open-endedness against television's complete closure when (on his late-1950s CBS radio show and later for the Radio Advertising Bureau) he constructed a gigantic chocolate sundae in Lake Michigan. He tagged his famous sound effects tour-de-force with the statement "Radio stretches the imagination." A young guest asked, "Doesn't television stretch the imagination?" To which Freberg replied, "Up to 21 inches, yes!" The point is that television visuals (and the magazine or newspaper illustration) appear to be so detailed that they leave little for the viewer to imagine. Their specificity does not allow much viewer participation in the generation of imagery, because most of it is supplied. That is "closure." Radio, on the other hand, is open-ended with regard to the listener's imagery.

Radio Is a Fertilizer of Fantasies and Daydreams

As a result of making low attention demands, while being pervasive in the physical and psychological space around the listener, and being open-ended with the listener's imagery, radio becomes a prime breeding ground for daydreams and fantasies. Consider this: no one sits down and works to come up with daydreams and fantasies. But daydreams and fantasies are a necessary and pleasant part of everyone's psychic existence. It takes a positive effort at concentration to keep them from happening. Left to its own devices, the human mind naturally slips into daydreaming and fantasizing. Ronald W. Roschke in his "Dream/Brain/Text: The Media-Brain Connection in Mental Processing of Texts" said:

> I would suggest that sleep-mode consciousness is *not* uniquely a property of sleep, but rather represents a way of thinking also accessible to the brain during its waking hours. The most obvious example would be the *daydream*. Although I am wide awake when I daydream, the quality of a daydream is more similar to a real dream than it is to waking consciousness. I am not aware of my daydream until it is over. I never find myself saying, "Oh, here I am going into a daydream." Rather, I suddenly realize that I have been daydreaming; my mind was off somewhere else. I was not attending to the situation around me. In fact, in many ways my mind did exactly what it does during sleep. What I was "seeing" was an image in my memory. My ego was really there, in that room with those people. I was hearing what they were saying. I could "see" them. But the quality of sight is like that of a nocturnal dream. It is a different kind of seeing from, say, looking at a picture. It is not really an hallucination but more like the

memory of an appearance. And yet, it is not simply the *memory* of a scene either, for in my daydream I can see things that I have never seen in "real life." New "memories" can be forged out of existing images as they are woven together into a matrix.[16]

The very *in*attention that radio listening allows is the *modus operandi* of the daydreamer. If the radio professional comes to understand that radio's strongest asset is the way it can be ignored, and realizes that the business of radio is to provide fertilizer for daydreams and fantasies, then inattention will stop seeming to be a threat. And it is shown later that dial-hopping, the behavior that drives programmers crazy in their quest to avoid tune-out, is only the means the listener uses to keep a certain daydream or fantasy going.

LESSONS ABOUT ENTERTAINMENT VALUES
FROM COMPUTER GAMES

Since the advent of arcade, home video, and computer games, electronic games have become another competitor for the listener's attention. If we could understand how the better of those games allow an exchange of the best efforts of a game designer with the best efforts of a game player, it might be possible to try to emulate that exchange in a radio format.

First, we must define what we are *not* talking about. We are not talking about games whose main objective is shooting, gobbling, or escaping—in other words, games whose main appeal is conflict and competition and whose main skill is eye–hand coordination. To put it another way, we are not interested in a game that mainly depends on positioning (the familiar joystick) and "zapping" (the familiar FIRE button).

Challenge and Control

It may seem arbitrary to dismiss such games because they were long the staple of arcade units and home video game cartridges. But these seemed to appeal most especially to children and especially to adolescent boys. Theorists have speculated that they may be zapping pimples, siblings, parents, teachers, or even the arms race as they hammer away at the controls. Whatever the object of disdain, it is clear that the conflict/competition appeal is finding expression in a safe (non-ego threatening) situation where the player can attempt to gain enough skill to ultimately control and overcome the adversary. Most such games are designed to increase the challenge of the action as the player's skills increase, with the scoring arranged to pay bigger rewards at higher skill levels. Thus, the beginning player knows that he or she will

---

[16]Roschke, R. W. (1987). Dream/brain/text: The media-brain connection in mental processing of texts. In K. H. Richards (Ed.), *Society of biblical literature 1987 seminar papers* (pp. 164–165). Atlanta, GA: Scholars Press.

be eased into the game, that the middle levels of play will be more difficult (but that his or her increasing skill should match them), and that the most difficult later levels can only be reached when he or she has mastered the intermediate ones. There is a combination of continually increasing *challenge* presented by the game, and continually increasing *control* as exercised by the player. These are the prerequisites for the "flow" experience, which is discussed in the next chapter. It is partly an attempt to gain that sense of *control* that keeps the kid pumping tokens into the arcade machines. It is difficult, but with enough practice, most such games can be mastered, and thus the player is rewarded with the sense that there is something in his or her life that he or she *can* control.

Fantasy Fulfillment

A sense of control is not the only prize video games provide. Fantasy fulfillment is clearly another strong appeal. William Hawkins, founder of Electronic Arts, a computer software company, said:

> A lot of people like playing with computers because they gain control . . . but at an emotional level it's a lot more interesting to think of situations where you're *not* in total control. That's what it's like when you're dreaming. At some level your mind is directing the action, but there is a feeling of helplessness. You can't alter the script; your brain won't let you. It will be like watching a movie for the first time, except that you'll be the hero and have to make decisions. . . . Everything you do in life is a situation in which there are separate players involved, and there are separate decisions you have to make. . . . There's a competitive feeling and maybe there's a score – but maybe there isn't. That's the kind of fantasy fulfillment you can get out of a computer, which is what we're really after.[17]

If Hawkins is right about the appeal of fantasy fulfillment, then radio has been on the right track for a long time. Because the only direct control the radio listener can exercise over programming is to turn the radio off or to change stations, good programmers have attempted to thwart even that limited amount of control by giving the listener reasons to stay tuned longer. It appears that the best of those reasons to stay would be ones promising fantasy fulfillment: through the music; through the presentational style; through features, contests, and promotions.

Perhaps the person who seeks pleasure in games is trying to achieve a temporary escape from the real world into a fantasy one, hoping to achieve a measure of control in the fantasy world that may be either greater or less than the control he or she has in real life situations. This person is different from the news/talk listener. The news/talk devotee seeks a temporarily deeper connection with the real world and all its problems, partly out of the sense that simply knowing about something is the beginning of gaining control over it. Yet the news/talk listener may also be deriving

---

[17]Hawkins, W., cited in Eckels, H. (1983, November). New game in town. *Technology Illustrated*, p. 18.

fantasy fulfillments in hearing about people, places, and events he or she could not possibly have known otherwise, and in which the "situations where you're NOT in total control" (in Hawkins' words) are the norm.

Hard to Master

When they are done well, both the fantasy-fulfilling music presentation and the situation-immersing news/talk presentation follow one of the prime rules of the video game industry: "make it easy to learn and hard to master."[18] Ideally, anything that means to be mass entertainment in America should be apparently easy to engage on its surface, while the content provides plenty of challenge. (This follows the "challenge-but-not-*too*-tough" formula for the "flow" experience, too, as is seen in chapter 4.) Another way of saying that is, the form (or format) should be familiar and nonthreatening, whereas what the format conveys (the content) should be endlessly novel and at least moderately difficult to master. In radio terms, that means that when the format is really working, it disappears. The content takes over. This is congruent with the precept that the business of radio is *in*attention, in the sense that the framework should be so transparent that only the content shows. The listener must be engaged at the level of a pleasant, voluntary competition – like playing a game.

The point has been made that it is not enough for a game to provide fast action leading to a sense of control. A good game might also provide a high degree of fantasy fulfillment. But are even those two enough? According to one of the gurus of video game design, Atari's Chris Crawford, most skill and action games are dismissable "as so much 'candy' that gives a quick thrill and nothing more."[19] In pop-music formats, much of that candy is in the music. Some people have even called the adolescent-appeal music "ear candy." Other format elements can be candy, too: jingles, promos, contests, announcer chatter, even the news when it's really soft features. There is nothing inherently wrong with ear candy; we all have at least a slight sweet tooth. But a station which doesn't provide much substance isn't going to attract and hold an adult audience for long. In other words, fantasy cannot be total escape, and escape never means blandness. Formats that do their best to be inoffensive wind up being unengaging because they offer too little challenge to the listener.

Something You Walk Away With

Then what *are* the elements of a video game appealing to an adult? Chris Crawford mentioned these: ". . . something to challenge a mature person with a sense of judgment . . . computer games, or any game really, should have a point, should mean something, and should have something you walk away with. It should make

---

[18]Ibid., p. 14.

[19]Immel, A.R. (1982, June). Chris Crawford: Artist as game designer. *Popular Computing*, p. 57.

you a better person."[20] Crawford said that the best games blur the distinction between learning and entertainment. Indeed, software publisher Electronic Arts has asked of magazine readers in its premiere advertising, "Can a computer make you cry?" A partial answer to that query is provided by the company's advertising brochure, which states "We are learning, for instance, that we are all more entertained by the involvment of our imaginations than by passive viewing and listening. We are learning that we are better taught by experience than by memorization. And we are learning that the traditional distinctions – between art and entertainment and education – don't always apply."[21]

MAJOR POINTS

1. As a mass-entertainment medium, radio provides relaxation and work accompaniment, information, socialization, and companionship, but the unique thing radio does is to encourage *in*attention.
2. Radio can take lessons from video game designers. Video games offer challenge, control, and fantasy fulfillment, but most of all they are something that is easy to learn yet hard to master. There has to be substance, not just sweet candy. The best games give you something you walk away with.
3. Radio listening is not done for escape so much as for relaxation.
4. Stephenson said that mass media such as radio allow the individual an opportunity to exist for him or herself rather than for the public.
5. Radio listening affords the simple pleasures of play: taking pleasure in being absorbed in novel fantasies and moods.
6. Radio is low demand, aurally encompassing, and open-ended with regard to the listener's imagery.
7. Radio is best thought of as a fertilizer of fantasies and daydreams.
8. Dial-hopping is the technique listeners use to keep a certain daydream or fantasy going.

---

[20]Ibid., p. 57.

[21]*We see farther* (1983). An advertising brochure from Electronic Arts (not paginated).

CHAPTER 4

What Radio Audiences Want

Audiences are the target of a lot of research. For example, a survey found that 40% of men read on the toilet, whereas only 14% listen to the radio there.[1] Format-oriented books about radio programming tend to treat audiences as different flavors of demographic pie – that is, they describe what kind of audience tends to be generated by which kind of programming. This chapter explores audiences from a "consumerist" standpoint. It looks at the listener's needs, desires, and expectations, some of them quite apart from the programming radio typically provides. Given the near-infinite variability of human nature, it would not be sensible to expect to find even a simple majority of radio listeners fitting most of the attributes that are described. Matching up formats with the listeners they generate is not the idea of this chapter. Instead, this chapter describes what drives people to listen and respond to radio in the first place, by paying primary attention to human needs, desires, and expectations.

FANTASIES AND DAYDREAMS

It is generally agreed that one of the entertainment functions of the mass media is to provide a means of "escape" from the real world, or, more positively, a means of relaxation through immersion in something else. The end of the last chapter stated that the real business of radio is to serve as a fertilizer of fantasies and daydreams. If so, then the question might be asked, what are the daydreams that people commonly indulge in anyway? A survey commissioned by the advertising agency D'Arcy Masius Benton & Bowles questioned 752 men and 798 women about their emotions, drives, and thoughts. The results under the heading "Have You Ever Imagined Yourself . . ." are shown in Table 4.1.[2] A pattern begins to emerge in the

---

[1]Allen, M. (1984, June 10). How do you rate (or do you care?)." *The Manhattan Mercury*, p. El.

TABLE 4.1
Daydreams[2]

	Men	Women
Saving someone's life	77%	75%
Finding a cure for cancer	28%	42%
Winning an Olympic medal	43%	24%
Accepting an Academy Award	18%	26%
Being President of the USA	26%	14%
Appearing on the cover of *Time*	17%	17%
Escaping from a prison camp	24%	08%

table that shows men being more interested in risk-taking (note the prison camp escape difference) and athletic prowess (the Olympic medal), whereas women seem to be more interested in the caring that is shown in developing a cure for cancer, and in the social acceptance that is reflected in winning an Academy Award. These trends are borne out by another question that asked, "Which of these fantasy activities would you love to try?" (see Table 4.2):[3] In Table 4.2, note that men continue to be risk-takers (hot-air balloon trip, African safari, white-water rafting, manned space flight, and skydiving) to a greater extent than women. Men's sexual aggressiveness appears to be about four times greater than women's in regard to visiting a nudist colony, and about six times greater in terms of a sexual encounter with a stranger. Women, on the other hand, like to imagine themselves in social situations that offer glamour and prestige (gambling at a Monte Carlo casino, having dinner at the White House, attending the Cannes film festival).

Interestingly, when asked what their greatest source of pleasure or satisfaction was, fantasies were not in the picture. Combining the scores for both men and women, 36% said their greatest pleasure came from their children. Twenty-eight percent said their greatest source of satisfaction was their marriage, 21% chose hobbies, 19% said vacations, 18% mentioned friends, and only 17% chose sexual relationships as their greatest source of pleasure.[4] Clearly, there is a considerable disparity between the actual sources of the respondents' pleasure and the sources of pleasure that they dream about. Media that supply a chance to daydream and fantasize help to bridge the gap between wishes and reality. That is why radio's job is to be a Petri dish for daydreams.

Pleasure Seeking

A closer look at the *imagined* (fantasy) activities just listed shows that many of them have to do with the *excitement* of a challenging new situation. Meanwhile, those

---

[2]Fears and fantasies of the American male. (1987, August). *Men's Fitness,* p. 48. (Copyright © 1987, *Men's Fitness* magazine, used by permission.)

[3]Ibid., p. 48.

[4]Ibid., p. 50.

TABLE 4.2
Fantasies[3]

	Men	Women
Visit mainland China	54%	45%
Gamble in a Monte Carlo casino	44%	52%
Have dinner at the White House	41%	51%
Fly in a hot-air balloon	48%	39%
Go on an African safari	54%	33%
Camp in the wilderness	53%	31%
Go white-water rafting	47%	23%
Attend the Cannes film festival	32%	35%
Participate in a manned space flight	44%	20%
Appear on a TV talk show	28%	27%
Have a sexual encounter with a stranger	31%	05%
Go skydiving	24%	10%
Visit a nudist colony	23%	06%

surveyed reported that the greatest sources of *actual* pleasure or satisfaction included children, marriage, hobbies, vacations, and friends – the sort of ongoing, low-key activities that might come under the heading of *relaxation*.

Fantasy, excitement, and relaxation are the three types of experiences that people typically seek in order to feel good, according to Harvey B. Milkman and Stanley G. Sunderwirth in their book, *Craving for Ecstasy: The Consciousness and Chemistry of Escape*. Milkman and Sunderwirth have explored the psychological and physiological reaction to mood-altering situations and to drugs in order to discover the actual sources of a person's pleasure – pleasure so intense that the seeking of it can become compulsive. For instance, while we tend to think that drugs are addictive, Milkman and Sunderwirth asserted that

> People do not become addicted to drugs or mood-altering behaviors as such, but rather to the sensations of pleasure that can be achieved through them. We repeatedly rely on three distinct types of experience to achieve feelings of well-being: relaxation, excitement, and fantasy; these are the underpinnings of human compulsion.[5]

Later, the authors use the term *satiation* interchangeably with relaxation, and *arousal* as a synonym for excitement.

Satiation/Arousal/Fantasy

Milkman and Sunderwirth defined each of these three types of ecstatic craving more closely. Those who seek relaxation/satiation might do such things as eat exces-

---

[5]Milkman, H.B., & Sunderwirth, S.G. (1987). *Craving for ecstasy: The consciousness and chemistry of escape* (p. xiv). Lexington, MA: Lexington Books. (Reprinted by permission of the publisher from *Craving for Ecstasy* by Harvey Milkman and Stanley Sunderwirth).

sively, watch TV endlessly, or use sedative (depressant) drugs. Such people are looking for tranquility, and ways to reduce their discomfort. Sometimes the discomfort they feel is their own hostility, and these behaviors provide a means of controlling it.

People who seek arousal actively confront a world they feel is hostile or threatening. To compensate for feelings of inferiority, they repeatedly demonstrate their physical or intellectual ability. Such people are often boastful and have an inflated sense of themselves. According to Milkman and Sunderwirth: "The sky diver's adrenaline rush is remarkably similar to the short, exhilarating jolt from a line of cocaine. Excessive risk takers often mix danger with drugs."[6]

Finally, people who crave fantasy sometimes involve themselves in mystical or occult practices, and tend to make too much of accidental, random circumstances. They may seek a greater sense of spiritual or cosmic unity. Marijuana and hallucinogenic drugs are favored by such types.[7]

Receptive and Active Fantasy

Milkman and Sunderwirth, in their later chapter on "Mental Excursions," make a distinction between two types of fantasy:

> *Receptive* fantasy is the concentration on thoughts or pictures that have been produced by others, for example, watching television, reading a novel, or visiting a black-light poster display. *Active* fantasy is the production of images and thoughts that emerge spontaneously from one's own psyche. These may be highly representational and reality oriented, such as a person visualizing how to approach his or her employer, or they may be highly abstract and unrealistic, such as imagining the creation or destruction of the universe.[8]

Without direct references to radio in the aforementioned passage, Milkman and Sunderwirth have nevertheless differentiated between the two fantasy modes in which today's radio broadcasting–and especially music–is perceived. For those who see music on video services such as MTV and then hear it on the radio, the mode is *receptive* fantasy, because such listeners are essentially replaying the video in their heads when they hear the audio. On the other hand, music that has either not had video connected with it or music whose videos have been forgotten may beget *active* fantasy, in which the listener develops images and thoughts from his or her own mind.

The Radio "Connection"

Although radio listening is not specifically mentioned by Milkman and Sunderwirth, because it is one of the most pervasive of the mass media, it is an

---

[6]Ibid., p. xiv.
[7]Ibid., pp. xiv–xv.
[8]Ibid., p. 122.

important source for fantasy, arousal, and relaxation. Dolf Zillmann and Jennings Bryant have identified both "excitement" and "relaxation" as ends desired by mass media consumers.[9] Veteran communications researcher Percy Tannenbaum has said "the basic element of entertainment is some heightening of emotional arousal or excitation . . ."[10] And research by Bryant and Zillmann into the arousal caused by both informative and entertainment television messages led to the development of an implicit continuum of stimulus categories and hierarchies, with the opposing ends labeled *nonarousing* and *arousing*. They found that nature films that emphasized grandeur were decidedly at the nonarousing end of the scale. Action drama, comedy, and game shows tended to be moderately arousing, whereas highly violent and fear-evoking drama were highly arousing.[11]

In considering only pop music on the radio, it is striking that there have always been strong *fantasy* elements in lyrics about sex and romance, *arousal* in the rhythm of most rock songs and in the lyrics of some, and *relaxation* in the slow ballads featured by the "easy-listening" formats. Radio talk has also featured all three types of experience: *fantasy* in the identification derived from imagining the fun, great-looking disc jockey who plays your tunes, *arousal* in listening to other people's quirks or opinions on a telephone call-in show or in hearing a newscast, and *relaxation* in enjoying the familiar, consoling voice of a trusted local personality.

PLEASURE AS PRODUCT, NOT BYPRODUCT

So, radio stations are already supplying many of the mass-mediated sources of fantasy, arousal, and relaxation. The point is, they may not realize how much some of their listeners crave such experiences. To really be in the radio business is to be intentional about providing fantasy, excitement, or relaxation – or in some cases, all three. Fantasy, arousal, or relaxation are not byproducts of radio listening. They *are* the product. The question then becomes, how can radio assure that the listener experiences at least one of these pleasures? Fantasy, excitement, and relaxation are all complex concepts. A programmer cannot just put on a new record and assume that, say, arousal will result. Other audience behaviors and other programming factors will help determine that outcome.

The Opponent-Process Model

One of the most basic of those audience behaviors, according to Milkman and Sunderwirth, may be

[9]Zillmann, D., & Bryant, J. (1987). Exploring the entertainment experience. In J. Bryant & D. Zillmann (Eds.), *Perspectives on media effects* (pp. 306–307). Hillsdale, N.J.: Lawrence Erlbaum Associates.

[10]Tannenbaum, P.H. (1985). "Play It Again, Sam": Repeated exposure to television programs. In D. Zillmann & J. Bryant (Eds.), *Selective exposure to communication* (p. 238). Hillsdale, NJ.: Lawrence Erlbaum Associates.

[11]Zillmann, D., & J. Bryant, J. (1985). Affect, mood, and emotion as determinants of selective exposure. In D. Zillmann & J. Bryant (Eds.), *Selective exposure to communication* (p. 157). Hillsdale, NJ: Lawrence Erlbaum Associates.

the repeated pairing of opposite emotional experiences, and their underlying physio-logical counterparts . . . Some researchers feel that such pairings by be . . . the sus-taining force behind all forms of human compulsion.[12]

This behavior, which is later referred to as the opponent process, is a theory advanced by University of Pennsylvania psychologist Richard Solomon. Solomon's opponent-process theory of human motivation suggests that a life event that creates a powerful mood or feeling also causes an *opposing* biochemical process. The feelings of euphoria or happiness provided by drugs or life experiences are the things that initially motivate a person's behavior. But such mood-altering behavior continues (sometimes to the point of addiction) because the person tries to avoid the unpleasant sensations that result from the opposing biochemical process.

In some addictions, for example, running, the initial experience of pain is followed by a highly pleasurable reaction, probably related to the release of pain-relieving endorphins. The addiction is maintained, at least in part, because runners develop a craving for the biochemical opposition to the primary activity. The opponent-process model may be used to explain the pleasure that some people apparently derive from inflicting pain on themselves or others, or from taking unnecessary risks through unsafe physical or sexual practices.[13]

Figure 4.1 shows what Milkman and Sunderwirth said is a predictable pattern of

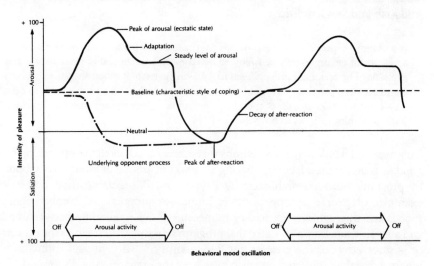

FIG. 4.1. "Opponent-Process" Model of Mood Changes (from Milkman & Sunderwirth).[14] Reprinted by permission of the publisher.

---

[12]Milkman and Sunderwirth, p. 104.

[13]Ibid., p. 105.

[14]Ibid., p. 106.

mood changes in a person who seeks alternating feelings of both arousal and satiation. The dashed baseline shows the person's typical style of coping with the world—neither aroused nor sated. The solid line shows the person's subjective feelings of arousal and satiation, rising above and dipping below the baseline. The dashed and dotted line shows the opposing biochemical process that was triggered by the rising sense of arousal—it is a sort of "mirror-image valley" to the peak representing arousal. The opponent biochemical process is what eventually brings the person "down" from the arousal peak. Milkman and Sunderwirth explained it this way:

> The peak of arousal intensity corresponds to the maximum state of biochemical excitement achieved during a risk-taking activity such as skydiving. The potent adrenaline rush, subjectively experienced as an ecstatic state, is followed by a period of adaptation in which the intensity of the pleasure declines, although the person continues to enjoy the exciting sensations of free-fall. Shortly after landing the diver feels a satiation aftereffect, the quality of which is very different (opposing) from the primary hedonic state. It is a sense of blissful relaxation, often bolstered by group celebration and alcohol intoxication.[15]

Note that the curve works for less hair-raising activities, too. What the skydiver experiences in a few minutes is experienced over an entire day by an alpine skier—arousal in skiing the mountain, satiation in the hottubs and taverns of *apres ski*. Say Milkman and Sunderwirth:

> A prolonged experience of stress and physical immobility from a traumatic automobile accident, for example, may be followed by an extended rebound of invigoration and euphoria. The opponent process leads to a waving pattern of mood alterations, which varies between people in terms of frequency and intensity. Some people seem to exist on a constant roller coaster of mood change, while others remain emotionally bland with only minor ripples in how they feel.[16]

Milkman and Sunderwirth's assertions that ecstasy is achieved not by seeking some "middle-ground" mood, but by striving for peaks of arousal or satiation is supported by program-choice research done by Bryant and Zillmann. Although they cite examples of people seeking positive, humorous programs to combat negative moods and thus achieve "excitatory homeostasis" (an equilibrium between under- and over-arousal), they also stated that program selection "often serves the evocation of positive affect of the greatest possible intensity."[17] Bryant and Zillmann also reported that their subjects "tended to overshoot the excitatory middle ground . . ."–

[15]Ibid., p. 105.
[16]Ibid., p. 105.
[17]Zillmann, D., & Bryant, J. (1985). Affect, mood, and emotion as determinants of selective exposure. In D. Zillmann & J. Bryant (Eds.), *Selective exposure to communication* (p. 173). Hillsdale, NJ: Lawrence Erlbaum Associates.

that is, they overcorrected for the mood they were trying to attain.[18] It appears that few people want to live the life – nor listen to programming – that deviates little from some flat-line average.

BODY RHYTHMS

The mood-alteration pattern described here is the product of (generally) conscious, willed sensation seeking. But there are subtler mood swings that occur throughout everyone's day as a result of biological changes tied to "body time." Radio runs by the cliche "clock on the wall" that tells real time, and the arbitrary "clocks" that control radio's music and commercial presentation. Meanwhile, radio listeners are generally unaware of the program director's (PD) format "clock." Instead, the listener pays conscious attention to real time, while he or she is generally unconscious of the control being wielded by his or her own body time. One of the better short treatments of the way body time works is by Lee Weston. His book is titled *Body Rhythm: The Circadian Rhythms Within You.* Weston was careful to separate his discussion of body time from the notion of "biorhythms." Most scientists do not find much factual basis for biorhythm claims; on the other hand, the concepts of chronobiology, circadian rhythms, and photoperiodism all have strong scientific backing. *Circadian rhythm* is the most commonly used term in the scientific community to describe the natural rhythms of the body, rhythms that keep a person in synchronicity with the world around him or her. Circadian rhythms are repeated daily. The 24-hour solar day is probably the primary "clock," according to Weston,[19] but organisms can also anticipate changes in *seasons* by sensing changes in the length of daylight. This latter capacity is called *photoperiodism.* Both circadian (daily) rhythms and photoperiodic (seasonal) rhythms fall under the more general term of *chronobiology* – the way any living organism lives with and reacts to time cues.

The PD as Chronobiologist

One of the things radio programmers need to develop is a greater sense of chronobiology. Once it is understood that the body reacts to time cues that cause us to think and feel and do certain things at certain regular times of the day and even at certain seasons of the year, then slavishness to either real time or to music "clocks" begins to seem arbitrary in both cases. Rather, the trick is for the programmer to try to find out what abilities and moods the average listener has at various times of the day and at various seasons of the year, and try to program to them.

Daily Rhythms

So far as the programmer is concerned, the most important rhythms are the daily, circadian ones. Some general findings have emerged from years of research by many different scientists. Among the general conclusions are these:

---

[18]Ibid., pp. 172–173.

[19]Weston, L. (1979). *Body rhythm: The circadian rhythms within you* (p. 11). New York: Harcourt Brace Jovanovich (copyright © 1979 by Lee Weston, reprinted by permission of Harcourt Brace Jovanovich, Inc.).

- When a person (males and females have similar rhythms) first arises from sleep, the person's mood is quiet, and distractions are not easily tolerated. Sensory perceptions are low. This would seem to indicate that listening to the radio – as a distraction – is not something most people really want to do *immediately* upon arising.
- Memory is best in the morning. It begins to slacken about noon, suggesting that oldies and nostalgia segments may work better in morning time slots.
- Mental skills such as number manipulation are best around noon. There is a measurable decline in the afternoon. Contests that require the listener to recall and use numbers might be best scheduled in the late morning.
- Many people feel like taking a short nap after lunch. If you wanted to program to complement that mood, you would play quieter music and have mellow announcing. To counteract it, your music should be livelier and your personalities more "forward."
- Sensory perception is at its peak in the early evening. This suggests that commercials that make strong use of sensory imagery will have greatest impact at that time.

These findings may not have direct application to every shred of music and every commercial message aired on the radio, because they are quite broad, but it seems wise to at least keep the general principles in mind.

Rhythm Durations

Although most of the traits just described recur at about the same time, in younger people that time may be shifted toward the night, whereas it remains in the daytime for adults. In addition, a person's rhythms tend to shorten with age. According to Weston:

> Since younger people have longer free-running rhythms, they unconsciously want to stretch their rest-activity cycle and tend to become nightowls. Their parents, whose rhythms have shortened, favor the daytime.[20]

Thus, all of the "time-of-day" findings may occur skewed more toward nighttime for younger listeners. Weston said that shifting the time when a circadian rhythm begins and ends is not too difficult, but changing its length is very hard to do. For example, it is possible to change the time when the usual patterns begin and end (as happens when travelling to a different time zone), but the length of each cycle is likely not to vary much. So, it may be hard to pinpoint the exact time to start radio programming so that it coincides with the development of a given need in the listener, but once the activity is begun, the duration is easier to suggest. For example,

---

[20]Ibid., p. 40.

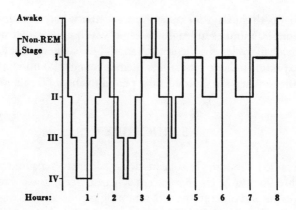

FIG. 4.2. The nightly sleep cycle (copyright © 1979 by L. Weston, reprinted by permission of Harcourt Brace Jovanovich, Inc.).

Weston gave details of an experiment that tracked the intervals during which test subjects *consumed* various items. People lived in isolation in a room where food, drinks, and cigarettes were available. Without day–nighttime cues, their eating, drinking, and smoking tended to fall into a rhythmic pattern with an interval of 96 minutes.[21] Weston said the 96-minute interval is close to a pattern found in sleep rhythms. But he also pointed out that during times of stress, or right after such events, the eating/drinking/smoking interval shrank to about 60 minutes.

The 90-Minute Hour

One conclusion that can be drawn from the aforementioned study is that relaxed listeners "consuming" the programming on a radio station might expect the programming to follow a cycle based not on the hour, but on 90 minutes. On the other hand, listeners subject to stress (perhaps in morning and evening drive?) might feel more at home in a clock-like 1-hour cycle. The "sleep cycle" that Weston mentioned is explained by him further, with reference to an accompanying chart (see Fig. 4.2). The term "REM" refers to a sleep stage in which there is rapid eye movement; the term NREM is a stage of nonrapid eye movement.

According to Weston:

> The first show of the night is brief. Typically, REM sleep lasts only about ten minutes the first time around. After it is over, the descent through the stages of NREM sleep begins again. The entire trip, going down from Stage I to Stage IV and coming back up, plus the ten-minute short-subject in REM, takes an average of about ninety minutes. Depending on the length of a night's sleep and individual sleep cycles, most people have four to seven such trips in the course of a night.[22]

---

[21]Ibid., p. 70.
[22]Ibid., p. 54.

It is striking that both the daytime consumption patterns and nighttime sleep cycles start out at about 90 minutes in length. Weston was quoted earlier saying that the duration of circadian cycles is difficult to change. This suggests that listeners might normally be expecting radio to program to them in roughly 90-minute cycles, except during those times when stress reduces the period to about 60 minutes.

STRUCTURE

Although the radio listener might subconsciously desire to consume radio programming in roughly 90-minute chunks (except when stressed), the desire to be able to perceive a structure and order to the programming is generally acknowledged. And although there are stations that feature an apparently random or structure-free method of presenting music, no station goes so far toward randomness and chaos that they cut off songs in the middle, or air only the last 12 seconds of a newscast, or announce their call sign by picking letters out of a Scrabble set. Thus, even so-called "free-form" stations still have a lot of structure in their presentation; they simply allow more leeway in music selection.

Long ago, Aristotle realized that there is pleasure in orderliness rather than chaos, and that what we have come to call classic drama derives its impact in part from a certain wavelike structure that seems to move toward chaos, then return back to normalcy. And even though radio drama per se is not the subject, Aristotelian dramatic structure is shown later to have a lot to do with a listener's expectations about "what happens when" on the radio.

Aristotelian Structure

The four elements of dramatic structure outlined by Aristotle millenia ago can be expressed in today's terms as exposition, development, building to a climax, and resolution.

Exposition is factgiving; backgrounding. In a drama, it is the journalistic five Ws and an H that begin to inform us about character (who), action (what), time (when), place (where), motivation (why), and method (how).

Development is the interweaving and deepening of the threads that were spun in exposition. This is the "entanglement" stage in a dramatic story. In modern parlance, "the plot thickens." Often at this stage, events are set in motion that can only lead to a later climax. Or to put it another way, there is in the development stage the creation of inevitability.

Building to a climax/climax is a phrase that today carries heavy sexual overtones, but in the case of much popular music, that is probably appropriate. The orgasms that Aristotle talked about were more often intellectual than physical. The high point of the dramatic action was supposed to result in a purging of the pity and fear the audience had built up during the development and the build to the climax.

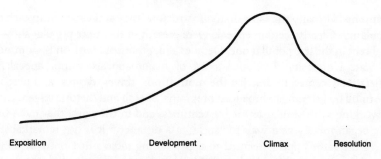

| Exposition | Development | Climax | Resolution |

FIG. 4.3.   Graph of Aristotelian dramatic structure.

The resolution is the time after the climax when all the threads that have come apart during the development and build to the climax are knit back together and life returns to something close to normal (see Fig. 4.3).

Because very little of modern radio programming is comprised of dramatic shows–and especially not Greek tragedy!–Aristotelian dramatic structure may appear to have low utility in describing what a listener expects from radio listening. But as is shown later, the wavelike form of Aristotelian dramatic structure does correspond well with the rising and falling rhythms of certain music presentation systems. And most individual songs are designed to be fairly close to the Aristotelian model.

The reader should especially compare the graph in Fig. 4.3 of Aristotelian structure with the Milkman and Sunderwirth graph of opponent-process mood changes (see Fig. 4.1, p. 39). In both, there is a buildup to a climax, the peak of arousal, then a short "shelf" period following the peak that is less intense but still arousing, and finally the period of resolution/satiation. Maybe one of the reasons dramas constructed along classical lines are effective is because they tap into the opponent process that is apparently so basic to human physiology and psychology. Or to turn it around and look at it from a cultural perspective, maybe millenia of dramatically poignant life experiences have conditioned us to desire (or have caused us to induce) psychologically and physiologically intense experiences in everyday life. Either way, whether noting the dramatic parallels to psycho-physiological behavior, or the similarity of physical responses to ancient dramatic patterns, the message about radio listeners is: people enjoy the wave-like, opponent-process pattern. Later chapters explore ways to make it an important part of programming structure.

APPEALS

Back when radio was (like television today) comprised of individual programs, rather than one continuous program of music, it became apparent that although two programs had virtually the same dramatic structure, they still varied from each other in popularity. Clearly, certain appeals were present in the more popular show that were absent in the less popular one. Decades ago, professor Harrison B. Summers of Ohio State University developed a list of major appeals, minor appeals, and modifiers that seemed to describe the motivations, drives, desires, and needs that people fulfill by listening to broadcast programs. Speech and rhetoric researchers had been working with similar terms for centuries, and in the sense that radio broadcasting began merely as a way to "speak at a distance," it is not remarkable that many of the same appeals seemed to apply during radio's first network heyday. Today, the terms (amplified by Joseph M. Ripley and Lawrence W. Lichty) are still good descriptors of why shows are popular with audiences, especially in television. The major appeals both attract a listener's attention, and then reward the listener for having paid that attention. A case can be made that the greater the number of major appeals that are well-presented in *any* broadcast program, the greater chance that show has of succeeding.

> Major Appeals: Conflict/Competition, Comedy, Sex Appeal/Personality, Information, Human Interest
> Minor Appeals: Sympathy, Affiliation, Nostalgia, Acquisition, Importance, Involvement
> Modifiers: Beauty, Credibility, Originality

Lichty's and Ripley's list of appeals is probably not exhaustive, nor is it immutable. As society changes, the appeals are bound to change with it. For example, some otherwise well-adjusted students have described television car crash scenes in which there is much smashing, twisting, explosion, and general destruction in the "beautiful" appeals category. And some appeals are stronger in the obverse: the very *in*credibility of Superman, for instance, is part of the charm. (We willingly accept the premises because they satisfy our daydreams.) A textbook on persuasive speaking is likely to list dozens of "motive appeals," such as pride, loyalty, reverence, dependence, achievement, authority, and adventure. But almost always, the Lichty and Ripley list has at least one term that is a good descriptor of the reasons people listen to broadcast programs – which reasons are entirely different from why they buy a product or subscribe to a service.

OTHER AUDIENCE NEEDS AND DESIRES

Maslow's Needs Pyramid

Except for the classification into major appeals, minor appeals, and modifiers, Lichty and Ripley did not attempt to build a hierarchy of appeals in the way that psychologist Abraham H. Maslow has advanced his now-famous five-step classification of human needs. In Maslow's scheme, a human being must largely fulfill physiological needs before he or she begins to try to fill safety needs; in turn, safety needs have to be fairly well squared away before he or she can worry about belongingness and love needs; those have to be in good shape before he or she can strive for esteem needs; and finally, if most things are under control, he or she can go for the self-actualization jackpot, where he or she realizes full potential as a distinctive human being.

Esteem Needs

It is interesting to note that the radio (and television) media work most obviously on the middle three of Maslow's levels, satisfying safety, belongingness, and esteem needs at the same time that our adequacies in these areas are brought into question. Professionals in psychology are seeing increasing numbers of people with low self-esteem, perhaps as a result of the separation of the worker from the finished product, perhaps as a consequence of measuring worthiness by disposable income. Whatever the causes, it seems safe to say that audiences are probably seeking from the media (including radio) ways to enhance feelings of self-worth, and ways of receiving honest emotional reassurance, without being exploited in the process.

A sense of self-worth has to be based on realistic self-examination. This would seem to be at odds with the beginning premise of this book, that radio serves best as an incubator of fantasies and daydreams. By definition, these are fiction, not fact. But radio's lack of specificity, its open-endedness, means that the individual listener brings his or her own imagery and predispositions to the dream. Unlike television that supplies specific visual detail that may be far different from the viewer's own reality, radio draws on a combination of the listener's reality and his or her fantasies to construct what might sometimes be a more practical dream for that individual.

The Audience and Control

Scan the magazine racks at any newstand and you are going to see that what American readers are interested in today is control. Our society wants to learn how to overcome an increasingly pervasive sense of helplessness to manage the circumstances of our lives. For instance, there is a whole section of home handyperson or "do-it-yourself" project magazines. Their message is, you do not have to depend on someone else for what you need. The ultimate expression of that impulse is the survivalist magazines, ranging from those with an environmentalist's viewpoint all the way to those frankly rating which weapons will do the best job of blasting away your neighbors if they try to get into your bomb shelter. (The attitude seems to be, the world as we know it may be coming to an end, but I'll be damned if I'm spending my last few hours with either the Commies OR the Johnsons!) Then there are the diet books – the magazines that promise control over your own flab. And there are physical fitness magazines – do-it-yourself *to* yourself. There are consumer products rating magazines that promise you won't be as likely to get ripped off if you read them first. There are computer magazines that help you to feel less confused in that bewildering field. And business opportunity journals that hold out the hope of financial independence. The magazine stand's message is that you do not need to be stuck in your present circumstances; that you can have clout; that you are not helpless.

Another popular magazine section – the one dealing with video in all its forms – has the same message, and an additional one. It is important to notice that while there are perhaps a dozen highly visible magazines having to do with video-television-satellites-VCRs, there is not one dealing with radio. *Audio* is well-represented in the hi-fidelity/stereo/music area, but there is no nationally distributed magazine that deals exclusively with radio.

The programming choices available to a cable subscriber or satellite dish owner are usually made explicit through several different kinds of locally printed program guides, some available as newspaper sections, others avaiable free at checkout stands, and so on. But because most music-format stations provide the same service all the time, newspaper radio guides are usually not very specific about programming, and some newspapers do not print radio guides at all. One content analysis of radio–TV columns published in 1980 found only 12% contained an item about radio (even though there were 10 times as many radio as TV stations on the air).[23] As a result, radio stations are often forced to produce their own "guides," which generally do not have circulation nor impact comparable to newspaper TV sections.

There is one reason why there are video guides, VCRs, multichannel cable systems, satellite dishes, and thousands of places to rent videotapes: All of these other media offer the listener some amount of control over what they listen to, and when and where they listen to it.

The popularity of satellite dishes even in areas served by cable is explainable by the vast increase in program choices they promise. When either cable or satellite service is coupled to a VCR, then the viewer increases his or her choices not only of what he or she sees, but when and where. The viewer becomes the producer. And the producer's role is enhanced still further through the use of a VCR for time-shifting or playback of pre-recorded movies. For the radio listener living outside large metropolitan areas with their wide range of signals, the number of available radio stations is likely to be less than the number of cable TV signals. And few people use audio cassette recorders to "time-shift" radio programs (usually because what was on when they were not available to listen is virtually the same thing that is on when they are). It is very rare to find an audio cassette deck that has both a programmable timer and a radio tuner built in, as VCRs have. What is sold instead are audio dubbing decks, that allow the *audio* "producer" to record the specific tracks off of a recorded cassette onto a blank cassette in the desired order. But note that the source material is another cassette, not a radio station.

If the listener does not find what he or she wants on your station, he or she will

[23]Adkins, G.R. (1984). What would radio-television critics like us to understand? The critics speak. *Journal of Broadcasting, 28*(3),358.

either go searching for it on some other station, or will switch over to nonbroadcast audio sources or to video or even some other medium. But the consumer *will* be in control. There are now too many choices beside radio to ever act any other way.

Control: Appearance Versus Reality

The radio station that succeeds in this environment is likely to be the one that conveys the feeling of putting the listener in control of what he or she hears. The Top 40 pioneers of the 1950s tried to supply at least the appearance of control. They put in machines to make recordings of phone requests so that they could then select for airing those requests that matched their playlist and clock anyway. If you listened then, you had the sense that at least one lucky requester was getting to hear what he or she wanted, even if that song was not what you were after.

Stations that at least present the appearance of letting the listeners be in control will do better than those that do not. But the most successful ones will be those that really do attempt to alleviate the listener's sense of frustration and helplessness. And that concept has to be at work in all program areas, not just with music.

Because the radio station has already chosen the music, the listener will probably derive the greatest sense of control from what the announcers say, and from the other spoken content (weather, traffic, news). These elements can serve not only the classic "surveillance of the environment" functions, but can also help the listener to cope, by arming her/him with information. In the same way, disc jockies can supply attitudes and viewpoints and in the process may become surrogate "soapboxes" for the listener.

Attention To and Usage of Competing Media

The point was made earlier that the *in* attention that can be paid to radio is one of its great assets. Radio does not demand that the listener "hang on every word" in order to enjoy it. But it is interesting to note how the current younger generation of media consumers process (utilize) competing media. Today's younger listener has grown up with printed media, radio, and television. He or she is accustomed to using all of these media, and in some circumstances will use them simultaneously instead of serially. About 20% of the undergraduates surveyed in my radio-TV classes (admittedly not a random sample by any stretch of the imagination!) often use *three* media at once. Typically, the TV is on with the sound turned low so that either the radio or the stereo can be played. While that is going on, they read. The printed medium, then, has foreground attention, and the radio and television share secondary attention. Sometimes the TV takes attention away from the radio and the book. A particularly interesting TV scene, guest, or event will demand primary attention to the TV, so the radio's sound is turned down, the TV's sound is turned up, and the book or magazine is closed. After the interesting segment is over, the previous pattern resumes. But it is important to note that nowhere does radio get primary attention in this media triad. And while some of the undergraduates surveyed watch TV with mostly undivided attention, none reported listening to radio that way. And although radio's open-endedness demands some "work" on the part of the listener, radio listening (like TV watching) is still a physically passive activity.

Earlier, radio was shown to be an indulger of daydreams—a mentally active but physically passive situation. Radio's rhythms, its structure, the appeals of its program content all exist to attract and hold the audience's attention. But once that attention is given, however marginally—what else is in it for the listener?

The Rewards of Interaction

To figure out why people listen to the radio when they have other media to choose from, or when they do not need to listen to anything at all, try to find out why some people ride motorcycles when they do not need them for transportation, or why people spend lots of money to ride chairlifts up mountains in the winter cold just so that they can go through the torture of skiing back down.

When a person is out for a motorcycle ride or goes skiing just for the fun of it, the gratifications he or she gets from interaction with the machine or the skis are in some way analogous to the ones he or she gets when listening to the radio just for fun.

Riding a motorcycle or skiing a mountain are exercises in the laws of physics, and the factors of aesthetics—an unreeling of the vectors of time, space, and force. While time, space, and force are all quantifiable in a physics lab, they can also be identified as attributes of aesthetic experiences. Because these vectors are used throughout the rest of this book, we need to begin to understand them now.

The Rewards of Exploring Time/Space/Force

Why ride, ski, or listen when you don't have to? One answer is, to explore your relationship with space over a given unit of time while using only the appropriate amount of energy (force). In skiing and riding, that may *not* mean going as fast as you can. Some forms of motorcycle riding (trials, for example), require lightweight machines and very *slow* speeds but with high concentration on balance and control. And even the fast bikes do not seem fast after a while at sustained high speeds— because any stimulus presented for too long eventually stops being a stimulus. Instead, motorcyclists on fast bikes often enjoy stopping quickly and starting quickly—using the bike's braking and acceleration abilities to the fullest, just as skiers enjoy the combinations of speed and braking that puts them in control of the mountain. Similarly, a talented actor can take an audience through the full range of emotions with high believability, putting them in touch with ideas and images they might not otherwise have had. And as is elaborated later, a well-programmed radio station can move the listener in time and space, requiring from him or her (and also supplying to him or her) appropriate amounts of energy (force). It can give the listener a sense of control, perhaps over some of the programming, but surely over some aspect of his or her private life. It can increase awareness of where the listener stands in time and space. And it is a highly credible service all the while – functional, but not only that; amusing, but not only that either.

In a way, it comes back to control. What modern industrialized people often seek is the 100% closed loop between human being and the environment or the machine. What we want in an increasingly mechanized world, and one in which nature holds the final cards, is the sense that we are in control of the powers that are in control of us. Skiing and motorcycling do that. The participant decides when and where to go. When you point your skis downhill or twist the throttle, *you* decide how fast you move. It is a closed loop.

The Listener's Agenda: Enjoying the Process

When a person goes skiing or motorcycling, he or she is at least partly responsible for the outcome. The participant has an agenda. But with an entertainment event, the audience is not responsible for the outcome. The audience does not arrive at the entertainment event with an agenda beyond simple enjoyment. Turning on the radio is a singular event, but listening to it is an ongoing process. Processes or procedures (like skiing or operating a motorcycle) can be interesting in themselves, without reliance on additional content for enhanced enjoyment. Doing the procedure has intrinsic rewards that surpass whatever the extrinsic ones might be. Put simply, in riding motorcycles, getting there is more than half the fun or else you'd go by bus. (Downhill skiing does not even pretend to be a form of transportation; it is purely for giggles.) Unwinding a twisty road or a gladed trail your way is better than having someone unwind it for you.

The problem with some radio programming is that somebody else does unwind it for you. The disc jockey or automation system is driving the bus. The listener just sits and looks out the window. Without the sense of personal participation – of an energy exchange taking place in time and space – the radio listener becomes detached, passive, and a candidate for tune-out. Live concerts and theatre exist because the audience *wants* to sacrifice control for the uniqueness and electricity which comes from observing the risk and open-endednes of ephemeral experiences. Most TV programming (except breakings news and sports) lacks such electric anticipation. Talk radio is ephemeral, like theater. But most music radio repeats the well-known song, oftentimes accompanied by the obvious introduction. One of radio's attributes is that it is a low-demand medium. But *demanding* little is not the same as *offering* little. There needs to be the chance for audience participation.

THE FLOW EXPERIENCE

Process is the most fun to do because it results in the "flow" experience. Dr. Mihaly Csikszentmihalyi at the University of Chicago has studied activities that are intrinsically rewarding. When we are deeply involved in these activities, the feeling we get is a sense of "flow." "Flow" is the elementary reward in what we enjoy. The person in flow loses a self-conscious sense of himself and of time. He gains a heightened awareness of his physical involvement with the activity. The person in flow finds, among other things, his concentration vastly increased and his feedback from the activity enormously enhanced.[24]

The increase in concentration during a flow experience is not willed—it comes automatically. Sometimes people in flow report altered senses of time and space, so that an individual is able to be aware of his or her actions, but is not aware of that awareness. The challenging nature of the activity does not allow time for the individual to become introspective about his or her performance. The individual does not judge him or herself from the perspective of a third party. In fact, self-criticism seems to destroy flow.

And yet, clear feedback of some kind is essential for flow to occur. The racketball player knows immediately whether or not his shot was a good one—and there is not time to get neurotic about why it was not better. The same is true of surgeons and performing pianists. But, Dr. Csikszentmihalyi pointed out, the nonperforming artist must derive his or her feedback from "an internal sense of rightness. The feedback is not an end in itself, but rather, a signal that things are going well. The person does not stop to evaluate feedback."[25]

The radio performer is in the odd position of being involved in a public performance before an audience (like the pianist), but with virtually no way to get reliable immediate feedback. The radio announcer stuck in a studio must derive flow from that elusive "internal sense of rightness."

A flow activity cannot be too simple or easy, because that leads to boredom. Nor can it be too demanding, because that leads to anxiety, which also stops flow. And the way it is done correctly should be unambiguous, like a tennis shot that lands in-bounds but where your opponent cannot return it.

Can Radio Listening Be a "Flow" Activity?

Is radio listening ever a "flow" activity? If a person in flow "finds his concentration vastly increased," how does that fit with the concept that the business of radio is to promote *in*attention? How can a person be both inattentive, almost dreamlike, and also be concentrating deeply? The answer is, people do not pay just one consistent level of attention to radio. The level of attention in part varies with the person's state of arousal/fantasy/satiation. It varies by overall mood. It varies by time of day, and is affected by where the person is and what else they might be doing. "Inattention" and "concentration" are flipsides of the same listening coin.

For the radio listener, where is the "enhanced feedback" that flow activities offer? When radio demands so little of the listener, where can there be a sense of having met a challenge? The answer this time lies in smiles, frowns, laughter, and even

---

[24]Furlong, W.B. (1976, June). The fun in fun. *Psychology Today,* p. 35.
[25]Ibid., p. 36.

tears. There are mere kinaesthetic responses, but they are also a kind of feedback. They are feedback in the sense that they confirm to the listener his or her participation in the listening event, and through that, his or her kinship with the speaker or singer, or his or her synchronicity with the spirit of the music. Years ago, I pulled to the curb of a busy street to hear the rest of Steve Winwood's "If You See a Chance" the first time it came on the radio, to give full attention to all it was saying. The deep sense of longing that it brought was confirmation of a commonality with somebody else who felt he must strive against settling for less.

The flow experience from an activity like radio listening is likely to be short-lived. In most music formats, it lasts either as long as the song, or as long as the jock's entertaining chatter. The music progression that is proposed later allows the possibility of more sustained periods of flow.

Kinaesthetic Responses

Can processes be fun merely to observe (watch or listen to)? Yes, if the observation of a process can provoke in us kinaesthetic responses. Kinaesthesia is the sense whose end organs lie in the muscles, tendons, and joints. These sense organs are stimulated by bodily tensions; thus they are sometimes called "the muscle sense." In kinaesthesia, the capacity for sensation that we think of as the aesthetic sense is tied to bodily reactions. Laughter and tears are kinaesthetic responses. So are goosebumps or sweaty palms. You have these responses most often when you are actually doing something (skiers and motorcyclists grin a lot), but you can have them as an observer, too. Evoking a kinaesthetic response in a listener has to be one of the highest goals of the radio arts. To do so is to create "the willing suspension of disbelief"–to cause the listener to forget that what he or she is really responding to is a gaggle of wires and diodes in a box!

But of course, the radio listener at that moment is not hearing the technology of the receiver. Instead, he or she is listening past it, through it, as a participant in an experience where performer and listener are joined in a kind of communion. Just as the kinaesthetically involved listener is mindless of the radio receiver as a technology, so it is in the "flow" experience that some participants report having no sense of the place in which the activity occurred.

On the other hand, skiers and motorcyclists are consciously employing the vectors of time and force to explore space, often to achieve a heightened awareness of their relationship to it. Could it be that radio listeners, too, seek a certain set of spacial cues that serve to heighten the probability of kinaesthetic involvement? That question is answered in the next section.

MAJOR POINTS

1. Men and women differ in theirs fantasies, with men more interested in risk-taking, and women more interested in caring and social acceptance.

2. Both men and women claim their greatest sources of actual pleasure are their children, marriage, hobbies, vacations, and friends. Media that supply a chance to fantasize help to bridge the gap between wishes and reality.

3. Relaxation (satiation), excitement (arousal), and fantasy are among the underpinnings of human compulsion.

4. Fantasy, arousal, and relaxation are not byproducts of radio listening. They *are* the product.

5. The opponent-process model states that every life event that causes strong feelings or moods also triggers an opposing biochemical process. The result is a wavelike pattern of mood alterations that vary among people in terms of frequency and intensity.

6. The program director needs to take chronobiology and especially circadian rhythms into account when scheduling radio programming.

7. When relaxed, people tend to follow a 90-minute consumption cycle (a length like that of sleep patterns). This cycle decreases to a 60-minute one when under stress.

8. Aristotelian dramatic structure (exposition, development, building to a climax, resolution) displays a wavelike pattern similar to both the nightly sleep cycle and to the opponent-process behavior model.

9. The greater the number of major appeals (conflict/competition, comedy, sex appeal/personality, information, human interest) that are offered by a program, the greater the chance the show will succeed.

10. Radio concentrates on the three middle levels of Maslow's Needs Pyramid (safety, belongingness, and esteem), satisfying them at the same time that our adequacies are questioned. Audiences seem especially to be seeking ways of enhancing feelings of self-worth and of receiving nonexploitative reassurance.

11. The radio station that succeeds in an era where computer games, home-programmed media, and even self-help magazines all promise more control is the one which actually does try to involve the listener in helping to determine programming.

12. The *process* of listening to the radio can be rewarding if the listener has a sense of interaction employing the vectors of time, space, and force.

13. The ultimate interactivity is the "flow" experience, in which the kinaesthetic response of the listener simulates the completion of the (otherwise missing) feedback loop.

PART II

Formats, Soundscapes, and Voices

In this section, the reader should gain a greater awareness of production values and management procedures as they relate to formats, of the acoustic spaces in which radio happens, and of the part that the human voice plays in them. Chapter 5 looks at format invention and development, the production "glue" that holds a sound hour together, and the way a music format needs to be managed. Chapter 6 concentrates on the way differences in the sound space cause changes in recorded music, in announcing, and in production. Chapter 7 pays special attention to the human voice as a physical presence in that space, making gestures through speech.

CHAPTER 5

Format Structure and Management

In a 1969 speech, one of the two or three people most responsible for the advent of format radio – Gordon McLendon – said:

> I have always been a listener, concerned almost entirely with what came out over the radio. Nothing has ever happened to change me in all of those years, and I feel now as then that it is the programs, which come out over the radio loudspeaker . . . that are all that matter in the end . . .

This chapter needs to lead off with a short history of radio music formats. By taking a look at how music has been presented on radio for the past 30 years, we can begin to understand which assumptions and "rules" make sense and which need to be challenged.

A BRIEF HISTORY OF RADIO MUSIC FORMATS

Music and News

By the mid-1950s, with the dual threats of television stealing radio audiences and newly built radio stations increasing competition for the audiences that remained, radio programmers were in a frame of mind to try almost anything to keep radio afloat. For decades, radio stations had been the mass medium, trying to be all things to all people. But as the total listening audience began to shrink because of television's increased popularity and availability, and as more and more new radio stations came on the air, programmers realized that differentiation might be a way to attract audiences. The continued success of stations such as WNEW in New York seemed to indicate a possible direction. For decades, WNEW had programmed a music and news format, and had done reasonably well with it even against the network flagship stations in the Big Apple. But as both radio network programs and radio network station audiences defected to television, WNEW and stations programmed like it managed to maintain their audience. The apparent reason was that the music and news format did not demand long-term or high-level attention from the listener, as the typical dramatic shows on the networks did. Listeners could enjoy a few moments of music and a little news while they did other things. The music and news format—because it placed low demands on listener attention—could accompany lots of other activities. Instead of competing with television, head-to-head, it could fit into the moments when listeners were not available to watch TV because some other activity took precedence.

Countdown Shows

"Your Hit Parade" had been a radio network staple since the 1940s. And independent music and news stations had often featured listings of the popularity of current records, and even carried "countdown" shows that played the Top 40 or so songs that week. Audiences for the countdown shows, where only the popular songs were played, seemed especially strong. So it is not surprising that programmers working for some of the major chains of independent (non-network-affiliated) stations, such as those owned by Todd Storz and Gordon McLendon, adapted the Top 40-countdown concept and turned it into a continuous format. By playing only the 40 or so most popular records they were catering to what the audience had already proved they wanted to hear. The concept of the hit-oriented playlist had been born.

Top 40 and the Limited Playlist

The success of the general Top 40 concept led many stations to try it. The proliferation of stations all playing the same music inevitably resulted in an attempt at differentiation through refinement. For instance, on some stations, certain records were restricted to being played only in certain dayparts, when the target audience for that music was most available. But the most important concept in developing the limited playlist came through a chance observation, about 1957. As the almost legendary story goes, station owner Todd Storz and programmer Bill Stewart had been sitting in a bar in Omaha, and they had been observing the behavior of both the patrons and the staff in regard to the tunes they played on the jukebox. Not only did the patrons play the same few favorite tunes over and over, but, as the place began to close, they saw waitresses going over to the jukebox and dropping their own money in to play the same songs still another time. Shortly after that, Storz and Stewart went back to Storz's Omaha AM station, KOWH, and began to install a refinement of the limited playlist concept in which the most popular hits were repeated more often than the less popular songs. The concept of the limited playlist applied the behavior of those waitresses at the jukebox. The reasoning was, people wanted to hear the most popular songs more often than the less popular ones, so even though a station might call itself a Top 40 station, it would really only play about 30 records, and of that 30, it would play the top 10 far more frequently than 11 through 20, and so on. The ultimate outcome was a station like WMCA in New York, which went to a surefire list of just the top 10 songs, playing them over and over again, 24 hours a day. Listener fatigue set in pretty fast with just 10 tunes, but WMCA had positioned itself as a sort of "hit utility" – if the listener wanted to hear a megahit, all he or she had to do was tune over to WMCA and it would be played soon enough. WMCA's extremely limited playlist and very tight top-hit rotation was the exception rather than the rule. Most Top 40 stations played 20 or 30 records. But they repeated the top hits more frequently than the lesser ones.

Differentiation Via Oldies

Once most Top 40 stations had installed some form of the limited playlist featuring heavy rotation of the top hits, the need for further differentiation arose again. The only two obvious choices were to shorten the list a la WMCA, or to expand it. Most stations chose to expand it by adding oldies. Oldies (or "gold" as Top 40s often called the songs) were hits of the past. They had proven their popularity. The theory was that oldies were as safe to play as were the top hits. Unsafe songs were the new ones. Thus, although at one time in the 1960s, record companies were releasing hundreds of singles each week, only three or four were added by most stations, and they only added those when the songs had proved their popularity at some other station or in some other way (record sales, name value of the artist, etc.).

Eventually, most Top 40s were playing a selection of oldies. Some stations tried an all-oldies format, figuring that because all the songs had been popular, they should continue to gather good audiences. Most of these stations found that all-oldies did not succeed as well as they had expected them to. Past popularity was not *ipso facto* a guarantee of present-day listener appeal.

Differentiation Via Presentational Style

As "rock and roll" became "rock," and as pop music styles in general evolved, stations also began to differentiate themselves on the basis of their presentational style. Some stations emphasized the more mellow, soft sounds in rock, and some eventually went back to pre-rock and roll music to rerun the sounds of the big band era and the days when Broadway musicals and the movies were the major source of pop tunes. Some did not go that far, but did call themselves "Adult Contemporary" stations, which means that they played mostly current hit songs, but omitted the tunes appealing only to teenagers. Another group of stations played primarily cuts from albums, realizing that the rising popularity of album sales as compared to sales of single records appeared to signal that people wanted to hear certain artists, not just certain songs. However, most of these album-oriented rock stations have wound up playing fairly familiar artists, and they often program many familiar songs, although not necessarily ones that have been megahits.

As formats proliferated, the major factor discriminating one from another has been the addition of qualifying adjectives to describe the major music genres. In defining their music, stations generally want to appear to advertisers as if they were highly inclusive of many types of listeners, without falling into the trap of trying to be all things to all people. Thus, some of the terms the industry uses are *purposely* obfuscatory. Radio researcher Rob Balon has studied the differences between the buzzwords and slogans radio people employ and the terms the public actually uses to describe stations. For example, he found that the term "Hot Hits" for a CHR format was identified by listeners most often by the old term "Top 40." Two popular terms, "Magic" and "Power," turned out to be benign in their ability to describe the music, but very good for recall. On the other hand, "fresh," "mix," and "variety" seemed to be good music descriptors, along with "easy listening," "rock," "rock and roll," and "oldies." Balon reported: "[The term] oldies is so strong that I've seen successful Gold stations begin using the word and immediately gain a cume increase, because the audience can relate to the product. But "classic" isn't a listener word.[1]

Three Ways to Classify Formats

Because keeping terms "loose" is good for business, this book has no intention of trying to tighten them up. But it is useful for the sake of later arguments to attempt to classify music formats on the basis of whatever commonality they display. The terms listed here include a noun that identifies the category of style, form and/or content into which the music might be classified, if the standard industry terms were abandoned:

1. *Roots.* This method classifies on the basis of the origin of the music, often with the assumption that the category appeals to listeners other than those who generated it (examples: Reggae, classic country, folk songs).

2. *Targets.* A second system classifies on the basis of the presumed target listener to the music. Thus, the term *contemporary hit radio* (CHR) is contrasted to *adult contemporary* (AC) by the presence of the word "adult" in the latter term, which indicates that the music includes most of the modern hits found in CHR, but without the youth-appeal sounds that would alienate an adult listener (examples: big band, nostalgia).

3. *Presentation.* The third classification method describes one aspect of the music's presentation. In these formats, the music's "roots" are taken for granted while audience "targets" are tacitly assumed (examples: easy listening, beautiful music).

---

[1]Denver, J. (1988, February 5). What your slogan really means. *Radio & Records*, p. 42.

The terms *roots, targets,* and *presentation* are intended to be new umbrella terms under which traditional music format names may be clustered. They are not meant to be predictive. That is, it would probably not be enough to go into a market, listen around the dial for a while, and then decide that there needed to be a more "presentationally oriented" station, or one that paid more attention to the music's "roots." The three words are merely useful as alternative ways of defining radio's music; they are not candidates for format terms themselves. Indeed, by the end of this book, the case is made that adhering to the standard music format notions may no longer be the best way to program a station's music.

In a Rob Balon study of listeners' "top-of-mind" awareness of the characteristics of Adult Contemporary stations in the top 50 U.S. markets, 500 respondents were asked what came to mind first when the station's call letters were mentioned. Although Balon's focus was on the problems that loomed for stations that received many "don't know" responses, it is interesting to note that among the market-leading stations, the most mentioned responses were ones with a music *mood* rather than a music *popularity* orientation. Such answers accounted for the top 46% of responses in the study of market-leading Adult Contemporary stations. Specifically, the responses were "soft and mellow rock," 22%; "mellow music," 14%; and "variety," 10%. Lesser responses included the popularity term "oldies," 8%; the mood term "easy listening," 6%; and "Joe morning guy," 4%.[2]

Audiences Attracted By Various Formats

A study of contemporary radio formats by James T. Lull, Lawrence M. Johnson, and Carol E. Sweeny published in 1978 tried to construct a generalized demographic profile of audience types attracted by each of several formats receivable in the Santa Barbara, California area.[3] The format terms used then were *Top 40, Beautiful Music, Middle of the Road, Live Progressive Rock, Automated Rock,* and *All-News.* Today, the term *Middle of the Road* might be equated with *Adult Contemporary,* whereas *Live Progressive Rock* would likely be called *Album-Oriented Rock. Automated Rock* apparently included both hits and album cuts – it could be anywhere from an AOR to a CHR to a soft rocker today. (Interestingly, as is shown later, listeners often do think of "automated" as a format rather than as a means of presentation.) All News might well be a Talk-News format now. And the Country format was conspicuous by its absence.

In spite of the need for such updating, many of the findings are still worthwhile. Marital status, for example, was a good predictor of format preference, with Beautiful Music and News listeners mostly likely to be married, and Automated and Progressive Rock (AOR) listeners least likely. Geographic stability was also a characteristic of All News listeners, while Automated and Progressive Rock (AOR) listeners were least likely to have remained in a single location for the 2-year period

---

[2]Balon, R. (1988, November 25). What listeners don't know can kill you. *Radio & Records,* p. 30.

[3]See Lull, J.T., Johnson, L.M., & Sweeny, C.E. (1978). Audiences for contemporary radio formats. *Journal of Broadcasting, 22*(4), 439–453.

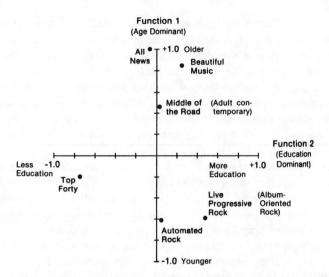

FIG. 5.1. Age and education-dominant discriminant functions (after Lull, Johnson, & Sweeny).

preceding the survey. In both cases, age was a common factor, with older people being more likely to be married and to stay in one place.

Education turned out to be the other important discriminating factor. Higher education levels were characteristic of Beautiful Music, Progressive Rock (AOR) and All News listeners.

The authors of this study offered a chart on which radio formats were located in space to reflect *both* the age and education dominant discriminant functions. Figure 5.1, using updated format terms and with such additional clarifying labels as *older, younger, more education,* and *less education* is based on the original chart by Lull, Johnson, and Sweeny.[4]

Electronic Media Habits Related to Various Radio Formats

Two of the three authors of the aforementioned study produced a follow-up to it which was published in 1981. This time, they studied consumption of other electronic media by listeners to each format type, and found these indices to be accurate at predicting which radio format would be preferred. For purposes of the study, *electronic media* were defined to include movies as well as records/tapes and television. Table 5.1 cross-lists five radio formats with the mean number of minutes per day spent with radio, TV, and records/tapes, and the mean number of movies viewed in theaters in the previous 3 months.

Table 5.1 shows the Album-Oriented Rock (AOR) audience listened to less TV but spent far more time with records/tapes and with movies than other segments of

---

[4]Ibid., p. 448.

TABLE 5.1
Radio Format Preference by Electronic Media Consumption
(From Lull, Johnson, and Edmond, "Radio Listeners' Electronic Media Habits"[5])

Format Preference	N	Radio*	TV*	Records/ Tapes*	Movies**
Top 40	77	124	178	54	3.4
AOR	153	188	90	92	5.1
Adult Contemporary	34	164	175	27	1.9
Beautiful Music	69	167	176	16	1.4
All News	20	130	129	26	2.5

*Radio, TV, and Records/Tapes expressed in mean mins. per day with each medium.
**Movies expressed in mean number viewed during the past three months.

TABLE 5.2
Format Preference and Selectivity Rank

Format Preference	Selectivity Rank
Top 40	2
AOR	1
Adult Contemporary	3–tie
Beautiful Music	4
All News	3–tie

the audience. AOR listeners also listened to the most radio in this study. Combined listening to records/tapes and radio exceeded 41/2 hours per day for the AOR listener. On the other end of the scale, Beautiful Music listeners spent the least time listening to records/tapes and also viewed the fewest movies.

Not reported in Table 5.1, but mentioned in the text, was the topic of selectivity. The authors noted that some listeners had developed media habits that reflected a desire to spend time with media over which they could exercise a choice as to content. (Recall the discussion of control and the desire to be your own "producer" in chapter 4.) This desire was seen in the significant positive associations on the time spent listening to records/tapes and the time spent viewing movies.[6] Table 5.2 shows a "selectivity" or "self-programming" ranking for the five given formats, based on the number of minutes of records/tapes listened to, or the number of movies viewed. What Table 5.2 suggests is that AOR listeners, while they tended to spend the most time with radio, also spent the most time programming their own music. This may be because they tend to be highly involved with music anyway, not necessarily because they are disenchanted with the way their AOR station programs it. Beautiful Music listeners, on the other hand, seem the most pleased to take what radio offers.

The result of changing Table 5.2 by deleting the All News format (the only one

---

[6]Ibid., p. 35.

TABLE 5.3
Format Preference in Selectivity Rank Order,
with Age-Dominant Discriminant Function Shown

Format Preference	Selectivity Rank	Age-Dominant Function
AOR	1	−.59
Top 40	2	−.21
Adult Contemporary	3	.46
Beautiful Music	4	.85

(In age-dominant function, −.59 = youngest; .85 = oldest)

which is not a music format), and re-arranging the formats in selectivity rank order, and expanding to include the age-dominant discriminant function that Lull, Johnson, and Sweeny found in the first study, is shown in Table 5.3.What Table 5.3 shows is a clear tendency for younger listeners to program their own music. Although for AOR fans that is not necessarily at the expense of radio listening, for younger Top 40 listeners it might be. There is no way to predict whether a generation of young listeners who are in the habit of programming their own media will revert to depending on radio programming for their music needs as they grow older, as beautiful music listeners now do. But "freedom of choice" is not something easily relinquished, so long as disposable incomes allow it.

More recently, the National Association of Broadcasters (NAB) commissioned a study on the psychographics of radio listeners titled *Radio W. A. R. S: How to Survive in the 80s.* (The second part of the published study is called *Radio W. A. R. S II: How to Push Listeners' Hot Buttons.*)[7] Among the findings were that AOR and Nostalgia listeners both thought of themselves as music experts; that Adult Contemporary fans were less involved with their station than any other listeners, while Country devotees were the most loyal; that AOR listeners often chose their station on the basis of peer group pressure; that Urban Contemporary listeners were the heaviest listeners (in this study) and also the most likely to use radio to change their mood.[8]

ARTS '82 National Music Preferences Study

The Radio W.A.R.S. study was both appreciated as "thought-provoking" and disdained for the simplicity of its methodology and findings. In the same year, the results of a potentially more useful survey of music preferences was published in the journal *Communications Research* and thus received much less fanfare among broadcasters. The study reported the results of a nationwide U.S. survey of music preferences that had been conducted in 1982 by the U. S. Bureau of Census for the

---

[7]Prepared by Reymer and Gersin Associates, Inc. Published by Research and Planning Department, National Association of Broadcasters, 1985.

[8]The psychology of formats. (1983, September 5). *Broadcasting,* p. 50.

National Endowment for the Arts under a grant to the University of Maryland Survey Research Center.[9] Known as ARTS '82, the survey consisted of over 17,000 interviews conducted with people ages 18+ across the United States. The data for the section on music preferences was based on a sample of 5,617 respondents. They were asked, "Which of these types of music do you like to listen to? Note that the question did not specify radio listening, concert listening, record listening, etc. – the type of listening was left to the respondent. The possible answers on the survey form were classical/chamber music, opera, Broadway show tunes, jazz, soul/blues/rhythm and blues, big band, country western, bluegrass, rock, mood/easy listening, folk, barbershop, hymns/gospel, other, and every type.

Two dimensions emerged from the statistical analysis that allowed each musical type to be placed in space relative to other types. The two dimensions were (a) "formality and complexity" and (b) "ecological or geographical base of the musical style."[10] The chart reproduced in the published article carried only the labels "Dimension 1" and "Dimension 2." I have supplied all the additional labels in Fig. 5.2. Dimension 1, formality and complexity, runs from high audience formality and performance complexity on the left (−) side, to low audience formality and performance complexity at the right (+) side. Dimension 2, ecological or geographical base of the musical style, has been relabeled "international or urban roots" at the bottom (−), and as "local or rural roots" at the top (+). I have also supplied two shorter labels – "uptown style" (−) and "downhome style" (+).

What is remarkable about this chart is that forms that are comprised of widely divergent content and that attract very different audiences may be at about the same point on one or both of the dimensions. Bluegrass and Soul/Blues/Rhythm and Blues are both perceived to be in about the same place along the dimension of low audience formality and performance complexity. It is the perception of their roots that separates them. Barbershop tunes and songs from Broadway musicals, suffer a similar dissociation on the higher side of the scale of audience formality and performance complexity.

Meanwhile, Barbershop and Bluegrass are perceived to be at initially the same place on the local/rural/downhome scale, even though they are separated by differences in familiarity and complexity. And Soul and Rock are thought to be at just about the same level of "uptown" intensity, although Rock is seen as less formal and complex compared to Soul.

It is interesting to note how music preferences in each of the four quadrants form fairly natural clusters: Hymns, Barbershop, Folk, and Big Band; Country and Bluegrass; Mood/Beautiful, Musical Shows, Classical, and Opera; and Jazz, Soul, and Rock.

---

[9]See Fink, E.L., Robinson, J.P., & Dowden, S. (1985, July). The structure of music preference and attendance. *Communication Research,* pp. 301–318. (Copyright © 1985 by Sage Publications, Inc. Reprinted by permission of Sage Publications, Inc.)

[10]Ibid., p. 310.

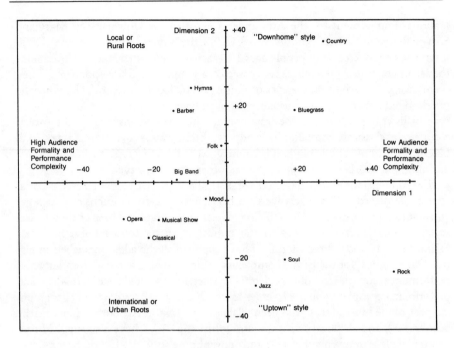

FIG. 5.2.   First principal plane for space created from the 13 music preference items.[11]

Of the 13 musical preference types, Rock and Country are positioned the farthest from the center intersection of the two dimensions, although both share the tendency toward low audience formality and complexity. It is evident that in order for a song to "crossover" from the Country to the Rock charts or vice-versa, it has to compromise its sense of roots, sounding neither rural nor urban.

The places where crossovers are most unlikely are from opposite diagonal corners. Barbershop or Hymns do not mix with Rock. Similarly, Country and Classical do not go together. By contrast, Classical and Rock have their "uptown" roots fairly close together, although the two formats are very different in regard to their complexity and formality. And Country and Hymns are fairly close to each other on the "downhome" dimension, although quite different in formality/complexity level.

Again, the chart in Fig. 5.2 is not specifically about radio listening–it is about music preferences in all kinds of listening situations. But it is based on a good national sample, and its formality/complexity and roots dimensions are a useful way of visualizing how formats based on these music types may be perceived. Most of all, the chart underscores that certain characteristics are common to what seem to be vastly different musical forms. That concept is important to this book, because

---

[11]Ibid., p. 311.

one of the main themes of the music selection process proposed later is that the traditional labels applied to music genres tend to be used as ways of excluding exposure to certain songs that would likely please the radio listener if given the chance to hear them.

The Symbiosis of Format Differentiation and Increased Ratings Detail

Why did the various music formats themselves develop? They may have been generated largely in response to increasingly sophisticated ratings reports that included more detailed demographic information. Top 40 blossomed in a time of very simple "headcount" ratings, when each station's overall market share was the most important attribute to be sold to advertisers. As a result, "losing" stations began to force the ratings companies to supply audience demographics in order to display subaudiences that the mass-appeal "losers" were winning. In order to better serve special target audiences, stations began "filtering" music that was on the hit charts, and the music trade magazines responded by developing specialized charts for easy listening, adult contemporary, and so on. The names of the charts coincided with the formats of the stations, and vice-versa. The symbiosis between chart names and station formats is important. For example, veteran record producer Jerry Wexler began his music career in the late 1940s writing for *Billboard*. He dropped the term *race music* and instead coined the familiar phrase *rhythm and blues*. We have to wonder if rock and roll would ever have become a national phenomenon in the 1950s if announcers of the day had had to use the term *race music* rather than *rhythm and blues*.

Once subaudiences could be more clearly identified, programmers began to develop formats that appealed to those audiences. This made possible such current phenomena as ethnic-appeal hits and ethnic-oriented music charts. But at the bottom of it all, every format exists first as a safety net: to prevent being wretched. If there is great entertainment along the way, that is a bonus. Formats do not assure entertainment; they only guarantee that something godawful will not get on the air.

PROGRAM INNOVATION

A Very Slow "Shazzam!"

Was it a "Eureka!" lightbulb-turning-on-over-the head experience that Todd Storz and Bill Stewart had that night in an Omaha tavern? Probably not. It is fair to say that the "Eureka!" event is a rarity in radio. Coupled with that, the true radio programming genius was, and still is, an endangered species. What there usually is instead is a group of people (not just one), working over relatively long periods of time (not overnight), making evolutionary (not revolutionary) changes in programming which (over the long term, and seen in the widest context), alter the content and presentation of radio programming. There is support for this less glamorous but more realistic viewpoint even in the limited playlist story. Storz was quoted in 1957 as saying that he "became convinced that people demand their favorites over and

over while in the army during the Second World War."[12] When I interviewed Bill
Stewart, he rebutted that idea, saying

> I think that is a little early. Maybe he originally got the idea at that time, but I don't
> think he ever put it into practice. I think that it was reinforced maybe by several things
> like this (the tavern experience). It was put into practice long after World War II.[13]

Keep Fixing What Is Not Broken

In this example, one of the crucial elements of the development of new radio format
elements is apparent: a gestation period, during which an initial idea receives tangible,
observable reinforcement. And although it is not obvious from the quotes just given,
a "Let's try it!" attitude on the part of station management is also essential if new ideas
are to succeed. It would not be stretching the facts too far to say that the program
directors and station managers who made a success of Top 40 just when television
seemed to be killing radio tried things in desperation that they would not have tried
had their stations been even moderately successful. It just may be today, when most
stations can find an important demographic to target for, and almost every FM station
in any realistic market can make money, success may be stifling format innovation
more than any other factor. A maxim to describe this might be that with format
success comes the narrow repetition of a formula; with format failure comes the wide
exploration of alternatives. The term *format failure* can be only a relative one. It cannot
mean that absolutely nobody is listening and never has; what is more likely is that
some of the people who used to be listening have left, and those who used to listen
a lot are now listening less. This is the present situation with most AM stations. But
today, mere "slippage" is failure nationally, because time buyers want to see a growth
trend, not shrinkage in audience. So the challenge in radio today is to find ways to
keep the format fresh and continue fine-tuning it. FM programmers may feel that
radical notions can wait for the future, when technological innovations, economic
problems, or shifts in audience behavior provide a greater threat to FM's current
bloom. But just as it is hard for the frontrunner in a footrace to pace him or herself
when there is nobody to catch up to, so is it difficult for most FM programmers today
to foster the sense of desperation that results in creative flux, and out of which comes
really new radio. The prevalent attitude of FM stations today, which parallels that
of an immortal but nameless engineer, is "Don't fix it if it ain't broke." AM's that are
still succeeding today *never quit* "fixing" things.

The Product Life-Cycle Model

If the flux of technological, economic, or social change are the primordial mud out of
which comes radio, and if within that mud there are occasional sparks of insight that

---

[12]Land, H. (1957, May). The Storz bombshell. *Television Magazine,* p. 3.

[13]Stewart, B. Interview with the author. New Orleans, Louisiana, November 4, 1971.

Copyright © 1972 by Field Enterprises. Reprinted by permission of Johnny Hart and NAS, Inc.

can–if the environment is hospitable–change old forms and grow new ones, then it seems useful to trace the development of a programming element from its inception through its maturation and decline. Dr. Richard J. Lutz, writing in *Radio & Records,* adapted a life-cycle concept for consumer goods to the life cycle of a record on a station's playlist. He used the standard stages in the life cycle of a consumer product to describe the introduction, growth, maturity, saturation, and decline of a record.[14] But the same concept can be applied to radio formats, as shown here:

The Progeamming Idea Life Cycle

Introduction–The programming idea is new, and only a few listeners are likely to have heard it.

Growth–The programming idea begins to gain acceptance, and there is rapid growth in the number of people who have heard it and like it.

Maturity–The number of listeners continues to increase, but not as quickly as in the previous growth stage. The station might be getting better ratings by now.

Saturation–The station featuring the new program idea enjoys its peak popularity at this stage.

Decline–The program idea begins to wear out as people begin to grow tired of it.

The Dangers of Maturity

One of the thrusts of Lutz's article was to warn music directors about a pitfall of call-out music research–namely, that for a record to be recognizable when only a 10- to 15-second chunk of it is played to the called party over the telephone, the record would have to be roughly in the maturity stage already.[15] If that is so, Lutz pointed out, then the station is giving up the possibility of introducing new records to its listeners, and eventually the station will be left with outmoded music. "Most

---

[14]Lutz, R.J. (1978, November 17). Media marketing: Right down the line. *Radio and Records,* p. 12.
[15]Ibid., p. 12.

consumer goods manufacturers believe that they must have products in *all* stages of
the life cycle in order to ensure long-run success," says Lutz. "Therefore, innovation
is the necessary lifeblood for the future."[16] The statement seems true for programming ideas as well as for records, especially when so much of the program
"innovation" on many stations is actually mere borrowing of ideas from stations in
other markets. Just as most stations hold back on many new records to see which
"opinion leader" stations add the song to their playlists, so do many program
directors take their cues on programming ideas from stations in other markets,
rather than developing their own ideas. The problem with "borrowing" an idea
from another market is that the idea may already be "mature" or even in the
"saturation" stage by the time it gets on local air. And the idea might even have been
an old one when it went on the distant station!

Because of What You Aired Yesterday, Today Has to Be a Little Different

Not enough people in radio programming are convinced that what worked literally
only yesterday may not work literally tomorrow. They are not concerned enough
with a long view that says, "How am I going to take very familiar elements and mix
them with enough novel ones to make the sequels original in their own right?"
"How am I going to acknowledge that *because* of what I did for them yesterday on
my radio station, my listeners have every reason to expect something a little bit
different today?" You can count the people who think this way (and have the clout
to do something about it) on the fingers of one hand. Because they have guts and
imagination, we call them geniuses and gurus. Without taking anything away from
these valuable industry leaders, it must be pointed out that the compliment does not
seem so big when you consider the competition.

The very format elements that a program director has become inured to (because
he or she has heard them so many time before that he or she really does not "hear"
them anymore) are the format elements that will become—or already are—tuneout
factors for the listener. A station should have some audio consistency, but not to the
point where it becomes predictable.

John Leader, in his "Programmer's Notebook" column in *Radio and Records,* wrote
about a conversation he had had with a PD who was worried about slipping ratings:

> Seems his station, which used to be considered "the hot newcomer," was now
> perceived as "the old-line rocker" since a newer station had recently blossomed in the
> ratings. We talked about a lot of things but finally settled on the fact that the new
> station sounded a lot "less professional" (his words) than his did and that puzzled him.
> I pointed out that maybe that was why listeners were leaving his station for the new
> one . . . not because it sounded "less professional" but because it sounded "less
> predictable" [my words].[17]

---

[16]Ibid.
[17]Leader, J. (1980, April 4). Programmer's notebook: Are you predictable?" *Radio and Records,* p. 18.

Clones

Often, a successful station in one market (be it AM or FM) is analyzed, and then an attempt is made to clone it for another market. The transplant fails a surprising number of times. Why?

When he was younger, one of my sons wondered why second movies rarely equalled the original in impact. By "second movies" he meant the films with a Roman numeral II (or III, or more) in their title. We mused over that for a while, and then we considered the *Star Wars* films. We agreed that the original *Star Wars, The Empire Strikes Back,* and *Return of the Jedi* were all good. My son pointed out that "George Lucas wanted to make more than one movie from the beginning. The first one is called Episode Four right in the titles."

Don't Just Imitate the Form – Understand the Function

Is that a clue? If you think you are only going to make one show – and then you discover that it is successful – maybe you feel compelled to make another that has the same success factors as the first. Only what are those success factors? Too often, moviemakers have fallen into the trap of imitating the form without understanding the function. Take *Smokey and the Bandit II.* Somehow, somebody got the idea that the essence of *Smokey* # 1 was car chases. There is no denying that smash-em crash-em is an appeal in the original, but so are some fine characterizations and a novel plot. They tried to do it again in *Smokey II,* not understanding that one of the appeals of the original was the very fact that it was so original! To have a similar impact, the sequels needed another character like Sheriff Buford T. Justiss, or a dog like Fred, or an idea as madcap as hauling a whole truckload of Coors to Atlanta at cruise-missile speeds. Hauling a cargo of something else to some other place at breakneck velocities is *not* being original. One of the strong appeals of the original is originality.

As already stated, radio is most definitely in the cloning business. The copying of formats and program ideas aside, the very nature of radio programming is repetitive – because the listener's routines are. But the listener is often turning to radio to provide entertainment and information that lifts him or her out of that routine. It is possible, because station operations also exist on a strict daily rhythm, to begin to believe that providing something that has a very familiar *form* (such as a rigid format) is the same thing as fulfilling the *function* of a radio station. Sometimes it is, but all too often, it is not. The very term *format* tends to deny the question of what function is being filled – the assumption is that if you play a certain format, the function *is* being fulfilled.

Programming consultant Lee Abrams, interviewed by *Radio & Records* in 1988 about the state of the AOR format, said:

> *Lee Abrams:* AOR is in what I call a mid-life crisis. All the passion is gone. We're "waltzing" – just going through the motions. No one is listening to records. The format is unbelievably boring.

R&R: But it all comes down to ratings, and they're still good.

Lee Abrams: That's right. Ratings equal money, and money is the ultimate tranquilizer. The attitude becomes, "We're making lots of money. Everything's cool." Of course, GE said that when they made lots of TV sets in the 60s. All of a sudden the Japanese came along and look what happened.[18]

Editors and Inventors

First, let us stipulate that most of the people who say they are doing radio programming are acting more as editors than as inventors. The great majority have adopted or adapted a format and a style and a music rotation that has worked for some other station, and they then conceive of their job as one of "fine tuning" rather than real innovation. The minority of people who are actually involved in trying out new kinds of radio programming are attempting to find or invent the programming equivalent of the Holy Grail. They are trying to invent the one format, the one music rotation, the one presentational style that will be good forever, once they find the key.

The problem with that concept is that it suffers from the same maladies as successful one-shot movies that then go into the cloning business. The very idea that you can "finally" get it right, once and for all, misses the point about originality completely. Nothing is ever "finally right" in radio. It is only right for today. Tomorrow it will be a day older, and the world will have moved on.

SPECIAL PROBLEMS OF AUTOMATED STATIONS

An automated radio station is – by its nature – one that operates from the premise that there *is* one formula/format that works the same way hour after hour. Only if the station positions itself as a "music utility" can that be true. The more the listener seeks other entertainment values, the more "bare bones" automation becomes a pejorative term. It has already been mentioned that savvier radio listeners can readily identify an automated station as such, and some even think of "automated" as synonymous with a type of format. They are sometimes right. Because many automated stations run the simplest of formats to minimize equipment expense and programming time, "automated" often equals "simplicity of presentation" in the listener's mind. (This is less the case with syndicated programming delivered live via satellite by such providers as Unistar and Satellite Music Network.)

Serving the Machine

IBM used to have a slogan that dealt with a lot more than just computers in this mechanized age. It went, "Machines should work. People should think." It applies

---

[18]Kojan, H. (1988, January 29). Abrams: AOR in serious crisis. *Radio & Records,* p. 44.

beautifully to computers, which are essentially "dumb" until people tell them to do something. But it also applies to a radio station, which is an assemblage of highly technical equpment all of which exists only to extend the human creations of a small number of producers to a large number of consumers. Recall that in radio's earliest days, the announcer's job was to introduce the songs played by a live band in the studio! The announcer was present as the music was being created. Radio airplay of phonograph records began to diminish the announcer's relationship to music making. And today, at an automated station, surrounded with machines that play the music, tell the time, turn on the network, and announce the music, it is easy for the staff to get the feeling that they are serving the machine, rather than it serving them—a sort of human sacrifice to the great god Go-Cart. But the IBM slogan still applies: "Machines should work. People should think." What they should think of is ways to communicate more effectively—both as entertainers via the airwaves and as managers via the interoffice memo.

Machines As Scapegoats

Automation often becomes the scapegoat for difficulties in management and pro-gramming policies—and especially for failures in communication—that would have been present in a live station, although the larger staff and the generally more complex hierarchy at a live station tend to conceal them.

The Typist As Program Director

Far too many automated station are actually programmed by the person who types up the logs, and not a true program director. It is the log typist/traffic person who determines spot rotations, where to fit in promos, and so forth. A discouraging number of these people have little or no concern with the station's sound—they simply need to get X number of spots played between 3 and 6 p.m. tomorrow. Yet, by generating the pre-log, they are the folks most directly in charge of the order of presentation on that radio station. No wonder it seems that the machines have taken over!

Going Live

Some automated stations operate live during some dayparts. One reason is to handle heavy spot loads or complicated network joins and news feeds. Just as often, the reason revolves around a morning "team" or format that presumably can only happen live. But the question then is, if the programming on the morning daypart seems more effective, why not use it all day long? ("It's 9 a.m. and back to automation. Do you know where your entertainment values have gone?")

Syndicated Production Collides With Local Production

The audience successes enjoyed by automated stations up to now have almost always been attributable to matching the right syndicated service with the music format voids to be filled in the given market. But with ever more stations on the air vying for increasingly distracted listeners, the right music mix alone is not going to make the difference. Today, with satellite-fed music that includes live jocks, there is the possibility of much more timeliness and topicality on the part of syndicated air personalities. A jock in Los Angeles or Chicago can work comments about today's world and national news, music stars, and so on, into his or her show, and convince us that this is happening live in the studio of our local station. The listener stands to be convinced, that is, until the station plays a local spot or promo. Then it can all go down the tubes. In too many cases, the disparity between network production quality and local production quality is ridiculous. The automated station, plugged into a satellite-fed network, sometimes sounds like the Jekyll and Hyde of the airwaves: great, then gawdawful. ("It's 9:14. Time for a network spot break. Do you know where all your production values have gone?")

Lack of Vocal Variety

Automated stations often also suffer from a lack of vocal variety, which tends to sound more severe than does the same deficiency on a live station. There are two reasons for this dearth of voices: small staffs mean fewer voices to do spot production, and many of the popular syndicated formats de-emphasize host chatter. There are a couple of possible answers, beside the best solution – hiring an additional production person. For one, salespeople could be more aggressive in getting client's voices on the air. (The same is true for whoever handles local PSAs and bulletin board items.) It takes more work and time to get a good reading, then still more to edit it for timing and cohesion, but making local people sound good wins lots of friends, some of whom have money to spend. A second answer is for the automated station to buy the services of a good voice in another market. Most syndicators can make available announcers to do time, temperature, IDs, promos, and so on. Unfortunately, they often want to sell the *same* voice that is heard on the music service they already are providing you. Don't buy the same voice unless the station has a very sophisticated automation system and somebody who can really program it so you can be assured that a "bumper" of some other material will be aired between the two different voice cuts. Because, after a lack of vocal variety, the next most prominent sign of poorly run automation is "matching voices" that don't match.

Staying Fresh

Then there is the question of how often a cart is freshened. Again, this is a problem for both live and automated stations, where the attitude often is "One good one is enough." And once more, the problem is exacerbated because there is less live announcing on an automated station. The trouble is, carts deteriorate very little with repeated use. Back in early Top 40 when spots were dubbed to acetate discs for playback, the day when the disc became too scratchy for the air was also the day the content got re-cut. Carts can be played hundreds of times with little degradation in sound; digital playback systems promise no deterioration at all. And some carts *will* be played that much. The people in charge have stopped hearing the elements that listeners hear all the time. It is the "mortar" not the "bricks" that needs the attention of the production staff and of management.

Attitudes

Attitudes are extremely important to the functioning of a radio format, and they are everything to an automation system. If the staff hates it, it is likely to sound horrible. If the staff understands what a well-run system can do to *improve* the sound of (especially a small-market) station, how it can give them time to be more creative, then the station is likely to sound pretty good. But some stations are so poorly managed that the staff actually practices a form of "sabotage" on the automation, purposely failing to encode carts with EOM tones, misprogramming the system so it plays the same jingle back-to-back, and so forth.

These days, the failure of an automated radio system to sound nearly as good as a live operation is almost never the fault of the machinery. It is much more likely to be the fault of poor management that somehow finds it easier to talk to computers than to people. As a result, some formerly-automated stations convert back to live operations. But killing the messenger has never made sense. "Machines should work. People should think." (It's 9:43 and your machines are working. Are your thinkers thinking?") And most of all, is anybody in management listening to the radio station like a listener?

THE PRIMARY TASKS

Management's primary task is to make it easy for a station's air and production staff to make the best possible programming. In the introduction to this chapter, Top 40 innovator Gordon McLendon was quoted. Todd Storz, also a Top 40 pioneer, shared the philosophy that building audience through careful programming was an important managerial role – in fact, he put it ahead of boosting sales.

Trying Things

McLendon and Storz deserve admiration because they were willing to "take a shot" – try things. In Thomas J. Peters' and Robert H. Waterman's classic management book, *In Search of Excellence* (which begat the NAB's *Radio in Search of Excellence,* also a fine effort), the number one point in their list of eight attributes of excellent companies (that is, ones that are "continuously innovative" – and therefore adaptable to new situations) was "a bias for action." In the early days of the Top 40 format, McLendon and Storz were frankly experimenting with the limits of radio. They did it in part because – at least at the outset – they did not have much to lose:

radio was thought by many to be a dying medium, killed by the onslaught of television. Just as a surgeon can take more risks on a cadaver than on a live patient, so were Storz and McLendon able to feel free to gamble a little. There was a prevailing attitude of "Gee, we've never done that before–let's try it!" More than any era since the beginning of radio broadcasting itself, the early Top 40 period was a time of rich experimentation and change. "Leaving well enough alone" would simply have been a foreign idea to Storz and McLendon. And because they encouraged program experimentation, between them and their staffs they came up with the Top 40 format that many people believe "saved" the radio industry.

The Staff as Source of Ideas and Productivity

At the stations he owned, McLendon had a system for regularly collecting new ideas from staff, and then redistributing those ideas back out to other staff members via a newsletter. He did not for a minute believe that all the good ideas came from top management in his office. McLendon certainly subscribed to another of Peters' and Waterman's eight attributes, called "productivity through people." The main idea here is that "The excellent companies treat the rank and file as the root source of quality and productivity gain."[19] At a substantial number of radio stations, the air staff and office personnel are considered necessary evils. (I know of a station that was designed with two floors: all of the programming and engineering staff are in a mostly windowless basement, while all of the sales and management staff are on the light, airy top floor with windows in every office.) These tend to be the stations where sales come before programming, rather than the other way around. In those places, the sales people are part of the elite, and their status tends to be resented by the balance of the staff.

If Programming is the "Product,"
Then Invention Must Be the Norm

It is too bad that in the past few years, broadcasters have begun talking about their programming using the term *product*. The consumerist viewpoint that is behind such a term deserves applause, but it unfortunately tends to mask the fact that broadcasting is a service business. (Products are tangible goods you can hold in your hand–services are not.) By extension, the people involved in radio are involved in a service industry, not a product business. More specifically, they are being called upon to make entertainment that is amusing and relaxing and fun, and informational programming that makes a complex world understandable. People involved in such endeavors cannot just be cranking out the same standardized product every day. For entertainment to be fun, and for information to be useful, all kinds of creativity, novel approaches, and invention are necessary. Those are the last things you want if your people are supposed to be bolting together Buicks, where you

---

[19]Peters, T.J., & Waterman, R.H., Jr. (1982). *In search of excellence* (p. 14). New York: Harper & Row.

want them all to look like Buicks when they roll off the line. But nobody is going to tune in a news show for the same news they heard yesterday, and no entertainment program or format can exist for long by repeating a limited set of elements. Yes, you do want some uniformity and consistency on your station: you want people to be able to recognize its sound as distinctive from all the competing signals, whenever they tune in. But you do not want that listener to get the feeling he or she has heard it all before, that this is a repeat. And to avoid that, your station must encourage the inventive ideas, the stabs at novelty, the flourishes of freshness. The people at your station must be seen by management as its most important asset – as important as the license to broadcast. The whole staff of the station needs to understand that management does view them "as the root source of quality and productivity gain."[20]

Another of Peters' and Waterman's eight attributes is "autonomy and entrepreneurship." They said, "The innovative companies foster many leaders and many innovators through the organization." And again: "They don't try to hold everyone on so short a rein that he can't be creative. They encourage practical risk-taking, and support good tries."[21]

Job Titles Versus Job Descriptions

This ties in with the earlier point about achieving productivity through people. One of the typical circumstances to be found in a radio station is a fairly tight organization chart, at least in terms of titles. As already deplored, some stations tend to pass out titles as rewards when they feel they cannot pay more. Doing so tends to further clutter the organizational framework. That might be livable if the majority of stations had – or encouraged employees to develop – realistic job descriptions. Most do not. Some stations assume that a program director does the work expected of a program director, but what that is – for sure – is probably never spelled out until he or she is called on the carpet for getting it wrong.

It may seem that a plea for job descriptions to fully flesh out the meaning of radio's numerous job titles would work against Peters and Waterman's (and my) general affection for loose organizations. Not really. Keep in mind, job titles are the problem, job descriptions do not have to be. The job description gives management and the employee the time and the room to really figure out, and then spell out, what he or she is supposed to do to meet the goals of the organization. The job description, then, can become one of the resources in meeting that goal. But the most important point is that resources, objectives, and goals all change over time, and so do people! It should not really be called "management by objectives" unless those goals and objectives are re-examined often in the light of experience. In the same way, managers should expect to rewrite the job description in concert with

---

[20]Ibid., p. 14.
[21]Ibid.

each employee at least once a year. The world around your station changes, and the employee in that world changes. If management is good, the employee is probably changing for the better, growing to be somebody who is more valuable now than when hired. Unless that job description changes, the station organization may neglect to supply the challenges that the person needs to continue to grow. How many people move from one station to another not because the pay is better or the lights are brighter, but because the old job offered no further challenge? Continual updating of job descriptions is a way to keep the challenges coming, especially if the employees suggest some of them for themselves.

Rewriting job descriptions on at least an annual basis is not only a good time to bring management's goals in line with the people resources at hand, but it is also a good time to provide some "strokes" to the crew, putting positives in writing. Further, it is also one of the few ways available to make an end-run around the pesky job titles. If everyone is really clear on what is expected and what the opportunities are, job titles are not necessary. Job titles are only like signs on restroom doors: helpful if you do not know your way around, but absolutely superfluous once you do. If management and staff together can write really complete, fulfilling job descriptions, then consider getting rid of job titles, so that employees become "who" again, instead of "what," and so that the job at hand – making terrific program- ming – becomes a job that everybody is involved in.

Toward Another Meaning for "Productivity" in Radio

When a radio station becomes "productive" in a time-sales sense (which means that it is productive from a commonly held management perspective), then the radio station may become less appealing to the people who work there, which in turn might bring a *decrease* in worker productivity. The reasons are these: (a) The more spots that are sold, the greater is the production load. The greater the production load (without an increase in staff help), the poorer the production job each sponsor receives on their commercial. All other things being equal, a spot with poorer production values will be less productive of sales results for the client. (b) Higher spot loads (should) cut down the amount of time that a jock can talk between records, so that when he or she is on the air, he or she sounds less creative and more like an automaton playing records. Thus, productivity increases (in the traditional sense) provide *dis*-incentives for typical air personnel to do their best work. What is needed is nothing less than a re-definition of station productivity – one that does not sacrifice quality and self-esteem for profits; one that instead finds a way to generate increases both in spot loads and in personnel involvement.

The Compaq Computer Corporation is a case in point. Compaq's stock tripled in value in 1987, and it became a member of the Fortune 500 club. Benjamin M. Rosen, chairman of Compaq's board of directors, said "Our strategy is to sell at a price that is roughly the same as IBM but to provide more functionality . . . . . . This is a switch on the common strategy of offering the same functionality for a lower price."[22] Assume that a station's commercial load is the "price." Stations usually do the traditional thing to compete with other stations: They lower the price of spots, which increases the spot load. Compaq did not do that. They kept the same price, but increased the product's functionality. That is what radio needs to do more often.

It is crucial to have strong people – and enough of them – in production. When the spot load goes up, the first person hired should be an additional production person. What should not happen, but does all too often, is for one or several of the jocks to assume responsibility for part (or for an additional part) of the production load. This is a no-win situation. Either the station has a jock who puts his or her best into spot production and then is tired when he or she gets on the air, or a jock who puts his or her best into an air shift and is tired when he or she does the spots. The answer is to hire someone to do only production. In addition to getting dependably top-notch commercial work, the station gets a very important bonus: never need a jock's voice appear in a taped commercial while that jock is doing a live show. More variety in voices means less monotony for the listener. And it saves the impact of the live jock's voice for live announcements. If your station has an announcer who can speak well, can ad lib, can be creative, and can keep it in good taste, then it is a waste of talent to confine that person to canned announcements, time, temperature, and titles. If he or she is really good, you can even charge extra for live announcements during that person's show. Recall that Arthur Godfrey had sponsor commitments more than a year in advance when CBS cancelled the best salesman network radio entertainment programming ever had.

The idea of taping something in production is to do a better job of it than you can hope to do live. The production should require such precision, such care, that only one "take" in a dozen might be good enough to air. The model should be the jingle companies, which spend thousands of dollars an hour to get an orchestra on tape, to make the perfect beds for later vocal overdubs. The instrumental track has to have enormous integrity, because it will be heard repeatedly. The same should be true with the production your station does. Do you want 'em good, or do you want 'em by sign-off tonight? In the automobile business, wanting them by sign-off gave us Corvairs and Vegas, not Toyotas and BMWs.

The Full-Time, Off-Air Program Director

This chapter must conclude with an argument for that endangered species, the full-time, off-air program director. Try out these four situations to see why: (a) If your station is automated, you listen for the transitions. (b) If you are the typical GM or the sales manager, you listen for what your advertisers would hear. (c) If you are a jock, you listen to other stations, because you're sick of yours. (d) If you are a newsperson, you're too busy to listen to anything but the police scanner.

---

[22]Compaq pits the compatible against big blue's breakaway. (1988, August 15). *Insight*, p. 42.

In each of these cases, who listens like the listener? Nobody, unless the program director specifically has that job responsibility. The PD probably does listen to check the music, and to monitor what the jocks say. But unless management has specifically asked the PD to be the listener's surrogate, that task tends to "slip through the cracks." And unless management keeps the PD's air work and production load light, he or she will get too bogged down in daily work to ever get around to listening like a listener. Oddly, the radio station can still go on sounding very professional. But it may be out of touch with its audience.

MAJOR POINTS

1. All current music-based radio formats are an elaboration of the music and news style that became the Top 40 formula.

2. Since the advent of Top 40, stations have sought to differentiate themselves on the basis of their oldies mix, and on presentational style. Three overall classification methods are "roots" (origins of the music), "targets" (presumed listeners), and "presentation."

3. "Hot clocks" have been devised as a means of codifying the presentation of certain kinds of music in a systematic way. Popularity has been a major component of every post-Top 40 format.

4. Nothing is ever "finally right" in radio. A format is only a safety net, not an answer forever.

5. With format success comes the narrow repetition of a formula; with format failure comes the wide exploration of alternatives. The successful station "pretends" that failure is ahead, and keeps fixing what is not broken.

6. The product life cycle, applied to radio programming, suggests that programming ideas should follow the same progression (introduction, growth, maturity, saturation, and decline) as popular music. A station probably needs to have ideas in all stages of the life cycle. Borrowing an already mature idea can be dangerous.

7. Because of what you put on the air today, tomorrow has to be a little bit different.

8. When one station clones the sound of another, too often the clone tries to imitate the form without understanding the function.

9. The special problems of automated stations include: making machinery the scapegoat for difficulties in management policy and communication, allowing the log typist to actually program the station, the disparity between the sound of syndicated and local production, a lack of vocal variety, mismatched voices, and failure to stay fresh.

10. Station managers can profit by looking to their staffs as a source of ideas and productivity. Constant invention and innovation needs to be the norm in radio programming.

11. Job titles often get in the way; job descriptions help everyone to define goals.

12. Most stations could benefit by hiring more people to do production. Commercials would get made with more care, and there would be more vocal variety on the air.

13. The off-air program director can better serve the station as the listener's surrogate, keeping the station in touch with its audience.

CHAPTER 6

The Structure and Appeal of Acoustic Space

THE LISTENING ENVIRONMENT

The three most revolutionary sound mechanisms of the Electric Revolution were the telephone, the phonograph and the radio. With the telephone and the radio, sound was no longer tied to its original point in space; with the phonograph it was released from its original point in time. The dazzling removal of these restrictions has given modern man an exciting new power which modern technology has continually sought to render more effective . . .[1]

A chapter that intends to produce greater awareness of the importance of acoustic space must include excerpts from the mind- and ear-opening book by R. Murray Schafer, *The Tuning of the World,* just quoted. Through the power of his writing, Schafer is able to make us imagine sounds and silences we have never known. Most of his book serves to awaken the reader to the noise pollution of industrialized society, a good part of it the result of mass-mediated sound reproduction. He does not go so far as to say we should shut off all radios and TVs and go back to crickets, but in reminding us of what a *natural* high-fidelity sound environment is like, he provides the historic baseline from which all *electronic* sound-making has departed. If radio production and performance people desire to attract and entertain listeners in today's soundscape, they must do so cognizant of the natural acoustic environment that mankind has inhabited for all of previous human history. Millenia of experience with that natural sound environment have become a part of our instinctive behaviors. When radio production and performance lack certain of the familiar

---

[1]Schafer, R.M. (1977). *The tuning of the world* (p. 89). New York: Alfred A. Knopf.

sound cues of the past, some listeners might react strangely, or might fail to react at all to certain sound stimuli.

Hi-Fi/Lo-Fi

What we think of today as high-fidelity sound reproduction might be very different from what Schafer means by the term. Quite early in *The Tuning of the World,* Schafer introduced the concept of hi-fi and lo-fi soundscapes, which he referred to in his later writings:

> A hi-fi system is one possessing a favorable signal-to-noise ratio. The hi-fi soundscape is one in which discrete sounds can be heard clearly because of the low ambient noise level. . . . In the hi-fi soundscape, sounds overlap less frequently; there is perspective – foreground and background. . . . In a lo-fi soundscape individual acoustic signals are obscured in an overdense population of sounds. . . . Perspective is lost. On a downtown street corner of the modern city there is no distance; there is only presence . . .[2]

The Shift from Discrete to Continuous

Next, Schafer explained the importance of the change from discrete, interrupted sounds to continuous, uninterrupted sounds, and pointed out the impact that shift has had on our perceptions of sound today. He said that the Industrial Revolution has introduced the continuous sound into the soundscape: a sound that has no beginning or end, but that drones on continuously. When a sound occurs more frequently than about 20 times per second, individual impulses lose their distinctiveness and blend into a single tone. Most such droning sounds emanate from our modern labor-saving machines. Examples include the whir of a refrigerator, the buzz of fluorescent lights, the throb of an automobile exhaust, the whoosh of an air conditioner, even the mumbling of an electric clock. These devices are so much a part of our lives today that we no longer are much aware of their existence. That fact even took Schafer by surprise:

> A few years ago, while listening to the stonemasons' hammers on the Takht-e-Jamshid in Teheran, I suddenly realized that in all earlier societies the majority of sounds were discrete and interrupted, while today a large portion – perhaps the majority – are continuous. This new sound phenomenon, introduced by the Industrial Revolution and greatly extended by the Electric Revolution, today subjects us to permanent keynotes and swaths of broad-band noise, possessing little personality or sense of progression.

> Just as there is no perspective in the lo-fi soundscape (everything is present at once), similarly there is no sense of duration with the flat line in sound. It is suprabiological. We may speak of natural sounds as having biological existences. They are born, they

---

[2]Ibid., p. 43.

flourish and they die. But the generator or the air-conditioner do not die; they receive transplants and live forever. . . .

The function of the drone has long been known in music. It is an anti-intellectual narcotic. It is also a point of focus for meditation, particularly in the East. Man listens differently in the presence of drones, and the importance of this change in perception is becoming evident in the West.[3]

This, then, is the aural milieu in which the producer of radio must expect the message or music to be heard: a soundscape in which there may be so many different sounds that they blend into indistinctiveness, and where the flat-line drone of machinery is the norm, even in the quiet suburban home. Note that when Schafer said "Just as there is no perspective in the lo-fi soundscape (everything is present at once), similarly there is no sense of duration with the flat line in sound," he was making a case about naturalistic sounds needing to exist in space and time as discrete events.

Signal Processing

Years ago, some radio stations tried adding reverberation to their program line in order to make their air sound seem more distinctive. Most of them have since given it up, because added reverberation disturbs both the space and time of the original sound, leaving the listener with less distinctiveness, not more.

Today, audio processing is often set up to deliver a bright, crisp sound, emphasizing upper midrange and treble frequencies. These frequencies have the ability to cut through most background noise well. But depending on the listening space, the bump in high-frequency output can make the overall tonal balance unnatural. In nature, treble frequencies are the ones most easily absorbed, bass frequencies being the hardest to attenuate. Thus, at considerable distance from the loudspeaker, a listener to a station using "bright" processing would hear more treble than that person would hear from a real sound source located the same distance from him or her as the loudspeaker. At a middle distance, especially against background noise such as that encountered in a car, the frequency balance is okay. But listening up close, as with headphones, results in excessive hiss and over-sibilance because of the strong upper midrange and treble. Thus, a radio station whose audio processing is "bright" is probably best listened to at intermediate distances in relatively noisy environments.

So-called "brick wall" compression and limiting is employed by many hit music stations to make them sound as loud as possible. Usually, one result is that the dynamic range suffers. Such stations, even if they play compact discs as their audio sources, sound very different from CDs played in the home.

---

[3]Ibid., pp. 78–79.

But there is another factor in considering compressed dynamic range, which has to do with whether the listener plays the radio as a foreground or a background experience. A listener to a foreground service such as an Album Rock format typically plays the music fairly loud. When that listener encounters a talk segment on a highly compressed station, it turns out to be unnaturally or even excruciatingly loud. An AOR station that marketed itself as a high fidelity outlet (wide dynamic range, low or no compression) might try running the music at peak modulation, then purposely backing down the level of talk segments so that they are a little less loud than the music. This heretical idea (having your commercials not quite as loud as the music) has the virtue of retaining your targeted music listeners through stop sets, rather than forcing them to reach for the radio to turn the volume down. Once their fingers are at the radio, they might change the dial. Quieter talk segments would give them less reason to do so.

The reverse situation might apply to Beautiful Music or New Age/New Adult Contemporary formats. Because the music on these stations is often heard at background levels, talk segments would be aired at peak modulation, and the music would be transmitted at a lesser loudness. Again, this is a way of super-serving the target audience.

I am aware that not fully modulating the signal decreases an FM station's stereo coverage area, and that some listeners choose a station simply on the basis of loudness. But these disadvantages may be outweighed by the chance to super-serve a narrow segment of the audience that currently finds the volume level of talk segments on their favorite station in sharp disagreement with how they like to hear their music. When they play cassettes and discs on their home and car stereos, they do not have these problems. Radio's loudness processing should not create any for them.

Headphone Listening

According to the Spring 1988 RADAR report, quoted in the NAB's *Info-Pak* for July–August 1988, almost half of all the radio listening being done today is taking place outside the home:

> Rising from 39% in Spring 1978, the share of radio listening taking place outside the home now accounts for 52% of all radio listening. The advent of mini-headset portables and high fidelity walk-along radios has fueled the growth in this out-of-home listening pattern. More listening is taking place not only in the workplace, but also walking to and from work as well as many other outdoor locations such as the ball park, beach and pool. The 13 percent rise in listening outside the home since 1978 is pretty evenly divided between the increase in drive time listening in cars (6%) and radio listening taking place in all other locations (7%).[4]

[4]Audience outlook: Radio audiences stable – But changing. (1988, July–August). *Info-Pak,* p. 7. (Published by the National Association of Broadcasters for members and associates.)

In regard to the increasingly prevalent headphone listener, Schafer said that the "head-space" created by earphones makes the hearing experience an utterly different one. When using headphones, sounds that would normally be located at some distance from the hearer instead seem to come from a point inside the hearer's skull. The headphone listener does not hear things as they actually exist in acoustic space. The whole universe of sound happens within the sphere which is the wearer's head[5] This is especially true of monaural sources, such as the human voice, which seem to come from deep inside the very center of the headphone wearer's cranium.

In a way, the wearer of headphones, whether listening to radio or cassettes, is living inside of a small yet ultimate acoustic shell. But even when heard through loudspeakers in a room, radio can act as what Schafer called a "sound wall."

Radio As a Sound Wall

Schafer pointed out that the castle garden of the Middle Ages was surrounded by an actual physical wall to enclose the sounds of its birds and fountains and to screen the sounds of the hostile world outside. Today, Schafer said, ". . . radio has actually become the bird-song of modern life, the "natural" soundscape, excluding the inimical forces from outside."[6] He pointed out that the portable radio listened to outdoors is often operating in a signal-to-noise ratio of about one-to-one, which drastically changes the way both the radio and the natural sounds are heard. Schafer concluded his discussion of the modern "sound wall" by pointing out that whereas walls used to be built in order to isolate sounds, these days sound walls are constructed in order to isolate. The high levels of amplification that some people employ to play back popular music are not meant to act as a social lubricant so much as a shield, allowing the individual to be alone, withdrawn, and disengaged from society. And with the prevalence of background music in public places, the sound wall has become omnipresent.[7]

Being cognizant of audiences in different environments with different needs for signal clarity and isolation or involvement allows the programmer to be intentional about serving those people. But it is difficult to imagine a level of signal processing that would satisfy both headphone and loudspeaker audiences, or a music-and-talk format that would please both background and foreground listeners. The programmer can *target* listening groups, but *delivering* specific groups is always more "iffy." In radio production, audio processing is largely a "set-it-and-forget-it" proposition, affected only occasionally and temporarily by records or commercials featuring echo, reverberation, or frequency processing of their own.

The case that Schafer made about sound walls almost portrays sound used in this way as a "force field." Sound walls keep unwanted sounds out, and isolate the hearer

---

[5]Schafer, p. 119.
[6]Ibid., p. 93.
[7]Ibid., p. 96.

to a limited acoustic environment. Headphones do this in an insistent, foreground way; sound walls do it in a persistent background way.

"Time" and "Force" Sound Parameters

The discussion of the listener's need for signal clarity, isolation, or involvement all have practical application in setting up the radio station's sound. The radio programmer can attempt to manage the *time* factors associated with the station's audio processing by consulting with the engineer who sets up the processing equipment. And the station might offer programming that works as an appropriate sound wall *force* for its target audience. That programming could range from background "elevator" music to foreground rock heard through speakers, to variations on these themes intended for listening in cars, to still further elaborations designed for headphone wearers.

Managing Perceived Acoustic "Space"

In radio production, controlling the amount of isolation or involvement is largely a format choice—and the choice of formats is also a long-term, generally unchanging situation. But if the audio processing *time* and the isolation/involvement *force* that a listener perceives are usually a compromise, the *space* need not be. Perceived acoustic space is a variable that can be under continuous control by the radio programmer. Indeed, perceived acoustic space and the rate of presentation are the two factors that can be most closely directed by programming people. Generally, only rate has gotten much attention.

In my audio classes, populated as they are by students who have used television from their earliest consciousness and who have only in their teen years discovered radio, it has proved helpful to use visual analogies to explain audio effects. They already know the "grammar" of TV as if it had been imprinted in their chromosomes; it is the supposedly simpler audio terms that are more difficult for them. Thus, to understand the importance of controlling perceived acoustic space, some analogies to television camera lens angles are useful.

A SENSE OF PLACE IN ACOUSTIC SPACE

TV Gave Up Space Exploration

If controlling the sense of acoustic space has been largely ignored in modern radio, at least it is also true that for about the past 30 years, television has not been working as hard as it might at exploring space either. Probably one of the reasons we still revere the so-called "Golden Age of Television" is because of the early style lenses that the cameras used until the mid or late 1950s, when the zoom lens came into widespread use. Prior to that, TV cameras had a turret with three lenses on it—a normal lens, a wide angle, and a telephoto. The camera had to be off-line in order to rotate the turret to a different lens. One of the effects of this was that a camera was forced to dolly in or dolly back in order to get closer to–or further away from–an object. In the process, other objects in the background were concealed or revealed by the relative change in size of the foreground object.

A zoom lens does not change the size of the foreground objects relative to the background ones. When it is zoomed in, they all grow at the same rate; when zoomed out, they all shrink at the same rate. And nothing is concealed or revealed behind them.[8]

So the net effect of using a zoom lens has been that it allows the camera to stay stationary, while the glassware in the lens does all the moving. Perhaps Golden Age television was more "three dimensional" in the sense that the viewer had a greater feeling of moving through space, toward–and away from–an object. When the camera got close to an object, it really loomed large compared to everything around it. And because the in/out camera movements are psychologically the most powerful anyway, the substitution of the zoom may have had something to do with diminishing the impact of later TV. (In 1988, ABC's use of tiny "point-of-view" cameras on skiers and lugers in the Winter Olympics at Calgary brought "the ultimate dolly" to sports coverage, while most prime-time shows continued to rely on the zoom lens.)

The Questions Raised by Zoom Lenses

If this were a book about the effects of television, then some of the next questions might be: What has 30 years of seeing things with zoom lenses done to our sense of community? Our sense of place? Our sense of being with someone, somewhere? If for the past 30 years television had been presented the way people actually see things (with a three-dimensional quality, with concealments and revelations in physical space), might our society be different compared to 30 years of television in which we get closer but things do not get bigger, and where the spaces behind things are left unexplored?

Because this book is about radio, the questions must be different. Television was enjoying its Golden Age at just about the same time radio was having its darkest hours in the 1950s. The rise of the Top 40 format happened in part because it was the only programming which seemed to find an audience in the face of the onslaught of TV. The earliest Top 40 disc jockeys were true personalities, and thus enjoyed considerable freedom to talk. Their inevitably less-talented imitators survived until programmers discovered that audiences could be increased by shutting up bad disc jockeys and playing more music. Eventually, most non-music programming (such as remotes, news, and of course commercials) came to be viewed as

---

[8]For a discussion of this effect and television camera movement effects in general, see Kipper, P. (1986, Summer). Television camera movement as a source of perceptual information. *Journal of Broadcasting and Electronic Media,* pp. 295–307.

tune-out factors to be minimized. Today, music format radio gets by with very little "talk" compared to radio as it was prior to Top 40, and very little of that talk happens in other than a studio environment. Thus, the predominant acoustic-space cues of modern radio come not from the announcer, but from the way the records are recorded. And too often, what is around that music on radio is the aural equivalent of a blue cyclorama curtain in TV: limbo.

Why Radio Sounds Like Limbo

The reason radio studios sound like "limbo" is because traditionally, radio control rooms and studios have been designed to be fairly "dead" to dampen the sound of the mechanical switches, solenoids, relays, and motors associated with radio production equipment. But these days, many of those switches are silent electronic ones, not noisy mechanical models. About the only noise still left in the modern control room is the broadcast cartridge player. Probably nobody *wants* to hear the sound of a solenoid slamming the pinch-roller against the capstan every time a cart is started, but is the only acceptable alternative dead silence? In its early years, television production people went through all kinds of contortions to hide microphones from view, even on talk and interview shows. Today, microphones are very much an accepted part of the picture. Why is radio still afraid of the minor sounds its sound-making equipment makes?

Control rooms and studios have also been designed to be neutral or benign in their effect on the frequency response of voices. The admirable idea has been to try to achieve "flat" (linear) frequency response, which translates to high fidelity reproduction. But these days, radio studios are virtually the only places where voices are heard that way. The more television has abandoned the studio for remote locations, the more it has gotten us accustomed to hearing announcers in all kinds of novel acoustic spaces. And it is the rare modern recording which seems to have been made in an acoustically dead studio. Many records today use chorus and reverberation effects to broaden or deepen the sound.

Questions Raised by Control Rooms

If being in acoustic limbo has been the case with radio for the last 30 years or so, then it must be asked, what has 30 years of hearing things from largely the control room perspective done to our sense of involvement in the community? What has the close-miked disc jockey done to our sense of being talked to by someone in an actual environment? If for the past 30 years, radio had instead continued to develop the announcer as a full-fledged actor in "the theater of the mind," or at least as a person at the site where the music was being made (as on the old big-band remotes), might our society be different compared to 30 years of radio in which only the musicians make such acoustic explorations?

Clearly, one challenge for announcing in the MTV era is for the announcer to create the same sense of *place* that the visuals do on carefully made TV. Usually, the control room mike, worked up close or at a middle distance–along with the very acoustic treatment of the control room itself–all make the announcer sound as if he or she is nowhere in particular.

The Ambience of a Remote

What is needed is a real acoustic sense of place, and of things that are happening in that place. Maybe more of modern radio should have the ambience of a remote, whether or not the announcer is actually doing one. The trick then would be to keep the atmosphere of the remote without losing the discipline of the studio.

One of the things that happens in a remote is that announcers and guests are sometimes *off-mike*. *Off-mike* is often thought of as a negative term, but it can be viewed as a positive effect, too. Because, when a person is off-mike, what is heard instead is the missing environment.

ABC television's coverage of the 1988 Winter Olympic Games was notable for more than its point-of-view camera visuals. The network was reported to have used more than 500 microphones overall, to be sure that there would not be any audio "dead spots" on bobsled runs, ski race courses, and so on.[9] ABC was trying hard to capture the total sounds of these wide-ranging events, just as for years football broadcasts had featured pickup of the sounds of scrimmage from a parabolic sideline microphone. In both TV and radio sports coverage, the sound of the competitors is mixed with the sound of the crowd, which is in turn mixed with the sound of the announcer. Notice that two of those three are environmental sounds. But also note that once the sports remote ends and the sportscasters "send it back to the studio," the sense of place in acoustic space largely disappears. That is why radio needs to have the ambience of a remote, even when it is in the studio. If the studio has been designed to sound "dead," it can also be processed to sound more "live." But most of all, many announcers must learn to sometimes work at greater distances from the mike, so that the sense of the space can come across to the listener.

Control of the important influence of the sense of acoustic space in broadcast music is considered in chapter 10.

RATE

It was mentioned earlier that the sense of acoustic space and the presentation rate are two factors that are very controllable by radio production people, and that only rate has gotten much attention. Actually, rate has been considered only in its largest, most obvious manifestations. Rate has always been a factor in music rotation systems (and is discussed at length later). Announcers speak at different overall rates

---

[9] Polskin, H. (1988, February 13). Keep your eye on pirmin zurbriggen–and other hot tips for your viewing pleasure. *TV Guide*, p. 8.

and thus suit some formats better than others. And the rate of individual program elements (such as commercials and jingles) has also been considered. In the mid-1960s, programmer Bill Drake decreed (for the stations he consulted) that the longest, least-produced spot should come early in a commercial cluster, whereas the shortest, most highly produced commercial should come last. The idea was to give the listener the sense of progressively shorter "talk" elements before returning to music, and heightened listener rewards achieved through the enhanced production. At about the same time, station jingles became available which provided a "tempo buffer" between a slow song transitioning to a faster one, and vice-versa.

Little consideration has been given to the "editing" rate of radio production – that is, how slowly or quickly the program elements are put together with each other. Again, analogies to television seem useful, to explain audio events to a generation that understands editing primarily from a visual standpoint.

Television Editing Applied to Radio

In television, the major editing effects are the cut, the dissolve, the fade, the wipe, and the key/super.

The cut is an instantaneous switch from one picture to another, and is by far the most common transition. The cut is like the segue in radio, except that the segue usually inserts a beat of silence between the full-up end of one element and the full-up beginning of the next.

The TV dissolve is very much like radio's crossfade – as the first elements are faded down, the next elements are faded up at the same rate. The replacement rate can be so fast the effect is like a cut (except with a slightly softer edge), all the way to a dreamy, languid transition lasting dozens of seconds.

The fade in TV is usually to or from "black" (although it could be any color). "Black" is TV's visual limbo. It is no place, no time, although time may be presumed to pass while in black. TV often goes to and from black between scenes, which is like a visual "new paragraph." Occasionally, TV will go to black and stay there for several seconds, often to allow time for what came before to be digested by the listener (e.g., several seconds of black after an obituary). It is a "moment of silence" for the viewers's eyes and mind. Overall, TV still uses more black than radio uses silence, because there are more dramatic moments on TV that demand such a visual pause. But radio too can benefit from pauses, as is pointed out in the next chapter.

Wipes and keys/supers are not really edits in the traditional sense, but ways of adding new information to the picture so that for a time the viewer's attention is shifted from the original scene.

A wipe is just a novel way of shoving one picture off the screen in favor of another. Today, radio counterparts of the wipe are not much in evidence, but back in Top 40's infancy, the playing of the next record would often be preceded by a highly produced intro which would proclaim "WQAM's Number Four-Four-Four" (with echo effect), or "WKKO's Rocket Riser!" Rarely was a song started without at least being announced by the jock, but featured music got the full production treatment. Short station ID jingles that gave the station's call letters just before or just after a song were called "stabs" or "shotguns," and these names are as good as any to describe the radio version of the wipe.

The super is like a dissolve held midway between two pictures, so that we see 50% of one and 50% of the other. The foreground elements in a super are transparent–we can see the background through them, which gives a wispy, dreamlike effect. (There is no audio equivalent because playing two records each at 50% volume is just audio chaos.)

The key also puts the elements of two pictures together, but in this case, the foreground elements seem opaque and thus they blot out the background elements in the other picture. Graphics of names, scores, and statistics are often keyed over the regular shot. In radio, the corollary to the key is the "drop-in" when it is used over some other element (not between elements). The key and the drop-in do not serve as transitions to something new, as the wipe does. Instead, the key or drop-in briefly adds information to the existing scene or sound, then returns to just that existing scene or sound without the additional information.

Radio Editing Rates

The previous introduction to the radio "editing" terms (segue, crossfade, silence, stabs, and drop-in) now allows a consideration of the editing rates that are inherent in certain well-established radio production procedures. Paying closer attention to editing rates could serve a station wanting to vary its editing between elements to achieve random variety, or that wanted to control editing rates to build a greater overall sense of rising and falling pace–to name just two examples.

The slowest edit is one where there is talk over a fade of the first element, talk over silence, then talk over the faded-up intro of the next element.

A slightly faster edit occurs when there is a fairly rapid crossfade between two elements (usually instrumental-to-instrumental) without any intervening talk.

Next fastest is an edit which is like the one above, but where talk occurs over the instrumental portions, usually in order to bridge between a talk or vocal segment in the first element and another talk or vocal segment in the second segment.

Faster still is a segue-with-talk: the first element ends full-up (no fade), followed immediately by talk over the faded-up instrumental beginning of a second element. This can also happen the other way around: the first element fades, with brief bridging talk over the fade until the second element is started full-up.

Fastest of all is the pure segue. One element ends with talk, vocal, or instrumental full-up, and the next element begins the same way, with only (at most) one beat between.

Most of the time, on most stations–even ones with very tightly controlled music presentation system–the editing together of the various other program elements is left entirely up to the discretion and ingenuity of the disc jockey. At the very least, this results in considerable disparity in the impact of the programming from jock to jock, even though they might play the same elements in the same order. At the worst, the way the program elements are edited together may work counter to the desired effect in controlling the order of the music and the commercials. So it seems worthwhile for stations to consider editing rates in their overall air presentation scheme.

This chapter has tried to develop the concept of the space between a listener's ears as a sound stage – a stage whose space is affected by the content presented, of course, but just as much by such factors as audio processing, the distance of the speaker from the microphone, the distance of the listener from the loudspeaker or headphone, the design of studio spaces, and the rate at which elements are melded together. In the next chapter, the stage receives its actor: the air personality.

MAJOR POINTS

1. Today we live and produce radio programming for consumption in what R. Murray Schafer called a "lo-fi soundscape" in which individual sounds are lost in a dense collision of other sounds.

2. According to Schafer, in an earlier time, most sounds were discrete and interrupted. Today, many sounds are like drones: one note, sounding continuously.

3. Audio processing that seeks to overcome the noise problems of the "average" listening environment by increasing upper midrange and treble is probably best listened to at intermediate distances in relatively noisy environments (such as cars), rather than through headphones or loudspeakers in a quiet room.

4. Today, said Schafer, the portable radio (played as a "boom box," or through earphones) exists as a "sound wall" that allows isolation, in the same way that stone walls used to be built to isolate sounds.

5. In radio production, controlling the amount of listener isolation or involvement is largely a format choice, and is thus not easily changed. But perceived acoustic space can be continuously controlled by the programmer.

6. The use of zoom lenses in television replaced camera-dolly movements that used to give a greater sense of exploring visual space. The radio control room/studio has helped radio to sound like "limbo." So has a generation of announcers who tend to work the microphone only at one fixed distance.

7. Television editing terms have audio counterparts: the cut = the segue, the dissolve = the crossfade, the fade-to-black = a silent pause, wipes = produced intros and ID jingles, and keys = drop-ins used over other audio.

8. Audio editing rates range from the slowest (talk over a fade of the first music segment, talk over silence, talk over the intro of the next music segment), to the fastest (pure segue – one elements ends full-up, and the next begins the same way immediately).

CHAPTER 7

Air Personality:
The Structure of Spoken Gesture

The focus of this chapter is on the announcer as actor, a performer in the theater of the mind. If that sounds like a throwback to the ancient golden age of radio drama, it shouldn't. Any radio performance still needs to have its roots in theatrical performance. In fact, the more our society becomes visually oriented, the more important the announcer as actor becomes.

THE CHALLENGE OF RADIO PERFORMANCE
IN A VISUAL ERA

Three decades ago, Edmund Carpenter posed the challenge for radio in the present television age, when the visual image has become the dominant one even for the hit music listener:

> The gestures of visual man are not intended to convey concepts that can be expressed in words, but inner experiences, nonrational emotions, which would still remain unexpressed when everything that can be told has been told. Such emotions lie in the deepest levels. They cannot be approached by words that are mere reflections of concepts, any more than musical experiences can be expressed in rational concepts.[1]

The question for radio is, how to convey those inner experiences, those nonrational emotions that cannot be put into words. The music does it in large part, and the

---

[1]Carpenter, E. (1977). The new languages. In E. Carpenter & M. McLuhan (Eds.), *Explorations in communication, 1960* (pp. 162–174). Quoted in Ohlgren T. H., & Berk, L. M. (Eds.). (1977). *The new languages* (p. 9). Englewood Cliffs, NJ: Prentice-Hall.

more a radio music listener has absorbed of MTV-type videos, the more those videos unreel again in the listener's mind as the radio supplies the sound track. Music videos seem almost to be textbook examples of visual gestures that "are not intended to convey concepts that can be expressed in words, but inner experiences, nonrational emotions, which would still remain unexpressed when everything that can be told has been told." Music videos provide the listener a very concrete visual stage for very amorphous, nonrational experiences. The visual stage is re-experienced each time radio replays the video's music. The question is, what happens to that stage when the music stops?

In the previous chapter, a plea was made that radio announcers and producers pay attention to preserving a sense of place in acoustic space – that when the music stops, some place with discernible spacial qualities can be heard by the listener. If an adequate acoustic place for speech can be assumed, then attention can turn to the actors who perform on that stage and what they do and say.

Radio Performers Are Salespeople

Earlier, a case was constructed that the listener expects radio to be very much in the entertainment business, so the idea of having "actors" on the radio is not a departure from that theme. However, radio is also in the selling business. Specifically, commercial radio is in the business of selling other businesses. Radio programming is entertainment, but it is also a sales vehicle.

Some people seem to think that these dual roles for radio are incompatible; that if you are really good at one aspect, then the other will suffer. These folks believe that a program with truly superior entertainment values will have trouble finding sponsors, or that the very presence of a sales effort alongside the effort to make good programs somehow contaminates the program production effort with "lowest common denominator" thinking. Not so.

The best radio is radio that sells. It sells everything: the music that is played, the people who play it, the news that interrupts it, the commercials that support it, the station itself.

Consider the singers who are popular with the mass audience. Most of them do not merely mouth the words and hit all the notes. They shape the words and the melodies to their own personalities, so that what comes out is a mixture of the song and the singer. And they do not just drop the song on your porch like a package from UPS. They do more than deliver the song. The really fine singers sell it to you, by investing themselves completely in the event. (Bruce Springsteen's concerts come to mind as an example.) Through the force of their personality entwined in the way the song is sung, the great performers make you care about the song, make you need to hear it to conclusion, make you believe in it, persuade you, suspend your disbelief. Ultimate communication is the singer, the song, and the audience merged into a single thinking, feeling entity. The success of the singer and the song becomes important to you – you want them to be great. You stop analyzing what is and is not working and simply get caught up in the moment, wanting it to go on, wanting to hear it again.

"Wanting to hear it again." That is, wanting to hear the song again. But what about the commercial that just aired? Does your station's audience want to hear it again too? Did the announcer make the audience suspend their disbelief and care about the product? Did the audience get caught up in the moment and wish for it to continue, wanting the announcer to go on being great?

If your answer is "No, of course not – these are commercials, not pop songs!" then you probably believe a stop set is an accurate name for what happens on too many radio stations: Much of the entertainment values inherent in pop music screech to a stop when the music ends and the spots begin.

NEEDING ARTHUR GODFREY AGAIN

In 1931, a young radio announcer named Arthur Godfrey was in a serious auto accident that kept him in a hospital for several months. He listened to the radio a great deal, and made an important realization. Most of the announcers of that day were not talking to an individual, but rather to a group. "Ladies and gentlemen of the radio audience" they would begin, visualizing a mass audience of thousands or millions as they spoke. They talked as if they were public speakers in a huge auditorium, exaggerating consonants for clarity, and punching everything out with lots of volume and intonation. They were more like platform orators than what we think of today as announcers.

Speaking to the Audience Individually

Godfrey realized that even if several people listened together (as families did when they gathered around the radio in the 1930s), an announcer actually was still talking to each person individually. Godfrey decided that he would talk to just one person at a time, even though he knew he would be reaching many others at the same instant. It should be noted that much of today's commercial copy uses "you" statements – or implicit "you" statements. Godfrey used "I" because it is a personal testimonial, like "word of mouth." The nameless announcer on the typical production spot usually is making "you" statements.

Once he had determined that radio listening was a solitary experience, even if done in a small group, Godfrey went on to develop a speaking style that would be congruent with this intimacy. He dropped his volume to a conversational level. He stopped intoning like a platform speaker. He did not exaggerate consonants for clarity – in fact, he dropped consonants and spoke like normal people do (example: "goin'" instead of "going"). His natural vocal timbre – rich and warm and resonant – made him sound like he was confiding in you. He talked like a neighbor, a companion. He was somebody you could trust. He did not talk down to you. He talked a lot like you did. This was no snake oil salesman. This was a friend. The public believed him, and they bought the products he talked about. Godfrey was probably the most successful radio network selling voice of his time, just as newscaster Paul Harvey is today.

EMULATE THE ANALYSIS, NOT NECESSARILY THE STYLE

The conversational style that Godfrey invented has waxed and waned over the years (it almost disappeared entirely in the hyperkinetic early days of the Top 40 format.) This is not meant to be a plea for more Godfrey-type, or Paul Harvey-type conversationalists on radio. But the same kind of analysis that Godfrey did can help any announcer to find a style for his or her particular daypart's boardshift, or for the 4 p.m. newscast, or for the spot he or she is going to do for the local shoe store. Among the questions to ask are: Who are your listeners likely to be? Where are they likely to be? What else are they likely to be doing? (Remember, radio is hardly ever given sole attention.) How long are they likely to stay tuned in?

Such audience analysis is bound to improve any speaker's effectiveness in reaching the intended audience in the desired way. But there are techniques to consider from both the field of public speaking and from stage acting that will work for any would-be radio communicator – even if the precise makeup of the audience is not well-known. A good radio announcer needs to be a public speaker who brings much of the drama of the stage to his or her utterances, and/or an actor who is especially effective at delivering monologues. Either way, the intent is to solidify the structure and deepen the appeal of his or her spoken gestures.

From public speaking, we are going to borrow the concepts of the four aspects of the speaking voice: rate, intensity (volume, loudness), timbre (distinctive vocal quality), and pitch. And from training in stage movement comes the concept of three distinct patterns that are reflected via the actor's body: a pattern in time, a pattern in space, and a pattern of force. When an actor moves from point A to point B, we can analyze his or her traverse in terms of (a) how long it takes him or her (time); (b) the amount of room he or she takes up with his or her body, gestures, and stride (space); and (c) how much energy he or she inve sts in the process, as revealed by his or her gestures.[2]

Time

We begin with time, which we will stipulate is the same as the rate of delivery. Obviously, an announcer usually has to get through a 30-second spot in 29.5 seconds. Godfrey was never very concerned with keeping his ad-libbed pitches timed to the second; they often ran over or under. But more important is what he did

---

[2]See Oxenford, L. (1952). *Design for movement* (p. 3). New York: Theatre Arts Books.

with time within the commercial. He would often take a very long pause, during which the listener could hear a complete breathing cycle. He was not speaking on a radio announcer's time, which is clock-bound. He was speaking on a listener's time, which is sense-bound. He paused to let things sink in, and he paused before important words to put some "sparkle" around them. Then he would steam through a sentence of mostly unimportant words, dropping consonants by the wayside, until he arrived at the next important idea, pausing before and after it again, to let it stand alone. Godfrey used variations in time (rate of delivery) to put the equivalent of white space around important words. A pause in the delivery made room around an important idea and helped it to stand out. Thus, in Godfrey's delivery, time (rate) also influenced space.

Pitch

The breathing space around important words was also influenced by the way Godfrey pitched his voice. He knew when to do a monotone and when to do a roller coaster of different pitches. He often avoided the falling pitch that typically marks the end of a declarative statement, and instead let his voice go up at the end, using the same inflection as when asking a question. Newscaster Paul Harvey uses this technique extensively, and several texts teach this trick to young actors, but not very many young radio announcers use it. That is too bad, because this technique leads the listener to believe there is more yet to be said. It keeps the audience "tuned in" to what is coming next, and adds a sense of expectation and curiosity. Godfrey used pitch to keep an important idea dangling in front of the listener, as if it were a kite in a strong breeze, bobbing and darting, but never coming to earth until the whole flight was complete. He used pitch to focus attention on the important ideas, giving them the space they needed in the listener's mind.

Timbre and the Distance From the Microphone

Godfrey was aware, as most announcers are today, that it is not possible to vary intensity (volume) as much in radio speaking as is possible in public speaking. (Talk too soft or too loud on the radio in the old days and you would either get lost in the hiss or you would blow out the microphone. Today, processing equipment will not *let* you be too loud or too soft.) So Godfrey made up for the limits the medium imposes on changes in intensity by accentuating changes in vocal timbre (quality). To listen to Godfrey do a spot is to hear someone who can run the gamut from warm, soft, and deep, to icy, hard, and nasal. He had a wonderfully flexible voice, but not any better than many today. What was more important than the physical components of his vocal mechanism was the way he apparently accentuated changes in vocal timbre by changes in his distance from the microphone. Icy, hard, and nasal works best when speaking loudly and at a distance from the mike. Warm, soft, and deep happens as close to the mike as possible without popping Ps and Bs. Godfrey used a lot of closeup, warm, soft, and deep timbre because he invented the style, but he could back off and holler, too. It is amazing how few of today's announcers know how to change their rate to get more emphasis, know how to vary the pitch to build expectation, and seem unaware of the vastly different psychological impact that talking just 3 or 4 inches closer or further from the mike can have. "Good morning again" said loud and distant from the microphone sounds like a greeting to a neighbor in the next driveway. "Good morning again" said soft and close to the mike sounds like a greeting to your lover on the next pillow. Godfrey used changes in timbre, and in distance from the mike, to affect the sense of psychological distance from him felt by the listener. Timbre and mike distance affected the sense of space, and substituted for radio's inability to project changes in vocal force.

Also consider this. When a person actually whispers in your ear, you know you cannot see the person's face, so you do not even try to actually glimpse the speaker. You visualize him or her in your mind instead. Similarly, when hearing a platform speaker, the speaker's face is too small to actually see, so again, you at least partly imagine it. But the middle distance that is typical of the voices on radio is also the typical distance for face-to-face conversation. And with that goes the expectation that you *can* see the speaker. Only the middle distance – the distance most used on radio – has the expectation of actually seeing the speaker. It is the one distance that demands pictures that radio cannot supply. Microphone distances that are either much closer or much further away allow the listener to imagine the speaker, and imagination is one of radio's fortes.

Space

You have noted by now that with Godfrey's (and by extension, any good announcer's) style, every aspect of the speaking voice affects the component of the actor's arsenal known as space. Godfrey succeeded not just because the listener knew who he was, and what he stood for, but also because the listener always knew *where* Godfrey was in relation to him or her. Godfrey's was not a disembodied mouth anchored forever at some middle distance like many of today's small-market announcers. Arthur was a whole person, because he could leap over the unimportant stuff and suddenly stop scrambling to admire the important material; he could hang that voice up in the air or land it squarely on earth; he could move himself very far from you or closer than anyone but your bedmate.

Godfrey's voice did not just happen in space – it *used* space, moved around in it, revelled in it, like our own bodies do. Godfrey's voice put his whole body across. He became, without any video to reinforce it, a physical character in people's lives. He had an aura of physical vitality, because he used the actor's tools of time, space, and force so well. A sizzling background instrumental music bed, or a well-timed sound effect, would have only detracted from the powerful impact his unadorned delivery had with an audience of millions.

Movement theorist Joseph Lange has said that certain actions or movements can evoke emotional reactions. For example, the physical act of jumping quickly backward as if to avoid a speeding car can evoke the emotions of fear, shock, and relief associated with the actual event. On a stage, careful blocking (placement and movement of objects and actors) can help the actor to portray his or her character's emotions, because good blocking puts objects and people where the actor can use them to best physical advantage. But in radio, there are no physical objects and rarely are there other people for the announcer to interact with. The only thing akin to blocking (in the sense of relational placement and movement on the stage) is the announcer's distance from the microphone. And most announcers never vary it.

Targeting and Selling the Listener

Knowing where the audience is, and knowing what else they are doing, is helpful. But it is not essential. If an announcer assumes, as Godfrey did, that he or she is not talking to homogenized masses but to each audience member individually, then listeners can be targeted one on one. There will always be some listeners who are not where the announcer would like them, or who are not devoting strong attention to the radio. It is up to the announcer to place the listener where the announcer wants him or her to be, and to get him or her to pay foreground attention to what the announcer is saying. That is done the same way a singer sells a song: by letting the singer's personality infuse the lyrics and power the melody. In announcing terms, that means not letting the copy or the clock dictate the effect on the listener, but letting the rapport the announcer wants to have with the listener determine it.

The listener comes to any given moment on the radio with no expectations at all. For the moment, think of the listener as a car, and the show or spot as a trip to be taken. The listener does not begin in any gear—he or she is in neutral. The announcer alone determines the speed to go, the route to take, and how often the car will be slowed to allow sightseeing along the way. It is the listener's car, but the announcer is driving it. And the listener will allow that to happen, so long as he or she cannot do it better for him or herself. But it takes nothing less than the force of the announcer's personality, entwined around the client's product or the station's format, like a singer wraps a song around his or her own psyche.

Your Neighbor As Salesperson

One more analogy. Too many radio announcers rank in the listener's mind along with itinerant door-to-door salesmen of the sort that keep pestering Dagwood Bumstead in the middle of a nice bath. They ring the bell insistently to get your attention, they launch into a wild-eyed pitch that will not keep you standing on the porch—dripping wet—any longer than necessary, and they go for the close in a hurry. They have a certain bravado because they expect to be rejected, and they need to sound "bigger than life" at least for their own egos. Why should you buy anything from a guy you do not know, who is here now but will be God-knows-where tomorrow? What reason do you have for believing him? What do you know about him? He can make all sorts of claims, but you have nothing but his breathless word for it. And he'll be back someday too soon pitching something else – maybe even a competing product. If Dagwood were really interested in buying the product, he'd probably ask his neighbor Herb Woodley for a recommendation. Dagwood's been talking with Herb over the back fence for decades. They have had their disagreements, but Herb is a known quantity. Herb is a companion, a confidante. Herb is who you would want to have selling your product. Herb is who you would want on your radio station playing records. Herb is any radio announcer who is him or herself first, and a voice second. Herb is Arthur Godfrey.

This needs repeating: It is not that all the world's radio announcers should try to imitate Arthur Godfrey. But radio announcers succeed best when they (a) try to become as much in tune with their audience's needs and expectations as Arthur Godfrey was; (b) become as much of a companion, friend, and trusted spokesperson as Godfrey became; and most important (c) never let the form of communication become more important than its function.

In the heyday of Top 40, AM hit radio's "bad boy" was Dick Biondi, the quintessential "screamer." Biondi yelled everything he said, which at the time was a revolutionary affront to the close-miked, soft-spoken types on traditional (non-Top 40) stations. When Biondi rared back and hollered, it was the vocal equivalent of a jump into hyperspace. Biondi succeeded on points (a) & (b), but the very act of shouting everything eventually seemed to become a formula. Later, Wolfman Jack succeeded well on point (a). On the point (b), he was a companion and friend (a la his role in the classic film *American Graffiti*), but he mitigated that trust by being an over-enthusiastic spokesperson for almost anything. On point (c), he employed his voice to great effect, using all three vectors of time, space, and force well (especially the last two), but after awhile, the vocal razzle dazzle seemed to settle into a formula and his style began to seem closer to shtick. The form took over. Yet Dick Clark has succeeded for three decades by adhering to the three points. In his case, selling any-and-everything has not seemed to hurt at all, perhaps because he brings the same measured earnestness to the music and performers he describes that he brings to a pitch for acne medicine. There must be at least 300 people in the country who have a vocal mechanism as good as Dick Clark's. But good announcing only appears on its surface to be about golden, pear-shaped tones, clear diction, superb phrasing, and the like. It really is about engaging another human mind in an efficient and imaginative communion. In that communion of two minds can come the kind of participation where the audience wants the singer to be great, cannot *wait* to applaud, and wishes like mad to hear it all again. Having sold him or herself, and the client's product, the announcer has gone on to sell you, the listener, on yourself: Yes, you are good enough. Yes, you can be more. Yes, the world is going to go on. And yes, together we can figure out what we are supposed to be doing in it.

TABLE 7.1
Traits of the Ideal Mate[3]

	Men %	Women %
Warm/loving	51	66
Sense of humor	57	58
Intelligent	50	37
Honest	30	43
Interested in same things I am	37	31
Good company	33	30
Dependable	24	35
Self-confident	20	17
Sexy	21	6
Enthusiastic	9	10
Optimistic	6	8
Serious	8	6

THE ANNOUNCER AS IDEAL MATE

The announcer just described is an idealized human being. So consider Table 7.1 that excerpts the answers to a survey that asked men and women "What do you look for when selecting the ideal mate?"[3] The top three responses (warm/loving, sense of humor, and intelligent) got substantially more than one third of the responses from both men and women. Traits such as honesty, shared interests, and being good company all hovered in the one third area. Traits that got substantially *less* than one third of the votes included being self-confident, enthusiastic, and optimistic. Now, ask yourself: If people do not think it is very important to spend their whole lives with a self-confident, enthusiastic, optimistic person, why is there so much self-confident, enthusiastic optimism among the radio personalities we want them to spend a few minutes with? If what people want in a person they can put up with for more than one night are traits like being warm and loving, having a sense of humor, and being intelligent, why don't we hear more of those? As we comic strip readers perform the voice of that wild-eyed salesman with the new gizmo on Dagwood's porch, we probably have him sounding self-confident, enthusiastic, and optimistic. But we don't believe him—perhaps *because* that is how he sounds about everything. At the bottom of it, self-confidence, enthusiasm, and optimism are all largely self-referential emotions. They mostly reflect the psyche of the speaker. They do not involve the audience in an exchange the way a warm and loving relationship does, the way a sense of humor rewards with laughter, the way intelligence lifts us up with insight.[4]

---

[3] Adapted from a survey by D'Arcy Masius Benton & Bowles, Inc., Fears and fantasies of the American male. (1987, August). *Men's Fitness*, p. 49. (Copyright © 1987, *Men's Fitness* magazine, used by permission.)

[4] Colleague Bill Adams and I (along with undergraduate student Bruce Steinbrock) are completing research into the audience's perception of radio announcers, especially focusing on the physical features

The Public Smile

We have all seen – and have come to suspect – the professional, public smile. We suspect it because we have seen that public smile vanish in an instant when the cameras were thought to be off. A radio voice that is only projecting self-confident enthusiastic optimism is a public smile, and we often do not believe it. (I would rather believe a grump like Larry Lujack any day than an eternally bright and cheerful Casey Kasem.) An announcer who is genuinely warm and loving, who has a sense of humor and is intelligent, will likely have a smile in his or her air voice that is generated spontaneously by a sense of interaction with the audience. It is not a pose. It is who the announcer really is at the moment.

ANNOUNCERS AS ACTORS

Playing Actions, Not Emotions

The truly effective radio announcer shares the actor's objective of accomplishing a true two-way communications exchange. Notice the term *objective*. Actors play objectives and intentions, not emotions. Playing emotions leads to stereotypes, which merely meet the audience's preconceived notions. That is why trying to convey self-confidence, enthusiasm, or optimism often does not work. Neither will an attempt to portray one or some of the list of appeals offered earlier. The appeals describe the results of programming decisions, results that audiences can perceive and react to. It is not sensible to ask somebody to *be* more novel or more nostalgic. Portraying nostalgia is a result of the actor *doing* something to achieve that situation, such as, "I'll try to regain a moment in my childhood." An actor cannot get to that moment through some form of the verb "to be," as in "be more pensive" or "be more moody." The verb "to be" followed by an adjective simply is not translatable into action by most people. The action itself must be defined, and then the adjective will be the result, the fallout from the action.

Actors following the Stanislavski "method" try to discover the reasons for their actions. They often start by expressing in a single sentence the smallest of their objectives – the ones that apply for just that given moment of the play. They then move on to larger objectives, such as the ones for a scene. Finally, the actor attempts to define his or her total goals – the "super" objectives in their interaction with others in the entire play.

that the listener imagines. The research procedure involves playing audio dubs of the soundtrack of videotapes of radio announcers doing their shows, then asking respondents to characterize the people they hear using a semantic differential scale, and other measures. One eventual goal of this study is the development of a checklist/model that could be used by would-be announcers as a self-evaluation tool, or by program directors as a means of analyzing prospective new staff members. The research was funded by a modest grant from the Kansas State University Faculty Development Committee. Video and audiotapes used were from the extensive collection sold by The Aircheck Factory, Wild Rose, WI.

Radio air personnel could benefit from a discussion with management about the station's smallest (moment-by-moment) programming objectives, all the way to the super objective of the station's total impact on the community. But the verb "to be" must be avoided. Instead, there must be a concentration on intentions and objectives—what the actor/announcer *wants,* moment-by-moment on that day for the station as a whole.

An Exchange of Effort

Part of the communication process is an exchange of effort on the part of both the actor and the audience. Perhaps the audience requires a greater effort from a live actor on a stage than from an actor on TV or radio, simply because the audience has made an effort to go to the theatre versus "just" tuning in. The radio audience has done less to hear the announcer, so demands less announcer effort. The whole listening experience, then, is both less demanding and less rewarding.

While radio announcers could hope that audiences would arrive at their radios fully ready to participate, previous chapters have shown that *in*attention is more likely. Thus, the burden of upgrading the communication exchange must fall on the announcer. And although an objective such as "achieving a communion" may be appropriate, there is one noun connected with the process that is useful to keep in mind: "quality."

Quality. Robert M. Pirsig, author of *Zen and the Art of Motorcycle Maintenance,* wrestles with the question of whether the quality of an object or an event resides in the thing itself or in the eyes of the beholder. Eventually, Pirsig came to the conclusion that

> Quality couldn't be independently related with either the subject or the object, but could be found *only in the relationship of the two with each other.* It is the point at which subject and object meet.
>
> That sounded warm.
>
> Quality is not a *thing.* It is an *event.*
>
> Warmer.
>
> It is the event at which the subject becomes aware of the object.
>
> And because without objects there can be no subject—because the objects create the subject's awareness of himself—Quality is the event at which awareness of both subjects and objects is made possible.[5]

In other words, quality is an exchange of one person's best effort for the best efforts of another. In radio terms, the best efforts of a producer of a program collide

---

[5]Pirsig, R. M. (1975). *Zen and the art of motorcycle maintenance* (p. 233). New York: Bantam Books.

with the best efforts of a listener to appreciate the program, and in that event, quality is realized. Too often, neither the creator, the owner, nor the user (to quote Pirsig's terms) feels a sense of identity with it, and hence it has no quality.

Intense Concentration

This kind of awareness is certainly much easier to accomplish in live theatre, where the actor and audience can see and hear each other. In live theater, there are moments when the audience so completely "loses the frame" that there is total belief in the reality of the onstage action. A kind of "tunnel vision" takes over, blotting out the proscenium, the lights, even other audience members. The mind's eye "zooms in" on the action, bringing the actors up close no matter how far back in the house the observer may be. And a hush overtakes the audience in a profound way–no one unwraps a candy, no one coughs, no one even moves. The communion is complete, both visually and aurally. Actors–without ever seeing the audience sitting in the darkness–report feeling "energy" coming from them at such moments. The actors can somehow sense the intensity of the audience's concentration.

It is the radio announcer's job to *imagine* such an intensity of concentration, and then to go ahead and *presume* it. The announcer does that by adopting the Godfrey-esque stance of talking with only person at at time–but really *talking with* that person, and doing that with the same care that you would take in talking with a person who mattered to you very much. In such real-life conversations, there can be the same timelessness and sense of being "in flow" that comes from wonderfully carved ski turns or from perfectly played sonatas–because there is an exchange of one person's best efforts for the best efforts of another. In radio, the best efforts of the producer/announcer/actor are perceived by the listener, who then is encouraged to put forth her/his own best efforts to appreciate the program. In that delicious collision, quality is realized.

With an idea of what it is radio announcers should strive to do, we can turn to the question of what they should say.

THE WEDNESDAY AFTERNOON FORMAT

Perhaps it is best to begin with the things to avoid. Programming researcher and critic Gary Bond wrote a well-focused essay on the junk phrases that pass for radio personality which he called "The Wednesday Afternoon Format," so named because of all the times he heard one disc jockey telling his afternoon listeners what day of the week it was–and even what year! Bond quoted the same jock delivering this all-too-common banality: "How are you doing today? Hope you're having a nice one. Nice to have you along. . ."[6] Some of these irrelevancies, said Bond, are the result of infrequent airchecking by program directors:

---

[6]Bond, G. H. *The Bond Report.* 3725 Yaqui Drive, Flagstaff, AZ. 86001.

Listen to the Wednesday Afternoon jocks and it becomes much easier to understand the number of talk restrictions that have evolved over time. Some programmers who are allegedly anti-personality are simply anti-crap. Restrictions have come about because of some believers in personality who had no personality. Programmers said, "If you're going to say nothing, I'd rather hear it in 4 seconds than in 40." That way, at least the jock is limited in the number of irrelevancies he can speak.[7]

Bond concluded his essay by pointing out how radio programmers' willingness to forgive banal and irrelevant chatter contrasts with TV:

The useless phrases that are continually repeated on radio throughout the country do not speak well for the medium. We should have the same respect for our medium as the television man who reacted indignantly to 5 seconds of black screen by saying, "I could have sold that time!" That respect calls for saying what is relevant and entertaining and avoiding filler cliches.[8]

Confirmation/Consistency/Predictability

Some people have read "The Wednesday Afternoon Format" and have reacted saying, "But people *want* to have information confirmed." This is true, up to a point. Confirmation is okay, but too much time spent telling me what I already know as if it were new information is the sin. As Program Director David Isreal said, "We've found people perceive lots of talk when there's little information."[9] Gary Bond made the point that many of the mistakes of the Wednesday Afternoon Format could be caught with simple airchecking. But sometimes, even airchecking does not work, perhaps because those in charge of radio programming do not listen to their stations the way listeners do.

I have had a problem for years with college freshman and sophomore broadcasting students imitating what they heard on the radio back home. What they often heard was the Wednesday Afternoon Format. When a student asks what *should* be included in an aircheck, the answer given by longtime Program Director and now Unistar executive Gary Taylor seems best. Taylor used to tell announcers looking for work on his stations what he *didn't* want in an aircheck: He didn't want the tried-and-true time and temperature, he didn't want the jock's name over and over, he didn't want the obvious title of the record and the name of the familiar artist; he wanted what was left. For too many would-be Wednesday Afternooners, nothing was. Those who still had something fresh and succinct to say might make it.

---

[7]Ibid. (no page number)
[8]Ibid. (no page number)
[9]Kinosian, M. (1988, July 22). Is less talk more appealing? *Radio & Records*, p. 49.

Zero Talk and Commercial-Free Hours

In an effort to be the station that has the most music and the least talk, many "more music" operations have tried playing up to an hour of segued songs with no introductions or back-announcing at all. One immediate result of such "zero talk hours" is the lengthening of stop sets when one finally occurs. If four or five spots are clustered together, a stop set becomes aptly named, for the entertainment generally does screech to a halt. Long stop sets thus become an open invitation for the listener to tune away. And the clutter of several spots in a clump makes it less likely that any given advertiser will stand out and be remembered. In the longer term, then, radio advertising runs the risk of being less effective for the client, except on high-rated stations in major markets where the sheer volume of listeners makes viable even an undesirable commercial position.

Some stations have promoted their music sweeps by calling them "commercial-free" hours, but W. R. Sabo, Inc., a radio marketing and programming advisory company, upbraided the industry for such phraseology in a trade ad. The bold headline read "DIRTIEST WORDS ON RADIO: 'Commercial Free'." The copy continued, "You can win big ratings without saying those dirty words. Great programmers get ratings with full spot loads. Profitable sales promotions. And with personalities who can bring customers to your retail advertisers."[10]

Selling the Music

Another result of "zero talk hours" and long music sweeps without announcing is that a great many casual listeners have no idea of how to ask for music that they have heard on the radio. The record industry tried to fight this trend with a "Play It and Say It" campaign aimed at programmers and announcers. Veteran programmer Bill Drake commented on this situation in a *Radio & Records* interview:

> Nobody should have to be told it's unwise for your audience not to know what the music is. Radio may say it's not in the business of selling records, but it *is* in the business of selling music. Stations must realize that by not selling the music there will be very little enthusiasm for it by the listener, which can translate to little enthusiasm for the station playing that music.[11]

Why Talk About the Music?

For many students, and lots of practicing announcers, the mainstay of disc jockey chatter that attempts to go beyond mere song title and artist identification has always been deeper information or further comment about the music being played. But depending too much on airplay music to provide grist for the conversational mill can be a trap. The trap has to do with the relative familiarity of the music. If a

---

[10]Advertisement by W. R. Sabo, Inc. in *Radio & Records,* January 22, 1988, p. 29.

[11]Drake, B. (1988, October 7). Drake: CHR is very healthy. *Radio & Records,* p. 28.

song is quite new, it is likely to provoke a strong listener response, as the melody and lyric begin the progression from being completely novel to being totally familiar. It is ironic that disc jockeys are *most* likely to have something to say about a song at this early stage of acceptance, just when the listener has plenty of responses of his or her own. To make matters worse, the jock is *least* likely to have anything to say about a song when it is older, just when the listener is also running out of responses. Thus, new songs can "speak for themselves" to listeners, while older ones would benefit the most from amusing interpretation by the disc jockey. It goes against human nature for a disc jockey not to be more excited by a new song than an old one, and not to have more things to say about it early in its lifespan than later. That is why the good announcers are actors: They can portray interest and excitement even when the music is very familiar. But the easiest way to avoid this problem is not to talk about just the music in the first place.

Two Audience Expectation Guidelines

These observations can be summarized as two "audience expectation" guidelines for disc jockeys: (a) help me when I need it, not when I don't; and (b) don't tell me what I already know. Any kind of predictability is tantamount to telling me what I already know.

If the same liners make the station too predictable, and talking about the music leads the jock into the trap of helping the listener when he or she does not need it, and telling the listener what is already known, then what *does* the announcer talk about?

The Associated Press's Broadcast Services division ran ads in radio trade magazines in 1988 with the headline "After 10 in a row, play today's hit single." A photo showed a disc jockey holding a singular piece of wire copy. The text of the ad continued, "Think of AP as an exclamation point at the end of a 27-minute music statement. A way to focus your audience's ear and brain; a way to set up a commercial break, a station promo, or a new addition to your playlist."[12] The remarkable thing about this ad is that it had to explain how disc jockeys might find uses for radio wire copy.

TALK ABOUT THE COMMUNITY'S STORIES

Ideally, the jock world talk about what the community is talking about. The really great announcers seem to know everything that is going on in their cities. But not only do they have the facts, they also have the feelings, the mood. And they convert those facts, focused through the lens of the community's moods, into *stories*.

The radio announcer who wants to become a true communicator needs to consider the behavior of ordinary people who are in an entertainment-seeking mood

---

[12]Advertisement by Associated Press Broadcast Services in *Radio & Records,* April 15, 1988, p. 13.

in public places – a mood that is similar to the one they are in when they hear a radio station in private. Announcers need to observe people at picnics, at taverns, on the beach, or in the park, and try to hear what they talk about. Once they get past the opening pleasantries, people are likely to begin to tell *stories*. Funny stories, lightly amusing stories, surprising stories, and simple narratives recounting the events of their lives. People do not generally engage neighbors in furious debate over "controversial issues of public importance," to quote an FCC programming guideline. It is usually impolite, indelicate, or dangerous to a friendship to do that. So people stick to telling stories for each other's gentle amusement.

Some people tune in only for stories. Garrison Keillor's enormously popular "News from Lake Wobegon" segments on American Public Radio's "A Prairie Home Companion" are an obvious example. The cassettes of merely the stories from the radio show have become big sellers. Or if you have listened to the legendary Wally Phillips on WGN, Chicago, you have heard someone who is both a conversationalist himself and someone who attracts other storytellers to speak on his program. We are back to that moment of communion – the ultimate radio communication: two people sharing their minds and hearts freely while thousands listen in. Almost every station has someone capable of holding up his or her end of a telephone conversation. It makes sense to put more of those actual two-way conversations on the air, if the announcer cannot achieve good listener rapport without it. But be sure he or she isn't just doing "The Wednesday Afternoon Format" with added call-in banalities. Calls with listeners still need to be topical, current, fast-moving, and involving.

Larger market stations often assign a producer to screen and edit actual calls to be used by the host of a morning show. Only a handful of stations continue the practice throughout the day, perhaps because the rarity of air talent with good two-way communication skills makes them expensive, or because paying an additional producer just to edit calls when the station is already paying an announcer seems inefficient. But Program Director Roger Gaither at Charleston, South Carolina station WKQB has encouraged his airstaff to put many listeners on the air all day long: "They don't have to be contest winners, either . . . They've learned that if they have something to contribute, they can be a part of the on-air activity at Q107. It makes Q107 feel like someone's friend instead of just another radio station."[13] A station not willing or able to make a commitment to all-day call-in communion could still move closer to the ideal of being a two-way conversationalist and storyteller by changing its "comment line" telephone call recorder to a line which takes calls from any listeners who have any kind of a story to tell. It could be a joke, an amusing anecdote, a believe-it-or-not, or merely a slice-of-life. The program director could screen the taped calls, then sprinkle them throughout the day, formatting them in some cases, or otherwise just dropping them in. The result is

---

[13]Denver, J. (1989, February 24). Station bonding. *Radio & Records,* p. 41.

likely to be a radio station that sounds more like a neighbor – with neighbors talking to other neighbors – instead of a second-rate nightclub with one tired, desperate standup comic trying to entertain continuously for 3 hours or longer.

The Need for Feedback

One of the probable reasons announcers in larger markets tend to build successs upon success while their small-market counterparts sometimes do not seem to get anywhere is that the larger market tends to generate more audience feedback that actually gets through to the announcer. There is a larger numerical audience, and therefore a greater chance that somebody will call in and say something encouraging.

Even though feedback in mass media such as radio is delayed as compared to live theatre, it is still an essential part of the communication process. It literally closes the loop. Every second, announcers send out the equivalent of verbal frisbies, and they do not get tossed back until minutes, even hours later – if then. In the meantime, the announcer has had to depend on training or ability as an actor in order to imagine the audience, approximate the timing, and assume the response. For the radio announcer, the "flow" experience is all imaginary, because he or she must provide his or her own feedback at the time he or she speaks. The delayed reaction from listeners, if any, is all just gravy.

Two-person announcing teams and "zoo crews" have been one useful method for announcers to *have* an audience, *know* the timing, and *discern* the response. These have sometimes led to excesses, where chatter or shtick goes on too long, or where there are too many "inside" jokes (because the "audience" in the station is not the same as the actual audience). And what worked for Wally Phillips in AM drive may not work in other dayparts when a more "background" service is desired.

There is some evidence that live laughter – and even "canned" laughter used judiciously – can increase the enjoyment of comedy and humor, because the supplied laughter is a cue that tells the listener how much he or she should laugh.[14] And as Andrew Crisell pointed out in his book *Understanding Radio,* laughter from a live audience influences the timing and delivery of the speaker's material for the best. But Crisell cautioned that a studio audience can also be counter-productive when the listening audience feels the show is being addressed to the *studio* audience instead of the radio listener. This is especially true in the case of visual jokes – things seen in the studio that the listener cannot see.[15] The listening audience in this case feels excluded rather than included – which is just the opposite of the desired effect.

[14]Zillmann, D., & Bryant, J. (1986). Exploring the entertainment experience. In J. Bryant & D. Zillmann (Eds.), *Perspectives on media effects* p. 318. Hillsdale, NJ: Lawrence Erlbaum Associates.
[15]Crisell, A. (1986). *Understanding radio.* London and New York: Methuen.

Reality Therapy

So the answer is to be in touch with the actual audience. Ideally, that could happen via an air personality's show being performed in a public place. Not every standard-issue disc jockey would like that, and there is still plenty to be said for the control which the studio allows. But if the show does not originate in public, at least it should be based *on* the public–what the people are thinking and feeling. The radio studio must not be the monk's cell. It must be a haven only for a while. The announcer who would be great must get out of the station and stay in touch with the real characters of the world, observing them as actors do in preparing for a role. Because, the irony is, only by really knowing who he or she is in relation to the world outside can that person be portrayed by the actor on the air.

Stanislavski said that an actor should answer these four questions: Who am I? Why am I here? What do I want? Where am I going? Maybe the secret of the best air personalities is that when they are on the air, they continuously answer those four questions for themselves, and for their listeners.

MAJOR POINTS

1. The best radio is radio that sells everything–the music played, the people who play it, the news that interrupts it, the commercials that support it.

2. Many of the entertainment values that listeners find in pop songs–especially the sense of interaction with the artist–needlessly disappear in commercial stop sets.

3. Arthur Godfrey adapted his announcing style to his new conception of the audience as millions of *individual* listeners. Today's announcers do not necessarily need to emulate Godfrey's style, but rather his analysis of the audience.

4. The stage movement concepts of time, force, and space are useful in analyzing an announcer's technique. Time (rate) is the easiest to control, but often announcers let copy or clock considerations take over. Force (volume) is limited by audio processing and transmission technology, but timbre (quality) changes are possible. Space (a sense of physical closeness or distance) is easily controlled, but is largely ignored as a tool by most announcers.

5. The best radio salespersons come across as neighbors, not carnival barkers. They do not overstate vocally.

6. When seeking an ideal mate, people look for personalities who are warm and loving, have a sense of humor, and are intelligent, far more than they seek people who are self-confident, enthusiastic, or optimistic. Yet the latter qualities are heard more on the radio than the former ones.

7. Good announcers sound that way because they are (in acting terms) playing actions and objectives rather than portraying stereotypical emotions.

8. The radio announcer bears the burden of upgrading the communication exchange from one of possible listener inattention to one of fairly intense concen-

tration. This is done by imagining the "flow" of a real-life conversation in which an exchange of efforts occurs.

9. The "Wednesday Afternoon Format" (a term coined by Gary Bond) is comprised largely of irrelevancies and filler cliches. It is too highly predictable. It probably talks most about music which is already familiar. And it violates two audience expectations: help me when I need it, not when I don't; and don't tell me what I already know.

10. The great radio communicators help to elicit and to retell the community's stories. They are not self-referential. They feel secure out of the studio, observing and staying in touch with the real characters in the real world outside.

PART III

Music Programming

The first part of this volume examined the makeup of the radio listening audience, attempting to expand the usual list of psychographic terms to offer new ways to think about attracting target demographics. The second section looked at formats, at radio's soundstage and at the voices on it. This section builds on that background in considering music programming – the major ingredient in many stations' recipes for success. A case is made here that most music format categories are too rigid and exclusive for today's audiences, and a different scheme for selecting music is explained.

In the second chapter of his book, *The Psychology of Music,* John Booth Davies wrote:

> Music is something of a mystery. Most people spend considerable amounts of time listening to music of one sort or another, and some people dedicate the major part of their lives to musical pursuits. Yet, unlike other activities such as reading, talking, or watching television, where the transmission of a more or less unambiguous message is readily apparent, music does not appear to pass on any message we can readily identify. Music does not really satisfy the requirements that would completely justify its being called a "language," since we tend to use the word 'meaning' rather differently in the context of music than in the context of language. In addition, music seems to have something in common with simple forms of sensory experience like warmth, taste, or the smell of jacket-baked potatoes. For example, one can, in a sense, appreciate the taste of a good steak, although the question 'What does it *mean?* is hard to answer. By the same token one can ask 'What does Beethoven's Fifth Symphony *mean?* and again be at a loss for a satisfactory reply. Any answer we might attempt would be couched in terms of our own reactions and feeling, and these are not identical with another person's responses to the same piece of music. By contrast, the message 'The

cat sat on the mat' is fairly precise in its meaning, and relatively unambiguous. However, it is not the kind of message that most of us would become excited about.[1]

When Davies said that "music is something of a mystery," he said a mouthful. How music works its special magic on a listener is indeed one of the most mysterious phenomena in aesthetics, psychology, and physiology, and this brief look at the area by a nonmusician does not do justice to the complexity of the problem.[2] But the ideas presented in this section about how music makes us over is later combined to develop a mood-evoking music presentation system. The arguments and viewpoints in each succeeding chapter depend on the cumulative effect of the material presented previously, so the reader is urged to read through this section consecutively rather than skipping ahead.

---

[1]Davies, J. B., (1978). *The psychology of music* (p. 25). London: Hutchinson.
[2]For more complete coverage of research on the psychology of music, see Deutsch, D. (Ed.). (1982). *The psychology of music*. New York: Academic Press.

CHAPTER 8

The Appeals of Radio Music

This chapter explores some of the research that has tried to establish how music affects the listener. It looks at general research into music's effects (some even pre-dating radio), and then at more recent research into how broadcast music affects listeners. All of the research material in this chapter is presented as a foundation for the music moods research that is offered later.

SONG POPULARITY

Most commercial music formats have one factor in common: They are all based on some measure of popularity. Because every modern format had its basis in the market-oriented Top 40 hits format, that is not surprising. And because no commercial station wants to play music that is *un*popular and thus drive listeners away, popularity with some root or target audience is almost always a key factor in developing a music format. At the core of the original Top 40 station's music policy was the then-radical notion that what the station should play was what the general public wanted to hear (what was currently most popular). From that concept came the idea of the limited playlist, in which the most popular songs are played more often than the less popular tunes, again in an effort to minimize mistakes.[3] Because various trade publications reported the relative popularity of current music, it was

---

[3]John Kluge, who in 1959 was chairman of the board and president of what was then known as Metropolitan Broadcasting Corporation (later Metromedia), was quoted as being skeptical of top-singles lists: "When I see one of those lists . . . . . . I'm always reminded of the fact that man is on top of animal kingdom charts because he makes out the list." [Metropolitan Soars with Kluge at Helm, (1959, May 25). *Billboard*, p. 8.]

possible to devise music "clocks" or "wheels" that prescribed which title to play when. Over the years, programmers have experimented with categorizing by such things as the tempo of the song and the sex of the artist, but what always winds up as the winning consideration is how popular the song is perceived to be. That is why a song's popularity has been a major factor in every format that has evolved out of Top 40 in the last three decades. But simple measures of popularity (sales, requests, jukebox plays) probably have never been adequate guides to choosing which music to air.

Airplay Decision Making

A research report by Eric Rothenbuhler titled "Programming Decision-Making in Popular Music Radio" reflects 9 months of first-hand study of the decision making at an AOR station in one of the top 50 markets in 1981. His report listed five ways in which the station he studied–and by extension, the rest of the rock radio business–operated more as a local outlet for the music being distributed and promoted by the record industry than as an entity making decisions based on the local audience's expressed needs and desires. First, the record distributors determined which records would be sent to programmers across the country, and when they would be advertised and promoted, thus drastically narrowing the field of choice. Second, the pitches of record promoters, and data and opinion from industry tradesheets were found to be influential in determining which records would be considered–records by unknown artists that did not have such backing were rarely listened to. Third, station programmers felt compelled to play the "consensus cut"– one particular song from a new album being promoted unanimously by record reps or in the trades, or the cut that other stations were playing. Unless there was either strong promotion or strong airplay for a particular cut, many stations hesitated to play the record at all.

Rothenbuhler's fourth and fifth factors are linked to the "gatekeepers" in the radio music business. The fourth factor was that people in programming positions tended to be hired not for their knowledge of the local community's tastes and needs, but for their knowledge of the format and the industry. The fifth factor was the strong influence, and sometimes absolute veto power, of the outside program-ming consultant. Rothenbuhler concluded that it was rare for local tastes and needs to be considered as decisions were made about which records to play. Information in the trades, from other programmers, and from program consultants were all felt to be more reliable and objective than the expressed desires of the local audience.[4] Rothenbuhler's findings are congruent with my belief that in the 30-plus years since the Top 40 pioneers decreed that their stations would play the music that the public wants to hear (rather than the songs the station owner or the announcer liked), there

---

[4]Rothenbuhler, E.W. (1985). Programming decision-making in popular music radio. *Communication Research, 12* (2), pp. 227–230.

has been a gradual abandonment of that apparently "populist" principle. Other stations might feel that Rothenbuhler's research would not have come to the same conclusions if he had studied *their* selection methods, but the inescapable truth is that for most stations, the selection process for hit music has become highly self-referential, with the main points of reference being what other programmers are doing. Relative to the 10,000 + U.S. radio stations, just a handful of people are determining what becomes hit airplay music. I would not criticize this concentration of control if it really seemed to be in the best interests of the radio industry, the music industry, and the public, but as later parts of this section show, that is not necessarily the case. A number of other factors are examined that can serve to supplement, or in some cases even supplant popularity as the controlling factor in structuring a station's music for airplay.

Why Is This Song Popular?

For the past 30 years, the main consideration in choosing music for airplay on a radio station that is trying to achieve a reasonable measure of audience acceptance has been "How popular is this record?" A record's popularity has determined how often it is played; this popularity has been the chief structural component of all radio music formats since the mid-1950s.

There is no denying that popularity of the song (and perhaps even more so of the artist who recorded it) is an important factor in choosing music for mass appeal radio airplay. But popularity, as important as it is, must finally be viewed not as an answer in itself, but as merely one of the most visible symptoms of many other factors that cause the audience to listen to and enjoy that song. It is sensible to ask "How popular is this song, and with whom?", but that does not go far enough. The question begging to be asked is *"Why* is this song popular, and with whom?" or *"What factors* make a song popular in the first place?"

It is actual observation of radio listening behavior that led me to the conclusion that the questions just raised are the ones that need to be asked today. In the past several years, there have been lots of opportunities to observe my teenage sons and their friends choosing the stations they listen to for music on the car radio. That radio has push buttons (to access pre-set stations chosen by the owner), and also signal-scanning (which simply jumps to the next strong signal each time a button is pushed). The more each teenager made listening choices, the more it became apparent that neither popularity of the song or artist, nor the prestige or reputation of the station were primary reasons for punching a button. When asked why they changed the dial, the answer was almost always some variation of the idea that the hearer just did not like that song. Sometimes factors linked to popularity were important: the song or artist was unfamiliar or too novel, or on the opposite end of the scale, the song was too well-known/burned out. (Occasionally, the song was okay but the artist was held in derision – often because he or she had become too popular with the mass audience. It seems that, at least with some teenagers, achieving mass popularity leads almost inevitably to a next stage where that very popularity places the artist in contempt.)

Pressed harder to explain why they liked a song, the teenagers usually said something like "I don't know, I just like it. Bug off!" But persistently asking "Why do you like it?" would sometimes elicit an answer that ran something like this: "I just like how it makes me feel."

This kind of ad hoc, moment-by-moment station selection is not just confined to the author's teenagers. Dolf Zillmann and Jennings Bryant have found that deliberate program choices are the exception—that

> the choice of entertainment is usually made "on impulse." The program that holds the greatest appeal at a given time and under given circumstances, for whatever particular reasons, is likely to be picked. The factors that determine this appeal tend to be unclear to the respondents. It would be the rare exception for respondents to engage in formal and explicit evaluative comparisons of the choices before them. It is more likely that they make these choices rather "mindlessly," without using reliable and never-changing criteria in their appeal assessments and ultimately in their choices.[5]

On the other hand, research by Zillmann and Bryant found that people form mood-specific preferences—that is, they behave as if they sort of "understood" what kind of programming they needed given the particular mood they were in.[6]

How Do Music Listeners Choose Their Stations?

Embedded within the rapid tuning behavior that is possible with a push-button car radio is the question "How do radio listeners search for stations, and how do they choose the one they ultimately settle on?" Carrie Heeter and Bradley Greenberg have identified three different "orienting search pattern attributes" that apply to the way people search through cable TV channels to discover a suitable program.[7] The three different search pattern attributes are processing mode, search repertoire, and evaluation orientation. These are worth a closer look for the implications they hold for radio station selection.

One of the search patterns Heeter and Greenberg identify is automatic processing, in which TV channels are searched in numerical order. In both radio and TV sets with electronic tuning, this is usually accomplished by pushing an "up" or "down" or a "scan" button.

The elaborated search repertoire mode is one that includes all or most TV channels. In radio, with would be the equivalent of "twirling the dial" from one end

[5]Zillmann, D., & Bryant, J. (1986). Exploring the entertainment experience. In J. Bryant & D. Zillmann (Eds.), *Perspectives on media effects* (p. 306). Hillsdale, NJ: Lawrence Erlbaum Associates.

[6]Ibid., p. 307.

[7]See Heeter, C., & Greenberg, B. (1985). Cable and program choice. In D. Zillmann & J. Bryant (Eds.), *Selective exposure to communication* (pp. 211–212). Hillsdale, NJ: Lawrence Erlbaum Associates.

of the scale to the other. The size of the "repertoire" of stations is chosen by the *listener* to be all-inclusive.

A restricted search repertoire would include only a limited number of channels, such as might be the case in tuning a push-button radio or one with a limited number of pre-sets. The repertoire of possible stations on these radios is restricted.

Then there is the crucial question of evaluating the choices offered. Heeter and Greenberg define exhaustive evaluation as searching *all* the channels in a given search repertoire before returning to the best choice – as compared to the terminating evaluation, in which channels in a given search repertoire are searched in order only until the first acceptable choice is found. In radio, the exhaustive evaluation would mean that *every* available/pre-set station would be briefly sampled, and only after that would the listener return to the best choice. In the terminating evaluation, the listener would stop an orderly search when the first acceptable option was found.

Especially among music listeners, the terminating evaluation is very common: search only until a desirable song is heard and stop on that frequency. The exhaustive evaluation is likely only when no desirable music is heard on the normal repertoire of stations, and the listener seeks to expand the range of choice.

A Program Choice Model

The whole question of choice is what the exhaustive and terminating evaluations come down to. Zillmann and Bryant have developed a choice model that explains a certain set of operations that people tend to follow in selecting among offered entertainment programs. The description of what people do in this choice model may seem to be "just good common sense" but Zillmann and Bryant have done us a service by writing it down very precisely. Their focus was more toward TV programming, but a shortened version of their choice model is still very useful for radio:

1. An arbitrary selection is made. A particular program is encountered by chance or by mindless probing . . .
2. If the encountered program is pleasing, it is accepted. If it is displeasing, it is rejected. Being pleased or displeased is considered an immediate affective [emotional] reaction that does not rely on elaborate cognitive deliberation. It is, so to speak, a gut reaction. The program either "feels good," or it doesn't. The affective response to an encountered program is a function of prevailing moods and emotions . . .
3. If the encountered program is accepted, respondents refrain from further program sampling. Should dissatisfaction set in, acceptance is withdrawn, and the inclination to reject will grow to the point where the program is abandoned and program sampling recurs. If the encountered program is rejected, program sampling continues.

4. Rejected available programs are entered into short-term memory. In continued program sampling, the sampled program is compared with those in memory. Essentially, this comparison is between the affective reactions that were evoked by the compared programs, and it takes the form of *better* or *worse*. Respondents will return to recalled programs that are deemed better than present ones. This return to better offerings can be applied successively until the program deemed best is reached. More likely, however, respondents will cease making comparisons (i.e., they will discontinue the sampling process) once a satisfying program has been found . . .

5. If programs or program components are known (i.e., stored in long-term memory), the anticipation of pleasure or displeasure that is based on prior responding to the programs (e.g., episodes of a series) or program components (e.g., actors with particular roles) enters into the comparison process. It expedites this process in the sense that little exposure to sampled programs is needed to render a verdict of accept–reject or better–worse.[8]

In the fifth point just listed, the "program components" in the radio situation are likely to be the remembered points of pop songs–that is, the "hooks." The listener recognizes enough of a song to know that other pleasurable or unpleasurable elements are coming up.

The fourth point suggests that the procedure of holding rejected programming in short-term memory with "better" or "worse" labels attached is the means a listener might use to settle upon the "least objectionable programming" when he or she just cannot bear to turn off the radio.

Factors Intrinsic to the Song

After punching around the buttons, quite oblivious to all of the research just mentioned, my teenagers settled on a song that they liked because of how it made them feel. Tied up in their phrase "I just like how it makes me feel" are plenty of popularity factors (peer acceptance of the song and the artist, participation in current fads or trends, etc.). But there is also the sense that "how it makes me feel" might have a lot to do with things that are intrinsic to the music rather than the social milieu in which it is heard. The question then becomes, are there certain factors in the music itself that cause people to have certain patterns of reactions to it? Because, if there are, and if it were possible to predict what those reactions might be from playing a certain song or set of songs, a new way of programming popular music on the radio could be developed. Ultimately, it might even be possible to program music in such a way that a station's listeners would arrive at a commercial cluster or stop set primed to receive the messages more readily because the preceding music would

[8]Zillmann, D., & Bryant, J. (1985). Affect, mood, and emotion as determinants of selective exposure. In D. Zillmann & J. Bryant (Eds.), *Selective exposure to communication* (p. 157). Hillsdale, NJ: Lawrence Erlbaum Associates.

have gotten them into the desired mood. But even if that Machiavellian outcome were never achieved, if a programmer could become really adept at evoking moods through the careful selection of the music to be played, the time spent listening to that station should theoretically increase. And Time Spent Listening (TSL) *needs* to increase. My sons are not the only ones who carry cassettes into the car if they are going to be on a trip longer than 10 minutes. They plug the cassettes into the AM/FM/cassette player because that way they can *guarantee* the mood that the known music on the tape is going to evoke. What they currently get on the radio is haphazard. As concerns the establishment or the extension of a certain mood, even the number one hit music stations offer no more than a pig in a poke.

RESEARCH ON HOW AND WHY
MUSIC AFFECTS US

By the late 1920s, researchers in the United States were beginning to investigate scientifically the ways in which music affects its audience. They were already confronting the problem of the wide variability in the backgrounds, environments, age, and susceptibility of different listeners, and the sticky subject of repeatability: that a second rendering of a piece can never be listened to again with the freshness of its first hearing, because every successive playing changes the listener's perceptions.

Esther L. Gatewood was one of the best-represented of the 1920s researchers investigating how music affected listeners. Her early studies with small groups found that musical enjoyment seemed to be derived from one of four sources: (a) physical/movement (either in the listener or in the music), (b) a feeling of simple satisfaction tied to melody, (c) associational factors (emotions and memories), and (d) ideational factors (such as the interpretation or analysis of the performance.)[9]

Relation of Sources of Enjoyment to Music Components

In her next study, Gatewood wanted to find out how those fundamental sources of musical enjoyment related to the elements of rhythm, melody, harmony, and timbre. For her material, she used 10 phonograph recordings of everything from ballet music and piano rhapsodies to Russian folk songs, American marches, and dance music (fox trots). (Keep in mind that this was likely to have been the limits of what was available on phonograph records in 1921.) The listeners were 35 young women volunteers. No precise age range is mentioned, but they seem to have been undergraduate women attending Vassar College. They were each given a data sheet that included the following question:

---

[9]Gatewood, E.L. (1968). An experimental study of the nature of musical enjoyment (continued). In M. Schoen (Ed). *The effects of music* (p. 104). Freeport, NY: Books for Libraries Press.

Which do you notice most?

> Rhythm
> Melody
> Harmony
> Timbre[10]

The responses to the question "Which do you notice most?" were largely divided between "rhythm" and "melody." Only in two of the 10 selections was "timbre" chosen as the dominant element. "Harmony" was not chosen in any of the cases.

Comparison of Most-Noticed Qualities With Effect on the Listener

The heart of Gatewood's research revolved around the comparison of these most noticeable qualities with the effect on the hearer. She reported:

> With what effect is each element most often combined by the hearer? Out of eighty-seven recordings [responses] of rhythm, it is combined thirty-five times with *happy* and thirty-three times with *excited, stirred,* a kindred feeling . . .[11]

This is an important early finding, because it points to the dominance of rhythm in developing feelings of excitement. Modern research also shows the commanding role rhythm fills in the development of feelings about the music. Gatewood found that "In almost every instance there is relation between rhythm and physical effect."[12] Harmony and timbre seemed to be most associated with music that made the listener feel "serious" or "rested." Melody was shown to have a great effect on associational factors such as memories.

Expectancy As a Basis of Emotional Response to Music

Musicologist Leonard Meyer offered another possible basis for our emotional response to music. He said that we bring with us a set of expectations about how things will likely proceed when we listen to music. If the music is congruent with what we expected, then we are in a relaxed state; if it is not what we expected, then we grow tense. Meyer said that the gratification we derive from listening is from the alternation of tension and relaxation that comes from our expectations being

---

[10]Ibid., p. 106.
[11]Ibid., p. 107.
[12]Ibid., p. 110.

frustrated and then fulfilled.[13] This is a classic psychological explanation of a gratification deriving from the release of tension, and its roots go back to Aristotle's *Poetics.*

Expectancies and Novelties

Music both satisfies our expectancies and also suprises us with novelty. Whether or not the listener expects something, or is surprised by something else, relates to two variables: how well organized the music seems to be, and how much knowledge or experience the listener has about the ways the music could be organized.[14] Psychologist John Booth Davies put the question in terms of *information,* saying that a highly redundant/high probability tune has a low information value, whereas a tune with much originality has high information value, in the sense that when a new event in the tune takes place, the listener's uncertainty about what will happen next is reduced.[15] But that did not answer the question of what kinds of music people liked. Davies predicted that people would prefer music that provided them with enough information to reduce their uncertainty about upcoming events in the music. Conversely, he believed that people would not like music that failed to reduce such uncertainty, either because it did not provide enough information (there was too much novelty), or because it provided too much information (there was too little novelty). Most people, Davies predicted, would like music that contained an intermediate amount of information: music that was both novel and predictable at the same time.[16] (Davies affirmed that the differences between listeners in the level of their previous musical experience would certainly cause them to experience the piece as having different levels of complexity, so that a person's liking for a song would not be entirely based on information factors inherent in the song.)[17]

Complexity Elicits More Attention

Davies also predicted that listeners would pay more *attention* to music that is slightly more complex than the music they would listen to just for pleasure.[18] Put in terms of pop music played on the radio, this seems to say that we pay closer attention to music that we have to work a bit to appreciate, but we tend to enjoy music that is a little simpler. On the other hand, each time a piece is repeated, the listener is likely to find it less complex. If the initial complexity seemed to be too high, the listener may well find that the music becomes more enjoyable. But where the initial complexity was too low, repeated exposure will make the music seem unchallenging and not worthy of attention, presumably because too little new

---

[13]Rosenfeld, A.H. (1985, December). Music, the beautiful disturber. *Psychology Today,* p. 50.

[14]Davies, J.B. (1978). *The psychology of music* (p. 75). London: Hutchinson

[15]Ibid., p. 89.

[16]Ibid., p. 90.

[17]Ibid., p. 96.

[18]Ibid., p. 98.

information is available.[19] Davies also said that a period of "intense exposure" to a tune may well cause us to be "fed up" with it, but that if the song is put away for awhile, the next time it is heard it is stimulating again.[20] He probably would question radio music rotations that put much emphasis on playing "recurrent" hits.

Familiarity and Novelty

A study by June E. Downey and George E. Knapp titled "The Effect on a Musical Programme of Familiarity and of Sequence of Selections" reported on the relationship of familiarity and novelty to the listener's response. They pointed out that certain individuals have such a strong need for familiarity that everything strange is viewed as unpleasant, whereas others are obsessive about experiencing the new or the bizarre and cannot abide the familiar. But for most people,

> Familiarity is in itself a pleasant feeling; it involves the *recognitive thrill* which is in part a feeling of safety, of being *at home*. . . . With too great acquaintance, however, familiarity lapses into triteness and pleasingness washes out. The only protection against such waning in value is a very rich content in the object.
>
> Novelty is a second factor which forces attention and brings in train the joy of adventure. In order that the *familiar* may not pass over into the *trite,* its contents must be so rich, so complex, as to insure continued discovery of new beauties, or subtleties not to be grasped from one presentation.[21]

The Appeal of Complex, Original Music

The quote just cited explains how the basic program appeals of familiarity and novelty apply specifically to music listening. The colorful language of the phrase "With too great acquaintance, however, familiarity lapses into triteness and pleasingness washes out" is about the best description we will ever get for what we would today call "record burnout." And the proposed cure is also worth noting: "In order that the *familiar* may not pass over into the *trite,* its content must be so rich, so complex, as to insure continued discovery of new beauties, or subleties not to be grasped from one presentation." That seems to be a call for music that is not necessarily assimilable in just one hearing. Instead, for many listeners, music should be "dense." In fact, what Downey and Knapp said about music might well be said about audio production and everything else in radio programming: If it is going to be heard more than once, it should be rich enough with detail and nuance that it can stand up to repetition.

---

[19]Ibid., p. 94.

[20]Ibid., pp. 95–96.

[21]Downey, J.E., & Knapp, G.E. (1968). The effect on a musical programme of familiarity and of sequence of selections. In M. Schoen (Ed.), *The effects of music* (pp. 238–239). Freeport, NY: Books for Libraries Press.

The Appeal of Obvious, Familiar Music

On the other hand, it is important to also take into account–as Downey and Knapp did–the fact that certain listeners will find anything out of the ordinary to be disagreeable. Often, younger teenage listeners fall under this description, because they are struggling to make statements about their individuality before they are really clear about who they are. Music that is too novel can be threatening to teens because it probably lacks peer approval. The form, the presentational style, even the names of heavy metal groups are a case in point. In spite of the high level of musicianship often displayed, it can be argued that heavy metal is a very narrowly defined genre, which allows little leeway for true experimentation. The lyrics and vocal style of many heavy metal groups suggest a surface alienation and reckless-ness, while the form of the melodic line, instrumentation, and performance tend to be comfortably familiar to teens. Thus, teenage listeners who adopt this music can, in effect, cloak themselves in a verbal aura of aloofness, angst, or danger while the other musical elements stay safely grounded in familiar, peer-approved territory. The result is often music that is remarkably strict in its adherence to form, while fulfilling the function of saying something like "kiss off!" or the impolite equivalent. Like the ballet, it is a form where all the possible moves have apparently already been invented; now the appreciation comes not from innovation but from the virtuosity of technical accomplishment in the presentation.

Those who remember the disco format will recall that one song tended to sound like another, just as some people feel "rap" music does today. And if most heavy metal music seems to take its cues from other heavy metal music, the same is also true of the pop love ballad. In any pop song, there is likely to be far more that is familiar than is novel.

Reliability

Percy Tannenbaum made the point that certainty is related to familiarity, in the sense that what is certain is preferred to what is uncertain. Certainty, when paired with familiarity, begets reliability, a very positive attribute.[22] Bedtime stories repeated endlessly to satisfy a child of course have great familiarity. Because they are the same every time, they also have certainty. The resulting *reliability* is why they soothe a child to sleep.

Perhaps instead of concentrating on the familiarity of airplay music, we should be looking at its reliability. Reliability carries with it the notion that the same *result* will be produced for the listener upon each rehearing, much as a bedtime story once did. The question to be asked then is different. It is no longer "Is this song familiar?" or even "Do you like this song?" Rather it should be "Does this song make you feel roughly the same way it did when it was new to you?" Reliability does not mean that a given song is good forever. On the contrary: because reliability takes *continued effectiveness* into account, songs that are familiar to the point of being over-played might not be reliable ones.

"Liking" and "Popularity"

A listener's "liking" for a song has much to do with appeals. It may also have to do with a song's "popularity" (its "hit-ness"), but "liking" and "popularity" are two different concepts. Most radio stations that play current hit music spend a lot of time tracking a song's popularity. The music director is usually aware of the general life cycle of a song's popularity, maybe even how a curve plotting that popularity is very like the curves of Aristotelian structure, sleep rhythms, and arousal/satiation, especially when early hearers and late hearers are averaged. But the music director may have given less thought to the concept that music popularity is a macro-time mood consideration – that the public's "mood" or attitude toward the music changes over the course of that song's advent, ascendency, zenith, and decline.

Consider the oldie, or some obscure jazz tune, or a dusty piano sonata. None is currently "popular" in the traditional meaning of the word. And yet there is high "liking" for these forms among certain listeners, quite apart from when they were hits (if they ever were).

Popularity should also be distinguished from "familiarity." Popularity is a state of being, whereas familiarity is the flipside of the appeal modifier known as originality.

Popularity Versus Familiarity

Familiarity is a strong and desirable component in the attraction of any song – perhaps not the song *en toto,* but at least the familiarity of the elements which make it up. Familiarity is almost always a factor in a song's popularity (or lack of it). In defining "categories of familiar music" in *Music and Program Research,* James E. Fletcher said of "current" songs:

> It is not always correct to characterize a "current" as new music, since popularity is based on resemblance to music already familiar to the targeted audience. Actually, fans expect only about fifteen percent of a song labelled "new" to be really new. If a familiar and beloved performing group releases a recording in another musical style, old fans often issue a strong negative reaction.[23]

Familiarity Varies With Time Spent Listening

Note that familiarity is a factor that varies depending on the length of exposure to the radio. With increased radio listening, familiarity with *all* musical elements also

[23]Fletcher, J.E. (1987). *Music and program research* (p. 17). Washington, DC: National Association of Broadcasters.

increases. When radio listening can be characterized as heavy, many elements begin to sound familiar to the listener. As a result, we would expect to find a higher novelty need, and greater risk-taking among heavy listeners, who would be trying to discover the unfamiliar. Among heavy listeners, a song's (or a performer's) popularity may be less important. Innovation theory suggests this happens sooner, and more often, among the "cosmopolites" in the population: those living in larger cities, having more education, and greater overall media exposure. Urban and suburban teenage listeners are an obvious example.

Please keep in mind that "novelty" or "originality" (and its flipside, "familiarity") are but two of the "content" appeals. Many more of those appeals are likely to be factors which contribute to a song's popularity.

Novel/Familiar "Hooks"

The term *hook* is widely used in describing a certain short melodic passage in a popular recording that is thought to be the novel element that sets this song apart from others in the listeners' minds, and thus augments the record's popularity. In call-out and auditorium research, it is often the hook of the song that is played for the listener. The novel elements are likely to be of any sort: production effects, vocal inflection, rhythmic change, unexpected timbres, and so on. The 1984 hit record "Jump" by Van Halen began with a synthesizer timbre that was then new to the public. That quality has come to be known as the "fat synth" sound because it was perceived as richer and bigger than previously recorded synthesizers. Clearly, some of the record's success was a result of that then-unique sound. Nothing quite like it had been heard before. Today, the sound is commonplace. Although a listener would easily recognize the "fat synth" hook, it no longer works as novelty, but rather as familiarity. That is what happens to pop music hooks. Because they generally are different in only one way, they do not offer the denseness and richness of more elaborate music. The *novel* pop music hook becomes *familiar* and eventually passes over into being *trite*.

THE PHYSICAL APPEALS OF RADIO MUSIC

We listen to music – from whatever source – because it moves us. Researcher Avram Goldstein of Stanford University found that of a test group of more than 250 people, 96% reported being "thrilled" by certain musical selections, which put music a full 26% ahead of sexual activity as a thrill supplier. Goldstein's subjects described thrills in terms of such physical sensations as goosebumps, chills, shudders, tickling, tingling, a lump in the throat, or crying.[24] The same research showed that although the intensity of response was different between one listening session and another,

---

[24]Rosenfeld, A.H. (1985, December). Music, the beautiful disturber. *Psychology Today,* p. 55.

people tended to have the same pattern of thrills every time they heard a particular piece of music.[25]

In an earlier chapter, the listener's desire for not just "feeling" but actual physical reactions to what he or she hears was outlined. Of course, the wish to experience kinaesthetic responses also applies to the music listener. Music performers often experience "motor" responses to the music they hear: the pianist feeling a phrase in the fingers, the horn player in the lips, and so on.[26] Rhythm is not the only source of these responses. According to Otto Ortman, kinaesthetic responses are also a result of

> the outline described by melodic motion, and the strain and relaxation involved in dissonance and consonance, as well as in *crescendo* and *diminuendo*. And, since movement is, perhaps, the most effective of all musical elements, kinaesthetic sensations are a very important type of non-auditory response. They, like the visual, are far more usual than is generally admitted, and form the true basis of many responses that are daily traced to auditory sources.[27]

Moreover, one does not have to be a performer of music to have such responses. As is seen in the next chapter, considerable research now exists that shows physical responses to certain rhythmic patterns and melodic lines to be virtually universal. But it is probably the rare instance in which broadcast music alone can cause a listener to laugh, cry, get goosebumps, and so forth. It is more likely to do so in a context, as when songs with similar (or perhaps contrasting) themes are played consecutively. Or when the song itself provides a strong context, telling a complete story with vivid images. Or when the listener provides from memory a nostalgic context for the song.

As has already been stated, the job of evoking kinaesthetic responses, of making radio participatory, is that of the total format, and should not fall primarily to the music played. It is the format as a whole, including commercials, and all the nonjock, nonrecord elements, that provides the total experience of the radio station in the listener's mind. But when music is the primary stimulus, and sometimes the only entertainment content of a radio station, the specific kinaesthetic effects it has on listeners are worth studying closely. That is the work of the next chapter.

MAJOR POINTS

1. Measures of hit music popularity do not go far enough. The question to be asked should be *"Why* is this song popular, and with whom?" Beyond that, what factors intrinsic to the *song* make it popular?

---

[25]Ibid., p. 56.

[26]Ortman, O. (1968). Non-auditory effects of music. In M. Schoen (Ed.), *The effects of music* (p. 254). Freeport, NY: Books for Libraries Press.

[27]Ibid., p. 254.

2. Early research on music effects found rhythm to be the dominant quality in developing feelings of excitement.

3. Complex passages elicited more attention, but repetition reduced that complexity and affected enjoyment. For some listeners, complex and original music will be prized, but for others, obvious and familiar music is more comfortable.

4. "Liking" and "popularity" are different concepts. The public's attitude toward a popular song changes with each hearing over the course of that tune's advent, ascendency, zenith, and decline. Oldies are "liked" even though they are no longer "popular," for example. Many popular songs are largely based on familiar musical ideas.

5. There is likely to be a higher novelty need and greater risk-taking among heavy listeners looking for unfamiliar music.

6. What begins as novelty in pop music over time becomes familiar and eventually passes over into being trite.

7. Listeners desire physical (kinaesthetic) responses to music.

CHAPTER 9

Music Moods Research

The preceding chapter showed why we listen to music on the radio by examining some of the basic appeals of airplay music. In that chapter, words like "effects," "feelings," and "enjoyment" were prominent. In this chapter, we focus more particularly on music as a generator of *moods,* and develop the theoretical structure for the mood-generating music progression that is offered in chapter 10.

RHYTHM, MELODY, PITCH, AND NOVELTY

What one of Gatewood's studies showed back in 1921 was that the effects that people report in listening to music spring from responses stimulated by certain musical elements, especially rhythm and melody. Although her sample was small and was confined to American college women, it did succeed in showing that not every response to music is a result of individual differences, but rather that there are musical elements that trigger responses more or less universally.

Years ago, psychologist Kate Hevner confirmed that listeners fairly consistently judged the same short musical excerpts similarly, basing their judgments on particular elements in the music itself. One of her findings was that people tended to describe music that was high-pitched as being playful and happy; low-pitched music was judged to be serious and sad (see Table 9.1). And although pitch was important in determining the mood, Hevner found *tempo* to be the single most important factor.[1]

---

[1] Rosenfeld, A. H. (1985, December). Music, the beautiful disturber *Psychology Today,* p. 51.

TABLE 9.1
Pitch a Factor in Determining Mood

High-Pitched Music	Low-Pitched Music
Playful	Serious
Happy	Sad

Pleasantness and Activation Reactions

Psychologist Julian Thayer of Pennsylvania State University, in a more recent study with Jeffrey S. Tanaka and Wayne Winborne of New York University, corroborated the earlier findings of Gatewood and others that listeners' reactions to music could be ranged on a "pleasantness" continuum from happiness and amusement on the one hand to disgust and sadness on the other; and on an "activation" continuum from tension and excitement at one side to relaxation and sadness on the other (see Table 9.2 on p. 132).[2] Thayer, Tanaka, and Winborne found that listeners' reactions were consistently related to the music's pitch and tempo. Specifically, pitch affected the pleasantness rating (note how this corroborates Hevener's findings about pitch), whereas tempo affected the activation rating.[3]

Either Very Exciting or Very Quieting Songs Preferred

As concerned the relation of pleasantness to exciting and quieting effects, Washburn and Dickinson found that listeners enjoyed music the most that moved them away from whatever their median state was, whereas music that was either much more exciting than usual or much more relaxing and soothing than usual was appreciated more than music that straddled the middle ground.[4] This has links directly to the ideas presented in chapter 4 showing that most people desire to be either aroused or satiated, rather than live in a median state between the two extremes.

Emotional States Accompanying Listening

A further step toward the consideration of the moods that instrumental music induces was taken in an article by Max Schoen and Esther L. Gatewood titled "Problems Related to the Mood Effects of Music." Eleven emotional effects were isolated, following study of over 20,000 "mood change charts" that reported on the behavior of a true demographic cross-section of listeners. However, the music was what we would today call classical and light classics, plus a march or two. Thus, it is not surprising that the most frequently listed emotional effect was "sadness."

[2]Ibid., p. 51.

[3]Ibid., p. 51.

[4]Washburn, M. F., & Dickinson, G. L. (1968). The sources and nature of the affective reaction to instrumental music. In M. Schoen (Ed.), The effects of music (p. 126). Freeport, NY: Books for Libraries Press.

TABLE 9.2
Pleasantness and Activation Continua

Pleasantness Continuum—Most Affected by Pitch
Happiness, Amusement < -> Disgust, Sadness

Activation Continuum—Most Affected by Tempo
Tension, Excitement < ->Relaxation, Sadness

However, "joy" was a close second, followed by rest, love, longing, and stirring. Dignity, amusement, reverence, irritation, and disgust brought up the bottom of the list.[5]

Desire for Mood Maintenance or Change

Schoen and Gatewood also were able to make some conclusions about which moods listeners generally wanted to maintain, and which they wanted to escape. They found that joyful, exhilarating music leaves the listener desiring more of the same, whereas sad, depressing music leaves the listener desiring a change, with milder, more restful music leaving the listener indifferent about what he or she hears next.[6] (See Table 9.3 on p. 133.) It is important to keep in mind this continuum—from joyful and exhilarating on the one end to sad and depressing on the other—because when combined later with Clynes' work, it is shown that certain rhythms and melody lines are predictive of the mood that will be produced.

Schoen and Gatewood also answered the question of consistency; that is, how many people desire music like their present mood each time, and how many desire music that is different each time? While cautioning that there were only two trials with 32 people, the investigators nevertheless found high consistency.

> If they chose music like the existing mood on one occasion they also did the second time. If, on the other hand, they chose music unlike the existing mood they again chose music unlike the existing mood. It therefore seems to be an individual variation which is consistent with the individual.[7]

Music Mood Novelty/Stability Seekers

This is also an important concept. It says that music listeners can be classified two ways: as what we might call "music mood stability seekers" and as "music mood novelty seekers." Neither the format nor the music can expect to change this basic

---

[5]Schoen, M., & Gatewood, E.L. (1968). Problems related to the mood effects of music. In M. Schoen (Ed.), *The effects of music* (p. 154).
[6]Ibid., p. 173.
[7]Ibid., p. 168.

TABLE 9.3
Desire for Mood Maintenance or Change

Exhilarating	*Restful*	*Depressing*
Generally a desire for continuation of this mood	Indifference as to succeeding type of music	Generally a desire for a change away from this mood

predisposition. There is some evidence that emotionally intense people seek novelty, complexity, and variety, but that the average level of intensity drops during each decade of life. The greatest drop in intensity is between the 20s and 40s.[8] In terms of current format radio listening, it would mean that certain listeners are going to be dial-hoppers no matter what: some of them (the mood stability seekers) going elsewhere because the station is not supplying a consistent enough mood, and others (the mood novelty seekers) going elsewhere because the station seems to be supplying too much of the same mood. No format (unless it makes music mood its first consideration) could hope to keep such listeners long term (see Table 9.4 on p. 134).

It is important to keep these points in mind: (a) Hearing *either* familiar *or* novel *music* could satisfy either the music mood stability seeker or the music mood novelty seeker. (b) Novelty of mood is not the same as novelty of music. (c) Stability of mood is not the same as familiarity of music.

It is essential to make the distinction between music *mood* stability/novelty seekers, and the very different idea of desiring either familiar or novel music – quite apart from the mood it creates. Theoretically, a music mood stability seeker could seek to achieve that stability through hearing *either* familiar or novel music. The same is true of the music mood novelty seeker.

Does a Station Need to Match a New Listener's Mood?

The research of Schoen and Gatewood has still more to say to the station that might decide to try to program in congruence with music moods rather than follow a standard popularity-based format. One of the questions which that station must answer is, given that every tuner-in comes to the listening experience with an existing mood, does the station's music stand a chance of changing or enhancing that mood? The answer from the research would seem to be "yes" – the existing mood of the listener is only a minor factor, because the music itself has "some dominant affective quality which awakens in the listener a characteristic response. The physiological increase or decrease of energy is directly dependent upon the music and is but little influenced, except in quantity, by the already existing mood of the listener."[9] So, although the majority of listeners – whether in an active or passive

---

[8]Studies portray the passionate, the impassive. (1987, March 26). *Kansas City Times*, pp. B-4, B-6.
[9]Schoen and Gatewood, Problems related to the mood effects of music (p. 170).

TABLE 9.4
Music Mood Stability/Novelty Seekers Contrasted

Music Mood Stability Seeker	Music Mood Novelty Seeker
Hops from station to station because he or she feels no single popularity-based format station supplies a mood consistently enough	Hops from station to station because he or she feels any given popularity-based format station supplies too much of the same mood

mood—prefer *succeeding* music to fit their existing mood, that finding seems to apply to the *continuation* of listening, rather than to the beginning of listening.

Application

Summaries of the research have already been supplied, but perhaps applications would be helpful to clarify the usefulness of all of the findings just discussed. (a) If a station sticks with a standard music format, it should expect to have some dial-hopping listeners of two persuasions: music mood stability seekers and music mood novelty seekers. But if the station attempts to program on the basis of mood, then (b) it can expect listeners to begin listening with a pre-existing mood. (c) Listeners prefer to hear music that matches an existing mood, even if that mood is passive rather than active. But the station is not trapped in the mood pattern of the majority listener, because (d) the existing mood pattern can be effectively changed through the music played. It is much more important for a station to build a mood from song to song (once a mood is established) than to worry about the pre-existing mood of new tuners-in.

MENDELSOHN'S MUSIC MOODS RESEARCH

In 1961, social scientist Harold Mendelsohn studied radio listeners in New York City for radio station WMCA, which at that time was running a pop music format. Mendelsohn conducted intensive personal interviews with 150 teenage and adult radio listeners in the New York metro area. The results of that study are so striking that they bear extended reproduction here. Note that the emphasis supplied to the words given here all came from Mendelsohn; the headings are mine.

Pop Music Listeners Accept Many Diverse Music Forms

A major finding of Mendelsohn's research was that people did not seem to have a taste for just one type of music to the exclusion of every other type. The one exception was a general distaste for strictly classical music. For the most part, every possible combination of nonclassical music received some acceptance from someone. . . . In other words, popular musical tastes seem to be highly individualized, and form no clear-cut pattern of persistent choice. It would be mistaken to visualize the listener to popular music as enjoying *only* rock and roll, or enjoying *only* "cool jazz," or enjoying *only* "show tunes" . . .[10]

Individual Mood Needs Are More Important Than Taste Predispositions

Mendelsohn's research more than 20 years ago made a key discovery that shows the linkage between (a) a lack of exclusive preferences and (b) the element in music that gives pleasure.

The key to understanding why there is a lack of exclusive preference where taste for popular music is concerned also helps unlock the mystery of what it is about popular music that is found to be pleasurable. The data in the New York radio audience study, and later on in the Colorado study, indicated that taste for a specific kind of music is generally more dependent upon the immediate *mood* of the individual than upon any immutable "taste predisposition." This is to say that popular music is enjoyed primarily because it either serves to *create* a desired mood; or to *change* an undesirable mood; or, to *sustain* and accompany an already established desirable mood. Where these mood needs are satisfied, pleasure is derived from a wide variety of musical forms . . .[11]

It would be hard to overemphasize the importance of this long-overlooked finding. The reason people do not have strong taste preferences for one kind of music to the exclusion of all other types is because the music is chosen to create, change, or sustain a *mood*. This finding has been further underscored by Zillmann and Bryant, who said:

The suggestion that entertainment preferences might vary with effects, moods, and emotions generally evokes considerable skepticism. It seems to be counterintuitive because people tend to believe that, if they are free to choose, they usually select whatever best meets their seemingly never changing taste.[12]

Desire for Variety

To be fair, radio format consultants have sometimes acknowledged the audience's desire for musical variety. But the typical response is often akin to this one which appeared in a radio trade publication:

[10]Mendelsohn, H. (1966). *Mass entertainment* (p. 121). New Haven, CT: College and University Press.
[11]Ibid., pp. 121–122.
[12]Zillmann, D., & Bryant, J. (1985). Affect, mood, and emotion as determinants of selective exposure. In D. Zillmann & J. Bryant (Eds.), *Selective exposure to communication* (p. 157). Hillsdale, NJ: Lawrence Erlbaum Associates.

Because variety is so much in demand, it might seem like the perfect time to alter our philosophies of targeting specific demos and increase variety in our music and programming mix, right? *Absolutely not!!!* The audience wants to sample different styles of music *but not on one station.* This common misconception springs from hearing listeners talk about their favorite music. They do want variety from their favorite station – a perceived variety – but only in the confines of a specific music genre.

Listeners who want to hear a variety of musical styles don't want it at the expense of altering their favorite station's sound. . . . With all the available options, they will tune in a station that superserves their desire to listen to a specific form of music.[13]

I think the programmer just quoted is offering the standard radio industry solutions. He may have based his thinking too heavily on the desires of the youngest radio listeners, who tend to have a high tolerance for song repetition and who develop strong affinities for certain peer-approved stations. The programmer was not thinking about the WMT-type listener, for whom the very inconsistency and lack of song repetition on the station is a drawing card.

Mendelsohn's crucial discovery decades ago was that people were not listening exclusively to certain musical genres. The style of the music was not nearly so important as the *mood* it created, changed, or sustained. But back then – as now – the major determinant of what music got played was popularity, formats based on popularity being the logical extension of the Top 40 concept. Mendelsohn's research went on to explain why radio listeners might feel compelled to tune around the dial to find the song they wanted:

It appears that two basic "mood needs" dominate the tastes and preferences of popular music devotees . . . the need for active mood accompaniment and the need for release from psychological tension. If the popular music fan seeks active mood accompaniment he will turn to music that in his words is "lively and peppy." On the other hand, if the popular music enthusiast's mood becomes fraught with psychological tensions, he will seek out the psychologically releasing music that he considers to be "relaxing." Curiously, "relaxing" music can be either pacifying such as waltzes or stimulating such as rock and roll.[14]

As we saw earlier in the work on "activation" by Thayer et al., there is a continuum – most influenced by a song's tempo – which runs from the pacific relaxation of waltzes to the exciting stimulation of rock and roll. Thus, the fact that relaxation from psychological tension can result from both quiet and exciting music is not so curious after all. Also note the consistency of Mendelsohn's discovery of the active mood accompaniment seeker who desires "lively, peppy" music with Schoen and Gatewood's finding 40 years earlier that listeners generally desire a continuation of an exhilarating mood.

---

[13]Pollack, J. (1988, December 16). Satisfying the complicated consumer. *Radio & Records*, p. 36.
[14]Mendelsohn, p. 122.

The Moods Questions That Need Asking

Keep in mind that two different studies by Mendelsohn "indicated that taste for a specific kind of music is generally more dependent upon the immediate *mood* of the individual than upon any immutable "taste predisposition." The word "popularity" does not appear anywhere in that sentence. Nor do any of the nouns or adjectives that describe contemporary radio music formats. Nowhere did listeners say that they primarily wanted music that was softly played and had a slow beat, or music that came from African or Caribbean sources, or that did or did not include pedal steel guitars. Yet for the most part, music research at radio stations continues to ask questions that deal mainly with the respondents' knowledge of the music ("Do you recognize this song?") or liking for the music ("Do you like this song?") Mendelsohn's research underscores the point that the real questions ought to be "How does this music make you feel?"

CLYNES' MUSIC MOODS RESEARCH

Frequent mention has been made of the work of Manfred Clynes, a musician and neuropsychologist. Clynes' contribution to the field of research into musically induced moods is important because he has been able to show that there are certain measurable, repeatable, *physical* reactions to given musical phrases. In addition, Clynes has presented evidence that these reactions are cross-cultural – that is, not dependent on Western rules and expectations about rhythm, pitch, timbre, etc.[15] He made a strong case that our reaction to musical phrases may be a result of biological determinants. Clynes said that there is a single common algorithm (or set of rules) in the brain for producing and recognizing certain kinds of dynamic musical expressions.[16] Clynes' research thus tried to answer the question "Are there dynamic forms that have an innate meaning, forms that can act upon the nervous system not in arbitrary ways but like keys in a lock, activating thereby specific brain processes to which we react in some sense emotionally?"[17] The answer in Clynes' research seems to be a clear "yes."

Non-Subjective Measurement Procedures

Unlike some of the research already reported, Clynes' work does not depend on subjective reports from listeners. Instead, Clynes' subjects learn to use a sentograph, a device that measures both finger *pressure* and the *direction* of any movement. Clynes

---

[15]For a refutation of this possibility, see Rosner, B.S., & Meyer, L.B. (1982). Melodic processes and the perception of music. In D. Deutsch (Ed.), *The psychology of music* (p. 320). New York: Academic Press.

[16]Clynes, M., & Nettheim, N. (1982). The living quality of music. In M. Clynes (Ed.), *Music, mind, and brain* (p. 51). New York: Plenum Press.

[17]Ibid., p. 47.

has devised ingenious experiments that trace the effects of both the rhythm and the melodic lines in music. Here is a description of how the sentograph is used in studying listeners' reactions to rhythm:

> a subject presses rhythmically with the pressure of a finger on a pressure transducer sensitive to both vertical and horizontal pressure. The seated subject as it were "dances" or "conducts" on his finger, keeping the finger in touch with the transducer all the way through, however, so that the rhythmic impulse is expressed as a pressure impulse produced by the arm. In this way pressure pulse contours are obtained that relate to specific sound rhythms . . .[18]

Predicting Body Movements From Rhythm

One of the things Clynes and Walker were seeking to do in the study just discussed was to see if a clear parallel could be drawn between rhythms heard and rhythmic body movements produced. If so, then it would be possible to predict (or even specify) which rhythms beget which body movements.

The Rhythmic Pulse As a Unitary Event

Clynes' research suggests that when the body's motor responses try to imitate a rhythmic pattern, it does indeed do so using a particular algorithm that contains *both* the activity and the rest, stored as a single form in memory. Clynes referred often to this "pulse." When the subjects in Clynes' experiments press rhythmically on the finger rest/pressure transducer, "pressure pulse contours are obtained that relate to specific sound rhythms . . ."[19]

This also works in reverse; that is, a person can be taught expressive finger pressure patterns that actually relate to the specific emotions being studied, but he or she learns them as simple motor skills. Then the subject is asked to match the patterns with a list of seven emotions that Clynes isolated. In Clynes' research, there is a remarkably high success rate.

Essentic Form: Fusion of Rhythm and Melody

Although it is common for musicians to talk of rhythm and melody as separate entities, it is also true that there cannot be a melody without some rhythm to propel it forward, and that rhythm by itself is not usually thought to be a complete musical experience. Clynes' research considers rhythm and melody as a single entity: the dynamic expressive forms that Clynes called "essentic forms." These forms, developed and confirmed by research, are more than simple tones or rhythmic beats, and

---

[18]Clynes, M., & Walker, J. (1982). Neurobiologic functions of rhythm, time, and pulse in music. In M. Clynes (Ed.), *Music, mind, and brain* (p. 173). New York: Plenum Press.

[19]Ibid., p. 173.

they are less than complete melodic phrases. To make an analogy, they are more than the individual words in this sentence, but they are less than the point of the sentence as a whole, and certainly less than the concept of this section of the book. Yet essentic forms are more direct in their impact. According to Clynes and Nettheim:

> Words denoting specific emotions, like the word joy or anger for example, may induce the mind to imagine aspects of joy or of anger to a various and controllable extent. The dynamic expressive sound forms for specific emotions have more direct power to induce this; and this so to the extent to which they precisely express that particular dynamic shape, i.e., one can say, the more "pure" an expression of joy or anger they are. In their pure form they require a special effort, a mental screen, to be ignored: it is difficult to remain unaffected in the presence of a true, authentic expression of grief, or of joy, as it indeed also can be in the presence of very sad or joyful music. Such gripping dynamic emotional "words," or essentic forms, are a means of emotional contagion in daily life, which may be used with a sense of putative power by demagogues and commercial advertisers, or as mutual emotional communication between persons; or in an autocommunicative way as in music and art where the communicative power creates its own rewards.
>
> Essentic form by itself appears to act directly to communicate its quality – no symbolic transformation is required, according to our theory and findings . . .[20]

Seven Emotions Isolated, With Their Expression Times

The seven emotions or sentic states that Clynes isolated in his studies are anger, hate, grief, love, sex, joy, and reverence. Each of these has its own unique expressive form. One component of the form is the length of time it takes for each expression to occur. That duration is its expression time. The times range from a low of 0.7 seconds for anger to a high of 9.8 seconds for reverence.[21]

TABLE 9.5
Expression Times for Seven Emotions (after Clynes, 1982)[22]

Shortest			*(Times in Seconds)*			*Longest*
Emotion:	Anger	Joy	Hate	Sex	Love	Grief	Reverence
Expr. time:	0.7	1.1	1.6	2.0[a]	5.2	9.0	9.8

[a]Not mentioned in text. Inferred from graphs.

---

[20]Clynes and Nettheim, The living quality of music. In Clynes, p. 51.

[21]According to Paul Fraise, "The slowest adagio in a 9/4 bar is no longer than 5 sec. and the longest lines of poetry have from 13 to 17 syllables, the time necessary to recite them being no longer than from 4 to 5 sec. . . . . . . According to Sears (1902), the average length of a musical bar in religious hymns is 3.4 sec. According to Wallin (1901), the average duration of lines of poetry is 2.7 sec." Fraise, P. (1982). Rhythm and tempo. In D. Deutsch (Ed.), *The psychology of music* (p. 158). New York: Academic Press.

[22]After Clynes and Nettheim, in Clynes, p. 56.

Inflection (Pitch Changes)

Another component of each form is what might be called its inflection. Clynes referred to it as frequency modulation – that is, the way the beginning frequency (the base frequency at which the tone begins to sound) is modulated up or down by increasing or decreasing finger pressure on the laboratory sentograph.[23] Figure 9.1 shows how vertical and horizontal finger pressure on the sentograph transducer were reproduced on a chart recorder.

Clynes also found that the modulation depth was very different for different emotions:

Love had only a small modulation; the sound has a steady secure quality. The downward modulation range though quite small (less than a semitone) was essential to the expression of this quality.

Anger an upward modulation range of approximately a minor sixth.

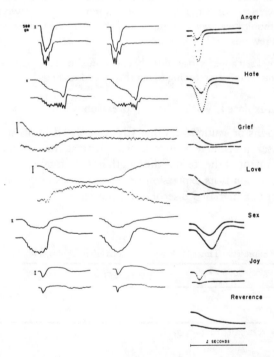

FIG. 9.1. Examples of "sentograms" of the essentic form of emotions (after Clynes, 1982, p. 55).[24]

---

[23]A soundsheet containing recordings of the seven essentic forms is included in a pocket on the inner back cover of Clynes' book *Music, Mind, and Brain.* It is helpful in understanding the modulation that becomes the "melody line."

[24]Clynes and Nettheim, in Clynes, p. 55.

TABLE 9.6
Modulation of Base Frequency During Expression of Each Emotion (After Clynes, 1982)[26]

Emotion:	Anger	Joy	Hate	Sex	Love	Grief	Reverence
Direction:	up	*	down	up	down**	down	up
% change:	59%	*	05%	14%	2.4%	21%	09%

*"one octave: biphasic 20% down then 61% up"
**note the very small modulation – almost steady.

TABLE 9.7
Expression Times and Modulation of Base Frequencies[27]

Emotion:	Anger	Joy	Hate	Sex	Love	Grief	Reverence
Expr. Time:	0.7	1/1	1.6	2.0**	5.2	9.0	9.8
Direction:	up	*	down	up	down***	down	up
% change:	59%	*	05%	14%	2.4%	21%	09%

*"one octave: biphasic 20% down then 61% up"
**Not mentioned in text. Inferred from graphs.
***note the very small modulation – almost steady.

Hate a very small downward modulation – the quality of its hard containment not permitting more modulation.

Grief a downward modulation range of about four semitones.

Sex an upward modulation range of approximately three semitones.

Joy initially a downward modulation followed by a swing upwards, which then subsides to the starting point. Total perceived modulation range – one octave – a third down, an octave up and a sixth down.

Reverence an upward modulation of approximately two to four semitones.[25]

Notice that each of the emotions has both a frequency direction (up or down in pitch), and a frequency depth. When these changes occur during the emotion's expression time is of critical importance in distinguishing one emotion from another, but for now, it is useful to just present a table showing the direction and depth of each emotion's frequency modulation (see Table 9.6).

Recall that what the words "up" and "down" referred to in Table 9.6 is the way the pitch of the original tone changes over the expression time, and that the percentage figure shows in a general way how much change there is.

For the purposes of advancing future arguments, Table 9.7 presents the two previous tables as a single table. Clynes did not present his results this way; the table is an amalgam of my own design.

---

[25]Clynes and Nettheim, in Clynes, pp. 62–63.
[26]Ibid, pp. 62–63.
[27]After Clynes and Nettheim, in Clynes, pp. 56 & 62–63.

Expressions in the Psychological Present

One of the things to note about the *length* of the essentic forms Clynes isolated is that none exceeds 10 seconds. That means, according to several psychologists, that all but the longest will probably seem to the listener to be happening entirely in the present moment. William Stern defined the psychological present this way:

> Within the "present". . . . . . falls the immediate aftermath or development of the experience, the perpetuation of which cannot yet be regarded as the product of an act of memory or recall. The "psychological present" has been assigned values of between five and seven seconds; even a trained expert musician will scarcely be able to extend it beyond nine seconds.[28]

Thus, Clynes' assertions that these forms operate in very direct ways, without the need for the listener to think about them, would appear to have good support.

Having developed this foundation of research into the moods and physiological responses that music engenders, we can now proceed in the next chapter to explore the specific elements of a mood-evoking music progression.

MAJOR POINTS

1. Research into the moods evoked by music shows that listeners prefer either very exciting or very quieting songs. Joyful, exhilarating music leaves listeners desiring more of the same, whereas sad, depressing music leaves the listener desiring a change. Restful music tends to leave the listener indifferent about what is heard next.

2. Music listeners can be classified two ways: as music mood stability seekers (who hop from station to station because they feel no single popularity-based format supplies a mood consistently enough), and as music mood novelty seekers (who hop from station to station because they feel any given popularity-based format supplies too much of the same mood).

3. Hearing *either* familiar *or* novel music could satisfy either the music mood stability seeker or the music mood novelty seeker. Novelty of mood is not the same as novelty of the music played. Stability of mood is not the same as familiarity of the music played.

4. A station need not attempt to try to match new listeners' moods, because the finding that listeners prefer succeeding music to fit their existing mood applies to the continuation of listening, rather than to the beginning of listening.

5. High-pitched music is generally perceived as playful and happy; low-pitched music is felt to be serious and sad. Perceived pleasantness is most affected by pitch,

---

[28]Rosing, H. (1984). Listening behavior and musical preference in the age of "transmitted music." In R. Middleton & D. Horn (Eds.), *Popular music 4* (p. 129). Cambridge, England: Cambridge University Press.

whereas the degree of activation (from tense to relaxed) is most affected by tempo (rhythm).

6. According to Mendelsohn, desire for a specific kind of music is generally more dependent upon the immediate mood of the individual than on some pre-ordained taste. Pop music is enjoyed primarily because it serves to create a desired mood, change an undesirable one, or sustain and accompany an already-established mood.

7. Relaxation from psychological tension can result from both quiet and exciting music.

8. Most music research continues to ask "Do you like this song?" or "Do you recognize this song?" The real question should be "How does this music make you feel?"

9. Clynes' research shows there are certain measurable, repeatable, cross-cultural physical reactions to given music phrases which have innate meaning for the hearer. These phrases ("essentic forms") are a fusion of rhythm and melody–more than simple tones or rhythmic beats, and less than complete melodic phrases.

10. Clynes isolated seven "sentic states" or emotions–anger, grief, love, sex, joy, and reverence–each having a typical expression time and inflection. All of these expressions fall within the psychological "present" moment.

CHAPTER 10

The Components of a Mood-Evoking Music Progression

R. Murray Schafer has pointed out that when classical composers repeated a theme numerous times, they did so not from a lack of inventiveness, but to impress the theme on the listener's memory. Schafer contended that the development of athematic musical style (that is, a style that lacks repetitions) a little after the turn of this century occurred at about the same time as phonograph records became successful with a mass audience. From that time on, said Schafer, the phonograph record provided the means for repetition. In his view, the ability to repeatedly play a recording is a means used by the listener to provide a certain comfortable sense of permanence in an era when rapidly changing events make the future seem uncertain. Schafer said that radio stations, by repeatedly playing the same few recordings, have catered to this human need for a greater sense of stability and security.[1] Yet I would argue that formats based on playing current hits actually work counter to this goal – that the ephemeral nature of artist popularity and the ever-shorter life cycles of hit records ultimately convey a sense of instability rather than steadiness.

This chapter builds upon the music and moods research in the previous chapters (as well as earlier material, especially on structure and appeals) to establish the structural bases of a mood-generating music progression. The term *music progression* is used because it is intended to be less encompassing than the term *music format*. A music progression merely means the order in which recorded music is presented to the listener. This chapter shows how the ordering of songs needs to be based on much more than an assessment of the tune's popularity. It also introduces and explains those additional factors that should be included in a music presentation system. A sample music progression is offered in chapter 12.

---

[1]Schafer, R.M. (1977). *The tuning of the world* (pp. 113–114). New York: Alfred A. Knopf.

MUSIC PRESENTATION BASED ON MOOD NEEDS

Problems and Strengths

At least two pitfalls in trying to develop a music progression based on "mood needs" become apparent fairly quickly. The first is that one listener's mood needs at a given moment are likely to be different from another's. A second is that how a piece of music makes one person feel may be somewhat different from how it makes another feel. There seems to be far too much chance of individual differences in both cases.

Yet the basis for some commonality also exists. First, we know that different audiences make themselves available to listen at different times of the day, and as a result, stations daypart accordingly. The findings about circadian rhythm patterns presented in chapter 4 suggest it may also be possible to track certain "mood rhythms" that coincide with the biological clocks we all share. And in chapter 9, it was shown that the music a station is playing at the time someone is beginning to listen is more influential on their mood than is the mood they had before tuning in. So, although the majority of listeners – whether in an active or passive mood – prefer succeeding music to fit the existing mood, that finding seems to apply to the *continuation* of listening rather than to the beginning of listening.

Second, we know that there are considerable variations in the way persons from the same demographic background will react to a given piece of music. Yet, research – especially that by Clynes, presented earlier – indicates that there are certain universal factors that work even across widely varying cultures that allow classification of certain musical phrases into mood categories.

Recognizing Listeners' Mood Needs

As we begin to try to structure a mood-evocative music progression, it is necessary to re-affirm that radio music listeners do not listen just to hear some abstraction called "music" – they listen for certain kinds of music that serve certain kinds of mood functions for the listener. Those mood functions are generally not simple, and presenting them well is not easy.

One of the things that killed disco as a format was its continual "upness" – not just in terms of the number of beats per minute, but its mood. It was always electric, always bright and glittery. And after awhile, that one mood, that one stimulus, stopped being a stimulus. The disco format needed ballads, blues, and harder rock in order to provide the contrast that would let us realize the good stuff at the heart of the format. Disco showed that providing a *single* consistent mood and style was not sustainable as a format, even though there were plenty of people who enjoyed the mood for the first few minutes they tuned in.

Ultimately, developing a music presentation system that recognizes listeners' mood needs becomes "a search for meaning" on behalf of the audience. But most stations do not attempt such a search. The audience brings its searching to the radio, and it hears meanings being sung at them in 3- and 4-minute songs, but the meanings come and go with no particular interpretation or flow from one song to the next.

Where Things Stand; Where We are Going

This is where things stand at this point: We have a programmer trying to devise a mood generating music progression. The appeals of the music itself (chapter 8) have been explored. The way music affects and generates moods (chapter 9) are familiar. Now the job is to figure out a method of presentation – a structure – that maximizes the music's appeal to a target audience having certain mood needs.

The term *format* is not used here because for most radio people it conjures up visions of "hot clocks" and other hit rotation systems. The arguments up to this point have tried to put to rest the notion that a song's popularity should be its major claim to airplay (re-read chapters 8 and 9 if you are not convinced). The structure being offered in this chapter makes popularity only one among several measures of a song's airworthiness. Thus, "rotations" take a back seat to other, broader systems of music presentation that allow for satisfaction of both the music mood novelty seeker and the music mood stability seeker. Structure is not the enemy of the music mood novelty seeker, any more than chaos is his or her ally. And the same is true for the music mood stability seeker: Structure is simply a consistent method for pursuing a desired outcome.

Once "hit-ness" is stripped away as the prime reason for airplay, most stations are left with very little else in the way of a structure for music presentation. The question then becomes, "What rational bases are there for choosing to play this song next?" Some of the answers lie in an examination of musical structure itself, from the smallest component parts of sound to the larger concepts of sound hours and dayparts.

Structure, as the term is used here, starts with the given that most human beings strongly prefer order over disorder. So intense is the drive that we sometimes try to impose an arbitrary order on events that may not have any internal consistency. That is what a hit rotation does: It imposes the arbitrary order of hit position in the Top 40 (or in all-time airplay, for oldies) instead of trying to discern the internal links among songs that would cause them to be played in succession.

The internal links among songs are themselves structural. At the same time, a discernible structure in a song is an appeal, of sorts. Because we take pleasure in orderliness, we also delight in the recognition of a familiar sequence or phrase. Thus, it is not surprising that virtually every popular song likely to be played on the radio has a structured – rather than a random – form.

Once again, the stage movement terms *time, space,* and *force* are the windows we look through to frame the discussion in this chapter. This is appropriate because, in many ways, the popular song is the ultimate spoken gesture. A system that seeks to present a series of spoken gestures so that they have a cohesiveness and integrity of their own is then just a logical extension of what the song itself already does.

TIME

Body Rhythms

We first consider time, and begin by looking at the heartbeat and breathing rhythms of the human body, which R. Murray Schafer has shown to be highly influential of our speech and music. Schafer said that the human heartbeat is the first and perhaps the most influential of all the natural body rhythms. Schafer said that before the metronome was invented, musicians determined the tempo at which music was played by reference to the speed of a beating heart. He contended that because of this rather obvious rhythm in our bodies, music with a beat that is close to that of the human pulse has a natural appeal. There is evidence that this is as much the case in stone-age societies as in modern civilization. To support that point, Schafer mentioned the work of Catherine Ellis,who studied the tempi of the music of Australian aborigines. She found the basic drumbeat was usually close to that of the normal human pulse. On the other hand, Schafer pointed out, so was the "Ode to Joy" from Beethoven's Ninth Symphony.[2] It is happenstance that Schafer mentioned the "Ode to Joy," but Clynes found "joy" to have an expression of time of about 1.1 seconds – virtually at the same rate as a slow-normal heartbeat.

Breathing is another body rhythm that is probably highly influential of the tempi we set in music. Schafer said that the rhythms of spoken literature and poetry are usually related to breathing patterns. Even more than the heartbeat, the breathing rate varies with exertion. Normally, a person breathes between about 12 and 20 times per minute, taking roughly 3 to 5 seconds for each complete inhalation–exhalation.[3] It is interesting to note that a breathing rate of 12 to 16 cycles per minute corresponds well to Clynes' finding of an expression time for "love" of about 5.2 seconds. This would put it on the long, relaxed end of the inhalation–exhalation duration.

Paul Fraise, in an essay on rhythm and tempo, made a strong case for walking as an important rhythmic component:

> The duration of the step is about 550 msec, and corresponds to a frequency of 110–112 per minute. . . . This frequency depends a little on anthropometric differences between individuals, age, and environmental conditions. This spontaneous activity, which is similar to a reflex, is a fundamental element of human motor activity. It plays an important role in all of the rhythmic arts.[4]

,

---

[2]Ibid., p. 227.

[3]Ibid., p. 227.

[4]Fraise, P. (1982). Rhythm and tempo. In D. Deutsch (Ed.), *The psychology of music* (pp. 151–152). New York: Academic Press.

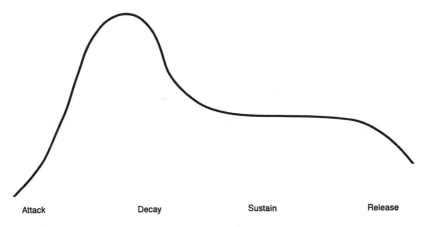

FIG. 10.1   ADSR sound envelope.

Time As a Structural Element in Sound:
The Sound Envelope

Next, we consider time as a structural element by making an analogy between the structure of a song and the "sound envelope" that describes the individual component sounds of the song.

Any sound can be described in terms of its sound envelope. A sound envelope is comprised of at least four parts: the sound's attack, the decay of that attack, the sustain of the main sound, and the release of the sustain. These four phases are often identified by the acronym ADSR standing for Attack–Decay–Sustain–Release. What ADSR values stand for is *timing* information: what is the duration of the attack, the duration of its decay, the duration of the sustain, the duration of the release?

ADSR Analogized to an Automobile

The terms *attack* and *decay* are really flip sides of the same coin, in the sense that they are the front edge and back edge of the initial part of the sound: the front bumper and grillwork on a car, as it were. Over time, the great bulk of the sound exists in the "sustain" portion, which could be analogous to the main body of the car. The release, although often much longer than the attack/decay, can be thought of as analogous to the tail lights and rear bumper. Thus, in micro-time, a sound has a fairly rapid onset, a long sustain, and a release of the sustain that can be of almost any speed.

ADSR Applied to Popular Songs

Popular songs have a similar structure. They generally do not take long to get the overall feel and direction of the tune established – usually no more than 10 to 20 seconds. The body of the song will generally last at least 3 minutes, but seldom more than 5 or 6 minutes. Most pop songs these days do not end abruptly, but rather they fade out over a period of 10 to 20 seconds, which is analogous to the release of the sustain. Using Mendelsohn's terms, the song's beginning creates a new mood (or changes an old one), whereas the body of the song serves to sustain the mood that the beginning has established.

Now consider the pop song again through the wider lens of Aristotelian structure. We trace the growth and development of individual songs, and the way those songs' internal timing and structure contribute to the growth and development of a sound hour.

ARISTOTELIAN STRUCTURE AND THE POPULAR SONG

Recall from chapter 4 that the four elements of Aristotelian dramatic structure are exposition, development, building to a climax, and resolution. An individual song will usually display most – if not all – of the elements of Aristotelian structure. The structure may be realized through the rhythm, the melody, and/or the lyrical content. Often, the instrumentation used, the arrangement, or the production techniques influence the sense of forward movement in the song. All of these factors are explored later.

An individual song may fit the Aristotelian model in a single sweep from beginning to end. These are likely to be "story" songs that recount what is already a dramatic event anyway.

More often, the chorus of a given song is a sort of climax, and the verse is the exposition and/or development that leads up to it. Later choruses in the song are often done with additional instruments or voices added, or are performed in a higher key, to increase the sense of climax.

The Lack of Resolution in Pop Music Structure

Often in popular music, there is little or no resolution – the climactic chorus is simply repeated and fades out. It is probably not too far-fetched to say that as music creators and listeners, we seem loathe to let go of our climaxes, and to admit that there is some period of time when we are on our way "down" instead of building up. It is the rare pop song heard on the radio that fades after a full resolution, rather than fading out the repeat of the climax. We tend not to notice this because the next song coming along generally begins at an exposition stage, which is at a low point in the building process, too. Thus, in much pop music, we really only deal with three of Aristotle's four structural elements: exposition, development, and building to a climax/climax. The next song's exposition substitutes for the last one's lack of resolution. Perhaps our pop music's failure to resolve completely is merely a reflection of our culture's anxiousness to get on with new things and to skip the weighing of what has gone before. It may be a reflection of our desire to "live in the

TABLE 10.1
Expression Times and Modulation of Base Frequency[5]

Emotion:	Anger	Joy	Hate	Sex	Love	Grief	Reverence
Expr. Time:	0.7	1/1	1.6	2.0**	5.2	9.0	9.8
Direction:	up	*	down	up	down***	down	up
% change:	59%	*	05%	14%	2.4%	21%	09%

   *"one octave: biphasic 20% down then 61% up"

   **inferred

   ***note the very small modulation – almost steady.

now" – to be in the state of "flow" where we relish not having the time to reflect on what has just happened. Or maybe the lack of resolution is a reflection of how our society turns to entertainment media like radio and recorded music to assist in achieving and maintaining a sort of perpetually climactic high, rather than dealing with the true ups and downs of life. Whatever the case, it is important for the programmer to realize that the resolution of the song playing now is usually in the exposition of the song that is to be played next.

Rhythms in Programming Sets of Songs

All of the structural elements just mentioned generally are presented at a consistent tempo *within* a song. When songs are placed in juxtaposition to each other, rhythms are likely to vary. Now, the case must be made that tempo/rhythms are an essential consideration in programming sets of songs during some smaller unit of time such as an hour. This is because there is a strong correlation between the mood of a song and the time it takes for that mood to be expressed. Recall from chapter 9 the discussion of Clynes' work on "essentic forms" – short phrases wherein rhythm and melody are expressed as a single entity. In that chapter, a table was offered that listed the seven emotions Clynes studied, along with their "expression times" (see Table 10.1). As was hinted earlier, expression times are at least partly tied to tempo, and in general, moods with longer expression times such as reverence and grief match up well with slow tempo music; moods with average expression times such as love, sex, and hate match up well with a wide range of medium tempos; and moods with short expression times such as joy and anger match up well with fast tempos. This makes logical sense as well: joy and anger are emotions that we experience "in the moment" with very little reflection or analysis, whereas we may only come to a sense of grief or reverence when we have devoted some time to thinking about the subject.

Combining Expression Times/Mood Categories
With Aristotelian Dramatic Structure

Although it was stipulated earlier that most pop tunes sustain the same tempo throughout a given song, certainly there can be great variety in tempo among a set

---

[5]After Clynes, M., & Nettheim, N. (1982). The living quality of music. In M. Clynes (Ed.), *Music, mind, and brain* (pp. 56, 62–63). New York: Plenum Press.

of songs. An analogy needs to be made again to the drama. There, an analysis of the length of scenes, or speeches, or the number of transitions, would usually show a rising curve that is consonant with the rising curve of tension as the drama develops, builds, reaches a climax, and then resolves. In other words, the closer to the climax, the shorter the speeches, the shorter the scenes, the greater the number of transitions. The overall rate of presentation speeds up.

Because reverence and grief have the longest of the expression times, it seems logical to assign to them the structural function of carrying out the exposition. Hate, love, and sex, with their average expression times, seem appropriate as the bearers of development; and joy and anger, with their quick expression times, seem best associated with climatic structure. As has been pointed out already, most pop music does not offer real dramatic resolution, and instead the exposition elements (reverence and grief) found in the beginning of the next song serve as the *de facto* resolution of the old one.

Thus, within a theoretical radio music hour that intended to run the mood gamut from low expression times to high and back again, there might be one or several sets or cycles of music such as the following: The set would begin (not necessarily at the top of the hour) in the slow expositional tempo associated with reverence and/or grief, increase in tempo as the mood shifts to the development phase featuring love, sex, or hate, reach a musical climax in the expression of joy and/or anger, and then begin the cycle again with the resolution/exposition of reverence and/or grief.

Adapting expression times to fit Aristotelian Structure allows radio music to be presented in a classic dramatic framework. However, the expectations that grow out of musical conventions should also be considered.

Phrasing

One of the attributes of a song, as performed, is phrasing. We think of *phrasing* — which is defined here as the inflection given certain musical passages by a change in the rate of delivery — as applying mostly to the lyric as sung. But phrasing applies to instrumental music, too. It starts with tempo or beats per minute (BPM) as a base, but then that basic rhythm is modulated by the melody line or the lyrics, so that certain especially important or poignant moments are emphasized. Phrasing is one of the elements that distinguishes expression times from BPM.

Just as phrasing is essential to the communication of important points within a song, so is it within a mood-evoking music presentation system. A sound hour that gave every tempo or expression category equal emphasis would wind up sounding like a vocalist who pronounces everything clearly but who — because of a lack of phrasing — seems devoid of commitment and verve. In other words, the mood-evoking sound hour needs to operate as an orchestra conductor does — using *two* hands. One marks the beat — the obvious, surface tempo, the beats per minute. The conductor's other hand gives the underlying emotion, the expression. In leading an orchestra, the two hands are sometimes complementary, sometimes at war. For example, a bass beat is continued with one hand, while the other diminishes, builds, or sustains a different line. Although the basic rhythm is what drives the music forward, it is the expression, the phrasing that modifies that forward motion and gives music (and by extension, sound hours) the desired impact.

Movement as Growth

We need to say more about the "forward movement" that takes place as a musical idea develops over time.

Music, like life, is usually perceived as moving forward toward some goal. The pulse of life is mirrored in music's rhythm. A single tone that sounds constantly has no meter, but once silences are interspersed, or other tones are mixed in, then we have no choice but to perceive a rhythmic pulse. And because rhythm happens over time, we understand that pulse to be an analog of some portion of our own lifespan. Every sound has a beginning, a sustain, and a decay, mirroring in microcosmic seconds the decades spanning our own birth, life, and death. While we live, we have no choice but to continue moving forward in time. We may have no idea of the goal our lives eventually will attain, but we can survey the past and discern the shape that our movement through time has produced. If in no other way than in the piling up of seconds ticking off the clock, our life is one of growth, whether we have willed it that way or not. So it is with music. Because music unfolds over a span of time, it is inevitably about growth—growth that is engendered by movement and that results in a certain shape. Jan LaRue in the book *Guidelines for Style Analysis* said:

> As we listen to a piece, its Movement leaves us with a host of short- and long-term memories that together constitute our sense of Shape in music, more or less defined and vivid, depending on the character of the musical material. At the first articulation in the musical flow ("articulation" is a better word than "punctuation," since it connotes both interruption and connection) the composer faces his first crisis: What should he do next? And although the choice seems infinite, it actually resolves into *four basic options for continuation:* recurrence, development, response, and contrast. Keeping these options in mind as a guiding hypothesis of Shape, we can more quickly recognize which procedure has been chosen; and in the course of the piece, we will gradually perceive a characteristic range or pattern of choices.[6]

Four Options for Continuation

What LaRue said about a section of classical music can be applied here to a popular song. And the same list of four options for continuation can also apply to a music progression. LaRue defined the four options for continuation further; listed here are my understanding of his definitions, with the connection made to radio music formats:

---

[6]LaRue, J. (1970). *Guidelines for style analysis* (p. 15), New York: Norton.

Recurrence–an immediate repetition, or one that happens after an intervening change.

Development–a continuation closely related by melody. (Development is not usually done in radio because melodies are not tracked. "Key" is the closest radio music programmers get.)

Response–a continuation unrelated melodically. (Rhythmic response continuation is common in radio music formats, but probably needs still more emphasis.)

Contrast–a complete change, usually following (and confirming) a heavy articulation by cadences and rests. (In the case of a radio sound hour, the cadences and rests could be something as obvious as a commercial set, or as subtle as an ID jingle which begins with one key or rhythm and ends with another.)

In his book *Emotion and Meaning in Music,* Leonard B. Meyer also discussed continuation, and was careful to distinguish it from repetition. Meyer underscored the sense in which musical growth must mean movement toward a goal, and how, when that motion is obscured, we expect change.[7] The idea can be applied to formats and rotations as well: so long as the listener can sense that there is movement toward some goal, he or she will not have a sense of repetition. Conversely, change (as an antidote to perceived repetition) will be expected when motion toward a goal is not clear. Meyer made the point in more detail later in his book:

A stimulus series, then, is well-shaped when its progress, its articulation into phases of activity and phases of rest, its modes of continuation, its manner of completion and closure, and even its temporary disturbances and irregularities are intelligible to the practiced listener and enable him to envisage with some degree of specificity and accuracy what the later stages of the particular musical process will be. Because good shape is intelligible in this sense, it creates a psychological atmosphere of certainty, security, and patent purpose, in which the listener feels a sense of control and power as well as a sense of specific tendency and definite direction.[8]

What Meyer offered in the aforementioned quote is a rebuttal to those who might argue that a mood-evoking music progression would be too "predictable." Music that is in some way familiar exhibits a coherent growth that becomes its shape. The shape, in turn, gives the listener a sense of security and certainty. Genuine predictability–being able to guess 100% correctly which song will be played next–goes against the necessary appeal of musical complexity which was discussed in chapter 8 (especially the work of John Booth Davies).

[7]Meyer, L.B. (1956). *Emotion and meaning in music* (p. 93). Chicago: The University of Chicago Press.
[8]Ibid., p. 161.

Expectation

Meyer also explored the concept of "expectation" in individual musical works, pointing out that expectation depends on memory:

> As we listen to a particular musical work we organize our experience and hence our expecations both in terms of the past of that particular work, which begins after the first stimulus has been heard and is consequently "past," and in terms of our memories of earlier relevant musical experiences.
>
> . . . As noted earlier, the norms developed in the memory are not rigidly fixed but change with the addition of each new memory trace: to the extent that the norms have changed, a rehearing of a work is a new hearing, yielding new insights.[9]

What Meyer said is congruent with additional points made in chapter 8: A song with fairly high complexity may not be as immediately enjoyable as a simple song; but with repeated hearing, the complexities become normalized and enjoyment increases.

There surely needs to be "continuation" in a mood-evoking music presentation system, but does there also need to be "expectation" (not just within each song, but throughout the hour)? The answer is yes, but again, positive expectation is not the same as negative predictability. Every week during radio's first network "Golden Age," it was absolutely predictable that Fibber McGee would open the hall closet and endure the ensuing avalanche of junk. But the audience looked forward to it with great expectation anyway, because the event fit the character and the storyline so well. Predictability did not detract from the audience's positive expectation. Waiting for the thunderous pedal of a huge pipe organ in the finale of the Saint Saens Symphony # 3 is part of the pleasure of sitting through the first movement and half of the second. The same expectancy is the fun of hearing the Big Bopper say into the phone "Do I what? Will I what?" (Expectant pause) "Oh, baby, you KNOW what I like!"

As it is with individual musical works, so it is with overall music presentation: positive expectation about what is to be aired next is fueled by the growth of what is being played now; the shape or mood of the present moment predicts the emotions to come.

SPACE

In chapters 6 and 7 it was argued that radio air personalities needed to be heard in real acoustic spaces – that the listener longs for audio cues that will allow him or her to imagine an actual place where the personality is speaking. The use of the

---

[9]Ibid., pp. 88, 90.

venerable "remote broadcast" is one way of supplying that aural ambience (although remotes have usually been offered more for their commercial than their entertainment value).

A sense of place in acoustic space in the music a station airs has been much less a consideration at most stations. More attention needs to be paid both to the sound of the space in which the music was recorded, and the sound of the space in which the radio listener is likely to reproduce that music.

Concert Halls

R. Murray Schafer made a strong case that concert halls have always influenced the way music is perceived. Pop music, when performed in large arenas or stadiums tends to emphasize bass frequencies and thus generates a sound that is diffused and enveloping. In contrast to that is chamber music, which is performed in smaller concert halls where directionality and high frequencies predominate. Dynamics, which are sacrificed for loudness in the arena seting, are also much more controllable in the smaller space. Schafer said that in music intended for performance in concert halls, a sense of distance is important. The "virtual space" of the dynamics of the music is reflected in the actual space of the hall. He equated quiet passages with sounds heard at the distant horizon, and loud ones with sounds played up close. Because the concert hall allowed music to be heard well even when played quietly, it became a place where silence was the normal mode of audience behavior. Music intended for concert hall performance thus became much more intellectual than it might otherwise have been, for the reason that focused listening and close examination were possible. Schafer even pointed out that the formal clothing worn to performances in concert halls helped to underscore class distinctions because of the social space it puts between those participating.

Schafer went on to show how the art gallery provided a similar refuge for those wanting to investigate the detail and the nuance of every facet of an artwork. He contrasted the concentrated listening which is possible in a concert hall with the much more diffused sound of music intended for performance outdoors, such as folk music. Folk music, he said, does not require the level of attention nor the focus that concert hall music does – the ear is allowed to wander over the aural landscape. The entire milieu of the concert locale thus becomes a part of the performance. Schafer predicted that the popularity of outdoor (and by extension, stadium or arena) rock concerts would bring about a decline in concert hall listening manners, "as concentrated listening gives way to impressionism."[10] (It is distressing to note how accurate a prophet Schafer was in regard to the deterioration of concert manners, although I would also blame television viewing. People can talk or even scream at each other in front of their TV sets and the video performance is not disturbed, so the same boorish behavior is carried into the concert hall.)

---

[10]Schafer, *The Tuning of the World,* p. 117.

Schafer said that arena concerts and much of the pop music heard on the home stereo is designed to flood the listener with sound, with little regard to distance and directionality. He identified this kind of listening condition with the classless society that is pop music.[11]

Spacial Cues in Recorded Music

Schafer made the point several times that pop music is seeking to immerse the listener in a blend of sound, rather than allow him or her to examine it from both an aesthetic and physical distance. But as already shown, the radio studio is also a place from which distance and directionality are absent. And what the disc jockey says is obviously not meant to be critically examined like a Mozart opera. The fact is, the music on radio – however much it lacks clarity and focus – is the only place where a listener is going to hear cues as to directionality and distance. And because at most stations music fills far more airtime than any other element, it is important to be *intentional* about presenting the spacial cues that are in the music; that is, there needs to be a rational scheme for the successive presentation of differing acoustic spaces. In regard to questions of distance especially, most stations have done the same with their music presentation that they've done in regard to moods: they jerk the listener all over the place from one song to the next. At one moment, we're in a huge arena hearing a rock band in concert; the next, we're "up-close-and-personal" with a love ballad. There is no sense of continuity and logical movement in space.

The Dynamic Sound Plane/Three-Stage Plan

In a later part of his book, Schafer described the work of a sound effects technician to illustrate what Schafer called the "dynamic plane." The dynamic plane is the aural equivalent of the concept of figure/ground in gestalt psychology, and it is also like the foreground/middleground/background of TV picture composition. The dynamic plane is a most useful concept that is employed later in analyzing acoustic spaces as heard in recorded music. Schafer quoted a sound effects technician as saying that the problem is always to select those few precise sounds which will best portray the scene while also supporting the narration or dialogue. To accomplish this, the technician had come up with what he called a "three-stage plan," whose goal was twofold: to restrict the number of sound effects to be included in the scene to a reasonable and practical number, and to determine just how recognizable and important each should be compared to the others.

> The "three-stage plan" divides the whole sound-scene (called "scenic") into three main parts. These are: The "Immediate," the "Support," and the "Background." The chief thing to bear in mind is that the "Immediate" effect is to be *listened* to while the "Support" and the "Background" effects are merely to be heard . . .

[11]Ibid., p. 118.

The "Support" effect refers to sounds taking place in the immediate vicinity which have a direct bearing on the subject in hand, leaving the "Background" effect to its normal job of setting the general scene.

Take, for example, the recording of a commentary at a fun-fair. The "Immediate" effect would be the commentator's voice. Directly behind this would come the "Support" effects of whichever item of fairground amusement he happened to be referring to, backed, to a slightly lesser degree, by the "Background" effect of music and crowd noises.[12]

The sound technician's three-stage plan of "immediate," "support," and "background" sounds is probably a better way to describe the dynamic sound plane in a popular music performance than "foreground/middleground/background." The reason is that "foreground/middleground/background" seems to force events into neat little thirds according to where sound sources would be arrayed *visually*. Visually, it's obvious that the lead singer in a band is in the foreground, other guitarists and keyboard players are generally in the middleground, and the drummer is usually in the background. But aurally, the mix does not necessarily work that way. When the lead singer stops singing and a guitar solo takes over, the guitar solo becomes foreground sound even though the guitarist might still be in the middleground visually. The terms *immediate* and *support,* because they do not refer to visual space, are thus better for describing what is aurally prominent and what is secondary. In the example previously given, the lead singer is "immediate," and then the guitar solo takes that position. The guitarist who had been performing a "support" function becomes "immediate" aurally.

Often, bands employ a small chorus of additional ("backing") singers who "fatten" the vocals or who sing the latest equivalent of "sha-la-la" or "doo wop doo wop" while the main lyric is being sung by the band members. Such a backing chorus would be an example of a "background" sound element.

Recording Site Ambience

Beyond the "background" in all cases is the ambience of the recording site. Oftentimes, how much ambience is perceivable is controlled by the distance between the performer and the microphone: the closer the miking, the less sense of acoustic place. Thus, there is often an interaction between "immediate" sound sources and the amount of ambience. If the "immediate" sound source is very close-miked, the listener generally receives less sense of place in the musical performance.

The Three-Stage Plan Can Describe the Listening Place

The terms *immediate, support,* and *background* are also useful in describing the listening place and situation where the radio music is ultimately consumed. An immediate

---

[12]Ibid., p. 157.

listening environment would be inside portable-stereo-type headphones, or with the volume turned up high on a relatively close-by loudspeaker system, such as in a car. Support would cover most other listening situations where the radio or stereo is being listened to intentionally, but where the volume level is "normal." Background listening would pertain just to those situations where levels are so low that the music is not really meant to be listened to in an intentional way.

In the "playback" environment, acoustic differences between rooms can have effects analogous to changes in mike-to-performer distance. Music played back in a room with very little carpet or furniture will be much more reverberant than in a carpeted, draped room with lots of overstuffed chairs. A close-miked immediate performer can sound quite intimate in the latter space – approaching the directness of the headphone experience. Played back over loudspeakers in a "starving college student's" bare flat, the intimacy would be mostly missing. Similarly, intimate-sounding performances remain so in a luxury car with plush carpets, softly cushioned seats, and sound-absorbent ceiling material, but would be more like the cold-water-flat experience in a VW with vinyl seats and rubber floormats. Thus, knowing where the majority of the target audience will be hearing the station at a given time of day becomes increasingly important. A 1988 study commissioned by the Radio Advertising Bureau and conducted by Arbitron found that nearly one half of all Americans listen to the radio in the workplace, over two thirds of adult listeners tune in the radio every time they drive their cars, and over one third of home radios are portables, including portable headphone stereo types.[13]

FORCE

In the previous portion of this chapter, the space in which a song was recorded, and the space in which it is heard by the radio listener, were both shown to affect the song's impact. And before that, BPM and expression time factors were shown to be closely tied to certain emotional states. In this portion, we look more closely at the *intensity* of the music both as performed and as perceived.

Intensity Factors

Timbre. Imagine a loud but close-miked, harshly spoken whisper. You will have to imagine it because it happens so rarely – which is good, because it is frightening. What is frightening about it is not that the voice is close-miked: we expect whispers to be that way. What makes it frightening is that it is loud and harshly spoken. The same words said quiety and sweetly might be soothing; spoken loud and harshly, we get the picture of someone just barely keeping a temper under control, speaking

---

[13]RAB/ARB survey shows heavy workplace radio use. (1988, September 30). *Radio & Records*, pp. 1, 26.

through clenched teeth, spitting out the consonants and half-growling the vowels. It's frightening because of the intensity of the performance, which is reflected in the vocal quality.

Or imagine an electric guitar. We can think of those played by Les Paul or Chet Atkins – or by Iron Maiden or Metallica. It's the same basic instrument in both cases, but with very different timbres or qualities. Again, the timbre or quality of the sound goes hand-in-glove with intensity.

Instrumentation/Presentational Style.   Some stations, in trying to focus and re-strict their music, make prohibitions. They might restrict pedal steel guitar because it sounds too "country," or strings because they sound too soft and sweet. But the instrumentation is not usually the culprit. More often the presentational style is. It is the *timbre* of a heavily distorted guitar or a raspy-voiced singer that are felt to be too "hard" for a station's sound. We know that tempo and melodic line are influential in engendering a mood, and that spacial factors contribute to the overall impact. But it is probably the instrumentation and presentational style (together producing a certain intensity of performance) that most affect whether – or when – a certain song gets airplay.

There is also the question not only of *what* the instrumentation is, but also of *how many.* Singing the same material, there *is* a difference in quality/timbre between the sound of the Mormon Tabernacle Choir and Peter, Paul, & Mary. Although there can be tremendous energy from either group, there is no getting around the potency of massed voices when singing loud. On the other hand, "beautiful music" albums with the 100 Guitars or the 101 Strings proved that more instruments do not necessarily result in a more forceful presentation when the content suggests a more quiet approach.

Instrument/Vocal Density.   Phil Spector, with his "Wall of Sound" production mix, showed that slow ballads like the Righteous Brothers' "You've Lost That Lovin' Feelin'" could have potency. The potency seems to come from the *density* of the instrumentation. In that recording, many of the sound sources are not "imme-diate" and up-front. Instead, they are in deep "support" range, even during the great climactic moments. The record has become a classic because of a strong vocal performance, the fine arrangement that builds so well to a climax, and because of the *density* of the instrumentation. This "rock" record features no less than a vocal duo, a chorus, strings, tambourine (reverbed), bongos, drums, and what sound like a vibraphone and a bass guitar. The intensity of the Righteous Brothers' vocal duet is matched by the density of their support.

A "Wall of Sound" is not the only way to achieve presentational impact. Many of James Taylor's, Paul Simon's, and Willie Nelson's most effective records could have been taped in a closet. Their engaging *lack* of vocal intensity is matched by a *spareness* in the instrumentation. The near-bombast of the Righteous Brothers arrangement would have been wholly inappropriate for their style. Taylor, Simon, and Nelson get their impact from the timbre of their voices, the simplicity of the instrumentation, and of course, what they say.

Lyrics

Up to this point, we have been dealing entirely with instrumental music in our discussion of how music evokes emotional reactions. Of course, most popular music has lyrics.

Lyrics seem potentially more difficult to deal with than instrumental elements for at least two reasons. For one, every word in any language in the world could conceivably be used in a song, making analysis and classification a hopeless task. For a second, the delivery of lyrics by a vocalist can greatly affect their impact, sometimes even altering their apparent surface meaning entirely.

But happily, lyrics are really easier to deal with than instrumental elements, because much of the time the words employed are rather limited—by the subject matter, by the need to rhyme or at least to fit the rhythm, and perhaps by the parochial imagination of some writers. The result is that the vocabulary that actually has to be dealt with is much smaller than the whole universe of words. Moreover, lyrics often are intended to say what they appear to say, so that a reasonably good guess about the feelings they will invoke is often possible from a fairly cursory hearing.

The Interpretation of Emotions Expressed Vocally

The research literature about the emotions evoked by vocal expression tends to be much more consistent than the research literature surrounding the evocation of meaning via instrumental music. In terms of ordinary speaking, most researchers agree that vocal expression alone can accurately convey emotional meanings. Put in terms of song lyrics, it could be said that there are certain emotional states connected with the words a lyricist chooses, and perhaps the same or a different set of emotional states attached to those words when heard by a listener. Thus, the effect of the words (as read, not spoken) might be very different among several listeners. However, when said aloud, those same ambiguous words can be expressed so that listeners usually correctly identify the emotional state the speaker was trying to convey, even if the listener does not understand the language the speaker is using![14]

Moreover, it appears that such familiar terms as *pitch, rate,* and *loudness* are good descriptors of the vocal characteristics that affect the expression of meaning. Researchers have found that listeners can differentiate between such feelings as contempt, grief, and anger on the basis of differences in rate, the length of pauses and speaking time, and the pitch. Vocal expressions of anger, for example, tended to be portrayed at a fairly fast rate; grief had many long pauses. Pitch turns out to be a

---

[14]See Sundberg, J. (1982). Speech, song, and emotions. In M. Clynes (Ed.), *Music, mind, and brain* (pp. 137–149). New York: Plenum Press.

reliable way to differentiate between happy and sad vocal expressions – happy ones are always higher in pitch than neutral or sad expressions.[15]

In an article by Joel R. Davitz titled "Personality, Perceptual, and Cognitive Correlates of Emotional Sensitivity," Davitz offered a table listing the characteristics that 61 subjects employed to describe what a voice sounded like when it was expressing each of eight emotional meanings. The emotions described were affection, anger, boredom, cheerfulness, impatience, joy, sadness, and satisfaction. Each of these was rated for the dimensions of loudness, pitch, timbre, and rate. The subjects were also asked to describe the speech's inflection (see Table 10.2). Some of these findings directly parallel the results already described in Clynes' research on the evocation of moods by instrumental music. I have constructed a table after the one offered by Davitz, employing the emotional terms used by Clynes, but substituting Davitz's vocal expression terms for Clynes' terms where appropriate (see Table 10.3). Either Clynes or Davitz might argue that "affection" and "love" are not equivalent, and neither are "sadness" and "grief." I have grouped them together because the similarities between the vocal expression and the instrumental expression are striking.

Clynes' work did not deal with timbre, and loudness was a factor only in the sense that over some period of time, the sound would range from zero amplitude to

Table 10.2
Characteristic Employed to Describe What a Voice Sounded Like When Expressing Each of Eight Emotional Meanings[16]

Feeling	Loudness	Pitch	Timbre	Rate	Inflection
Affection	soft	low	resonant	slow	steady & slightly up
Anger	loud	high	blaring	fast	irregular up & down
Boredom	moderate to low	moderate to low	moderately resonant	moderately slow	monotone or gradual fall
Cheerfulness	moderately high	moderately high	moderately blaring	moderately fast	up & down; overall up
Impatience	normal	normal to mod. high	moderately blaring	moderately fast	slightly upward
Joy	loud	high	moderately blaring	fast	upward
Sadness	soft	low	resonant	slow	downward
Satisfaction	normal	normal	somewhat resonant	normal	slight upward

---

[15]See Davitz, J.R. (1964). A review of research concerned with facial and vocal expressions of emotion. In J. R. Davitz (Ed.), *The communication of emotional meaning* (p. 25). (Copyright © 1964 by McGraw-Hill Book Co.) New York: McGraw-Hill. (Reprinted by permission of McGraw-Hill Publishing Co.)

[16]After Joel R. Davitz, Personality, perceptual, and cognitive correlates of emotional sensitivity. In Davitz, p. 63. (Reprinted by permission of McGraw-Hill Publishing Co.)

Table 10.3
Comparison of Davitz and Clynes on Feelings/Emotions, Rate Expression Times, and
Inflection/Frequency Modulation

Davitz/Clynes Feeling/Emotion	Davitz/Clynes Rate/Exp. Time	Davitz/Clynes Inflection/Freq. Mod
Affection/Love	**slow**/5.2 sec	**steady**/mostly steady
Anger/Anger	**fast**/0.7 sec.	**upward**/upward
Joy/Joy	**fast**/1.1 sec.	**upward**/*
Sadness/Grief	**slow**/9.0 sec.	**downward**/downward

*initial ⅓ octave down, then up an octave, then down ⅙.

some normal loudness and finally back to zero again at its conclusion. (Clynes was measuring the time it took to go from silence to full audibility and back to silence; he was not looking for subjective judgements of which of the tones were louder or softer.) In addition, because of the way he designed his research, Clynes did not feel that starting frequencies were critical, since he felt the same results could be obtained over a "moderately wide range."[17] (In his research, lower starting frequencies were chosen for the tones that expressed anger and hate, with a medium pitch level used for all others.) Thus, the dimensions that can be related are rate (which I pair with Clynes' "expression time"), and inflection (which here is related to Clynes' "frequency modulation"). In the resulting table, Davitz's vocal expression terms and findings are listed in boldface on the left, Clynes' terms and findings in normal print on the right.

Note that there is good agreement between Davitz and Clynes on the four identical or nearly equivalent emotions. In the next chapter a case is made that music can be tested on the basis of its vocal and instrumental rate/expression time, and on the basis of its vocal and instrumental inflection/frequency.

This chapter on time, space, and force factors has introduced enough new material that it may be helpful to conclude with several tables that summarize how the concepts presented here fit into the generation of music moods.

THE TIME/SPACE/FORCE COMPONENTS OF RADIO MOOD

The sets of factors that appear to affect the mood that is generated by listening to music on the radio can be summarized as: (a) performer or song characteristics, (b) general audience characteristics, and (c) individual listener characteristics. All three sets of factors involve the concepts of time, space, and force, but they have different meanings in each case.

Performer or song characteristics (see Table 10.4) refer to the traits that are inherent in the performer or in the song. Being inherent, they are stable. Example:

---

[17]Clynes and Nettheim, The living quality of music. In Clynes, *Music, Mind and Brain*, p. 62.

Table 10.4
Performer or Song Characteristics

Time	Space	Force
Song Rhythms	*Involvement Factors*	*Acceptance Factors*
BPM expression time	performer distance recording's ambience	instrumentation lyrics presentational style

the force factors of instrumentation and presentation style affect a station's acceptance of the song.

General audience characteristics (see Table 10.5) are traits that exist in the audience at large, taken as a homogenous mass. As such, they are a mix of stable and variable characteristics. Example: A cultural rhythm such as Mother's Day might call for more music with reverential expression times, whereas the Fourth of July suggests music with joyful expression times.

Table 10.5
General Audience Characteristics

Time	Space	Force
Communal Rhythms	*Involvement Factors*	*Acceptance Factors*
seasonal rhythms cultural rhythms	appeals structure	performer popularity song popularity

Individual listener characteristics (see Table 10.6) are the final set of factors. Because these refer to traits held by individuals, they are highly heterogeneous and vary widely. Example: The place in which a person normally listens will influence how involved he or she can be with the programming.

Table 10.6
Individual Listener Characteristics

Time	Space	Force
Personal Rhythms	*Involvement Factors*	*Acceptance Factors*
circadian rhythms lifestyle needs	listening place listening situation	familiarity drives for arousal/satiation

MAJOR POINTS

1. The ordering of songs needs to be based on more than popularity. A hit rotation imposes the arbitrary order of hit position, instead of trying to discern the intrinsic merits within a song, and the internal links among songs.

2. A slow-normal heartbeat is close to the expression time Clynes found for "joy." A normal breathing rate is close to the expression time for "love." These body rhythms are undoubtedly part of our reaction to music performed at these tempi.

3. Most popular songs exhibit a structure comparable to one cycle of sound expressed as the ADSR sound envelope, or to one dramatic action graphed on the basis of Aristotelian dramatic structure. In the latter case, note that most pop songs lack true resolution. The next song's exposition substitutes for the previous song's lack of resolution.

4. Moods such as reverence and grief match up well with slow-tempo music; moods with average expression times match with love, sex, and hate; and moods such as joy and anger match well with fast tempos.

5. When expression times are matched to the dramatic structure curve, reverence and grief match up with the slow, low curve of exposition. Hate, love, and sex are related to the more elevated part of the curve called development. Joy and anger are associated with building to a climax. Because of pop music's lack of resolution, reverence, and grief also match up with resolution, becoming the exposition of the next song.

6. LaRue's four options for continuation of a musical idea are recurrence, development, response, and contrast. These can be adapted to describe a mood-generating music presentation system.

7. Expectation is an additional factor in a mood-generating music progression. Positive expectation is not the same as negative predictability. Positive expectation about what is to be aired next is fueled by the growth of what is being played now; the slope or mood of the present moment predicts the emotions to come.

8. The music on the radio is more likely to have directionality and distance (spacial) cues than is talk on the radio. But music is usually presented in such a haphazard way that the listener is thrust "up close and personal" in one song, and is pulled back to concert distance the next.

9. The dynamic sound plane/three stage plan suggested in Schafer divides the sound scene into *immediate, support,* and *background* areas. This terminology avoids the bias of the visually oriented terms *foreground, middleground,* and *background*. It can be used to describe both the recording site and the listening place.

10. Among the factors contributing to the intensity (force) of a song as performed are the timbre of the vocals and instrumentals, the presentational style, the number of performers, and the density of the instrumentation.

11. It has been shown that the emotions expressed in lyrics can be interpreted even by people from other cultures who do not know the language. And the rate, pitch, inflection, and loudness of spoken expression help listeners to identify various emotions. Of these, rate and inflection correlate well with Clynes' findings in the cases of love, anger, joy, and sadness.

CHAPTER 11

Factors in MOST –
Mood-Oriented Selection Testing

Chapters 11 and 12 take the theory and reasoning in the previous part of this section and move them toward practice, toward the framework of a mood-evoking music order.

The station seeking to apply the strategies to be outlined here and in chapter 12 would do best not to use them literally, but rather to think of them as examples of the testing and thinking the station needs to do. The examples provided are not meant to be formulas, but instead should be viewed as the artifacts of research that has only recently begun, and that must be further refined.

The two problems any music programmer must solve are – given our target demographic – which songs do we play, and in what order do we play them? It comes down to questions of selection and order. Happily, the attributes of a song that recommend it for selection in many cases are also useful in determining when it should be presented.

Note the phrase "given our target demographic" in the previous problem statement. Some of the attributes of selection and order work best with a specific audience segment – they are not "one-size-fits-all." Before starting to apply the attribute tests, not only would you know your station's target demographic in terms of how many listeners are available in the typical age, sex, education, and occupation breakouts, but you would also have some sense of what that target audience's mood needs are, and how they might change from daypart to daypart.

In order to aid recall, easily remembered acronyms have been developed for the music selection factors and for the music presentation factors being offered. All the tests to be applied to selecting a song for airplay are called mood-oriented selection testing (MOST). The decisions to be made about when the song is presented are grouped under mood-evoking music order (MEMO). (In chapter 13, where a truly

Table 11.1
Factors in MOST

Audience/Listener Characteristics	
Time	(Song rhythms)
	Expression time
	Scale
Space	(Involvement factors)
	Performer-to-microphone distance
	Recording site ambience
Force	(Performer/song acceptance factors)
	Presentational style (timbre)
	Instrumentation (number, density)
	Lyrics

audience-sensitive format is proposed, mood-evoking respondent-interactive track-ing – MERIT – is introduced.)

The list of factors (see Table 11.1) to be included in this chapter on mood-oriented selection testing is based on a condensed version of the time/space/force components of radio mood found at the end of the previous chapter. That summary's separate categories of general audience characteristics and individual listener characteristics have been melded into a single list of audience/listener characteristics. This amal-gamation reflects the fact that a programmer can never have very much data about individual listeners as compared to information on the general audience. The audience/listener characteristics are used in chapter 12.

TIME (SONG RHYTHMS)

We begin again with time as the first area for testing, and specifically with Manfred Clynes' expression time terms.

Much of the moods research cited in this book points to a link between a song's rhythm and the mood it engenders in a listener. The salient point of Clynes' research for the radio music programmer is that the specific expression times for the seven emotions Clynes has isolated are expressed in *seconds.* They are quantifiable.

Finding the Expression Time

Programmers familiar with counting BPM need to "shift gears" to classify music using the Clynes expression times. First, the beats are not counted. Instead, the *length* of the *interval* from one "beat" to the next is timed. Note that the word "beat" in the previous sentence is in quotation marks. That is to alert you that the literal beat (the thump of the bass in the rhythm) does not necessarily equal the essentic pulse in Clynes' domain. Recall the portion on phrasing in chapter 10: the orchestra conductor leads a new slow theme with one hand while the other hand maintains the basic rhythm; or the singer holds onto a certain word and "wrings out" its meaning. In both cases, the expression time is likely to be longer than the short interval between thumps from the bass. In a slow ballad, a phrase of just two or three words might be a complete expression, whereas in a faster song, whole sentences can be a single expression.

It helps to keep asking the question, "Is this expression complete?" In the author's testing, respondents have been asked to simply say "Now!" whenever they feel that the expression is finished (that a new one is beginning, or that the old one is starting to be repeated). Some respondents seem to do better because they just have a good sense of musical phrasing – they let themselves get caught up in the flow. The worst are those who make literal counts without investing any of their own emotions. Averaging responses among several listeners is helpful. The averaged expression time will be in seconds or portions of a second.

USING CLYNES' TERMS TO SELECT AIRPLAY MUSIC

Clynes' studies using a Sentograph finger pressure transducer, and carefully pro-scribed melodic/rhythmic Essentic Forms, is *basic* research of the most valuable kind. Along with colleague Bill Adams and undergraduate students Ted Smith, Eileen Meyer, Jenny Jones, and Roger Burns, I have attempted to *apply* Clynes' findings to the problem of selecting music for radio airplay.

Pilot Study

The pilot study for this research surveyed 36 respondents. Their ages ranged from 18 to 24 years old, and the pilot group was about equally split male/female. Ten instrumental music selections were played, each 20 to 40 seconds in length. The music was chosen from a variety of stereotypic genres such as country, jazz, pop, classical, slow rock, and blues. Each respondent was instructed to use any adjective that came to mind to describe how the music made him or her feel. The respondents' words were then grouped under one of Clynes' seven terms. Words that were deemed to be reasonable synonyms of a Clynes' term were accepted, so that "rowdy," "partying" and so forth were grouped with "Joy," while "holy," "church" and the like were clustered with "Reverence."

The pilot study results showed substantial grouping on the Clynes variables. Relative frequency clusters on one variable (frequency/total responses) ranged from .33 to .78. This showed that respondents selected a synonym corresponding to the same Clynes variable names to describe feelings evoked by a song 33% to 78% of the time.

Study Using Music Representing Clynes' Terms

For a second, larger survey, the investigators decided to pre-select the songs to be played not so much on the basis of music genre as before, but on the basis of representing the seven Clynes terms. This second survey would test whether the respondents could make the same matches as we investigators did, even though we were familiar with classifying the music using the Clynes terms and the respondents were not. In effect, we were acting as if we were radio station music directors, and we considered the respondents as if they were audience members in an auditorium music test.

In the second survey, some of the songs were to be of a "pop" nature, whereas other selections would usually be classified as "college radio" or "alternative" music. Most of the music was unfamiliar at the time the survey was conducted. We specified these characteristics so that at least some of the music would resemble that considered for commercial airplay. On the other hand, the songs were to be relatively obscure, and by lesser known artists, so that the respondents would not apply past emotional experiences related to familiar songs and artists. Moreover, some songs were to be instrumental segments, while the majority were to include lyrics. (Clynes' work did not include consideration of lyrics, because his research dealt with much smaller forms. Most of the songs we tested did have lyrics because most pop songs have them.)

A list of the tested songs is given in Table 11.2.

Study Procedure

After selections were found that met the criteria, they were reduced into a sequence of 21 one-minute cuts. In all cases, the cuts were recorded starting at the beginning of the song. Unlike typical auditorium testing procedures, we did not just play the "hooks" (most easily remembered portions) of the music, because most of these songs had never before been heard by the respondents. Some songs took longer to settle into a pattern than others. However, after the first test it was found that 1 minute was far more than was needed to establish a basis for response, even with these mostly unfamiliar titles. As a result, the majority of the testing was done with cuts of about 30 to 40 seconds in length. (This is still far longer than the 15- to 20-second maximum cut length typical of auditorium testing, or the 7 to 10 seconds recommended by some research firms.) The selections were concluded by simply cutting them off at a "natural" ending of a phrase.

The selections varied from those that the researchers thought would evoke a strong, definite reaction, such as Joy in "Don't Live Your Life in One Day," to some the researchers guessed would cause no reaction, such as "Opus 4" – a cut comprised entirely of rhythmic speaking with no melody line. We even tried rock songs in foreign languages ("Im Nin Alu"). Certain selections were also chosen by the researchers specifically because they were complex; that is, because they did *not* elicit just a single response from us. Often these displayed a strong tension or opposition between the words and music. An example is the sexual yearning covered by an angry refrain in "Show Me Some Emotion." Some songs went beyond opposition and seemed to evoke two or three emotions simultaneously. Upon further reflec-

Table 11.2
List of Tested Songs

Number	Title	Artist
1.	Call Me Blue	A House
2.	Watermark	Enya
3.	Where Nowhere Is	Hoodoo Gurus
4.	Bella	Carlos Santana
5.	Show Me Some Emotion	Underworld
6.	Shiver and Shake	The Cure
7.	Opus 4	Art of Noise
8.	Camilla, the Old Old Story	Art of Noise
9.	Still in Hollywood	Concrete Blond
10.	Blue-Eyed Pop	Sugar Cubes
11.	I Don't Mind at All	Bourgeois Tagg
12.	What the Whole World Wants	Game Theory
13.	A Thousand Hours	The Cure
14.	Im Nin Alu	Ofra Haza
15.	The Telephone is Empty	Love & Rockets
16.	Apron Strings	Everything But the Girl
17.	Evening Falls	Enya
18.	All Day, All Night	The Other Ones
19.	(no title supplied)	Moneytree
20.	Don't Live Your Life in One Day	Howard Jones
21.	I Love You Lord	Phil Keaggy

tion, the researchers decided that some of these songs were comprised of several emotional "layers." One layer might be emphasized in the bass line, whereas the lead guitar represented another emotion. This layering is evident, for example, in "Camilla, the Old, Old Story," where the throbbing bass lines suggests Sex and the breathy melody suggests Grief.

Study Sample and Results

This second, larger survey produced 129 usable sets of responses. The sample was 36% male, 64% female. Of the sample, 4% was age 12–17, 74% was age 18–22 (mostly college students), 10% was 23–34, and 12% was 35 +. About 11% of the sample had completed high school, 83% was comprised of college undergraduates, and 6% had graduated from college or had advanced degrees. Eighty-two percent of the sample listed "student" as their occupation. Obviously, the sample was skewed by the presence of many female college undergraduates, so the results need to be viewed with that in mind.

The study participants were asked to listen to each selection and then indicate which of the seven Clynes terms was closest to how the music made them feel. An eighth choice, "no feeling," was also available. In all the testing sessions for this

Table 11.3
Clustering on the Majority Emotion for the 21 Songs Tested

This Many Songs	Were Clustered on the Majority Emotion	Greater Than or Equal To	This Percent of the Time
1			90%
3			60%
9			50%
13			40%
20			30%
21			20%

Table 11.4
Clustering on the Majority and Immediately Adjacent Emotion for the 21 Songs Tested

This Many Songs	Were Clustered on Majority or Adjacent Emotion	Greater Than or Equal To	This Percent of the Time
1			90%
7			80%
11			70%
15			60%
17			50%
19			40%
21			30%

survey, the selections were played in the same order. Future research will alternate the play pattern.

Chi-square analysis on the frequency of responses for a given emotion, computed for each song, shows with a 99.95% certainty that the choices were not random. In this study, the only variable was the musical selections. Although the respondents may have chosen the same emotional response to describe different songs, our results indicate that each response depended on the music, and not some other factor.

One of the things we hoped to show in our study was that each song inclined people toward some *specific* emotive response. The results tend to support this. Responses were clustered on the "majority" emotion (the emotion chosen by the majority of respondents) as much as 90% of the time for one song (see Table 11.3).

The results for the majority emotion and for immediately adjacent emotions were analyzed and can be found in Table 11.4.

By arranging our data from the slowest of Clynes' expression time terms to the fastest, we found that for over two thirds of our musical selections, 80% of the responses were grouped on, immediately adjacent to, or no more than two emotions

Table 11.5

Percentage of Respondents Who Chose the Same Clynes Expression Time Variable for Each of 21 Tested Songs

1.	61.9	8.	30.4	15.	52.9
2.	39.8	9.	50.4	16.	56.0
3.	52.5	10.	33.9	17.	47.6
4.	36.3	11.	39.4	18.	42.6
5.	50.0	12.	60.8	19.	33.7
6.	47.4	13.	51.6	20.	89.7
7.	25.9	14.	32.7	21.	36.4

Table 11.6

Percentage of Respondents Who Chose Either the Same Clynes Expression Time Variable or the Next Highest or Lowest Clynes Expression Time Variable for Each of 21 Tested Songs

1.	85.6	8.	34.8	15.	84.3
2.	70.3	9.	84.5	16.	74.4
3.	83.9	10.	45.8	17.	87.9
4.	68.2	11.	75.8	18.	58.3
5.	60.5	12.	88.3	19.	51.8
6.	70.7	13.	65.9	20.	90.5
7.	35.2	14.	42.9	21.	61.0

Table 11.7

Percentage of Respondents Who Chose Either the Same Clynes Expression Time Variable or the Next Highest and the Next Lowest Clynes Expression Time Variable for Each of 21 Tested Songs

1.	87.3	8.	65.2	15.	89.2
2.	96.9	9.	96.7	16.	87.2
3.	94.9	10.	57.7	17.	96.0
4.	78.8	11.	87.6	18.	92.2
5.	90.7	12.	95.2	19.	81.9
6.	94.0	13.	78.6	20.	91.3
7.	42.6	14.	58.2	21.	92.4

removed from the majority response. This data is represented for each of the 21 numbered selections in Tables 11.5, 11.6, and 11.7.

Tables 11.5, 11.6, and 11.7 showing the percentage of respondents who chose either the most popular emotive response for a song, the response corresponding to the next highest or lowest expression time among Clynes' terms, or the response two terms away from the majority response, may at first glance appear to be statistical manipulation to prove a point. But Clynes' own research encountered problems in mistaking one emotion for a similar one:

The errors in identifying anger were predominantly mistaking it for hate, and vice versa. No subjects mistook hate for anything else except anger. Grief was mistaken for reverence by 20% of subjects, and joy for love by 12%. The correct choice and these switched pairs of qualities accounted for 94% of the results in anger, 100% for hate, 92% in grief, and 96% in joy. The majority of errors were a mutually mistaken pair.[1]

Conclusions From the Study

Analysis of the second survey leads us to conclude that a given music selection being considered for radio airplay will evoke a similar emotional reaction from a significant number of listeners. The emotive responses were the same for a given piece of music for a statistically significant number of responses (based on the chi-square analysis).

Because the music was from more than one typical musical genre, we might also conclude that the emotional responses were not based on the genre of music played. This would be a less scientifically verifiable conclusion at this point because there was a limited number of genres represented. Further study should try to overcome this limitation. However, because "no feeling" was a choice available to respondents, and because that choice did not appear to predominate as a result of a music selection's genre, we may tentatively conclude that the genre did not affect how the music made the respondent feel.

Interestingly, songs 7, 8, 10, and 14, which have the lowest percentage of clustering, also averaged a much higher percentage of "no feeling" responses than the other 17 songs. The average "no feeling" for songs 7, 8, 10, and 14 was 35.7%, whereas the average "no feeling" responses for all other songs was 14.3%. Further study should try to verify a relationship between a lack of clustering and the "no feeling" response. The presence of both low clustering and a high percentage of "no feeling" responses would be a useful filter for songs that might be "dangerous" for radio airplay.

In summary, our preliminary research shows that our sample of students and the public was generally able to assign pre-selected segments of recorded popular music into categories labeled with Clynes' seven emotion terms. "Pre-selected" means that the music was pre-screened into categories that the researchers felt matched the Clynes terms. Thus, what was really being tested was whether the nontrained sample was likely to make the same music moods distinctions as the trained "radio professionals" doing the pre-selection. It appears so far that this is generally the case.

Of more importance is whether *non*-preselected music also can be categorized with good dependability. If detailed analysis of this and later studies shows this to be the case, then the implication is that focus group-type music selection sessions could employ the Clynes terms and the general methodologies just described to select airplay music on the basis of the moods that the music is likely to evoke in the majority of the audience.

---

[1]Clynes, M., & Nettheim, N. (1982). The living quality of music. In M. Clynes (Ed.), *Music, mind, and brain* (p. 57). New York: Plenum Press.

Relating Expression Times to Major, Minor, and Blues Scales

When the expression time is fairly different from the times Clynes found, or when there are other difficulties in classification, a simple correlation with major and minor scales is often helpful. To understand the correlation to be presented, we must briefly review rhythm as it relates to *melody*–a term otherwise avoided in this chapter because it is so vast and hard to nail down. (Most of the time, the "hook" in a pop song exists mostly around the melody.)

Pure rhythm–for instance, a drum solo–can exist apart from melody, but melody always goes hand-in-hand with rhythm. This is because once a first tone is succeeded by any other tone, the length of the first tone is made finite and comes to be perceived as some rhythmic unit. (See LaRue's discussion of "continuation" in chapter 10.) A succession of tones becomes a melody. Melody occurs absolutely on the basis of rhythm.

The first and main note on which a melody begins is known as the "tonic" of a key–the "main note" of the melody is (almost always) in one of 24 keys, such as E-flat or C-major. (Matching of keys is one venerable device for ordering the presentation of radio music, but order of presentation is the subject of the next chapter.) The terms *major* and *minor* are often interchanged with the word *key*, but a more-accepted word in music is *scale*. Since the 17th century, the two major modes in western music have been the major and minor scales. About 100 years ago, the blues added a third scale. Today, most U.S. popular music is in the major, minor, or the blues scale.

In 1935, Kate Hevner published a study that employed an adjective checklist to confirm the traditional attitudes that minor mode (scale) music was perceived as gloomy, depressing, or sad, while major mode pieces were judged to be happy, cheerful, joyous, and so on. She carried out her study to disprove an earlier one that had concentrated on the effect of just major or minor *chords*. Hevner's study put the major or minor chords in a musical context.[2]

Clynes' seven essentic forms, in my view, each carry an expectation about their scale. In Table 11.8, they are listed left-to-right along with my interpretation of expression time, in seconds (longest expression time to the left, shortest to the right). Table 11.8 lists the usually expected scale.

The majority of music listeners in the western hemisphere associate the major, minor, and blues scales with the given emotions as strongly as they associate high-pitched music with joy and low-pitched music with grief; or high-pitched, fast-rate melodies with small, light objects like birds, and low-pitched, slow-rate melodies with large, heavy objects like elephants.

Again, the reader must be cautioned that Clynes does not make these assertions

---

[2]See Hevner, K. (1953). The affective character of major and minor modes in music. In R.W. Lundin (Ed.), *An objective psychology of music* (pp. 145–146). New York: Ronald Press.

Table 11.8
Expression Times and Terms Related to Major, Minor, and Blues Scales

Reverence	Grief	Love	Sex	Hate	Joy	Anger
9.8	9.0	5.2	2.0	1.6	1.1	0.7
major	minor or blues	major or blues	major minor or blues	minor or blues	major or blues	minor

about major and minor scales, or the way one expression time flows into another. They are my interpretations and assumptions. Having the major/minor/blues scale correlation as an additional means of classification is just handy.

Once you have an average expression time in seconds (perhaps corroborating the apparent emotion using the major, minor, and blues scales), you should be able to label most songs with a mood they are likely to evoke.

Open-Ended Tests Uncover "Emotionless" Songs

In separate research, a small number of songs have been found that – when tested on an open-ended basis – do not evoke any emotion at all. That is, when the person is not presented with the Clynes list of seven terms, but is instead asked simply to tell what the song causes him or her to feel, a surprising number of songs left respondents feeling no reportable emotion. These might well be "dangerous" songs to play on the air. Using the previously explained expression time classification, such songs *would* fit under one of the seven emotional categories, even though actual listeners are unmoved by them. Thus, it seems sensible to balance the counting of expression times with additional open-ended testing to be sure the theoretically possible mood is actually perceived by the listener.

No other factor to be discussed in this chapter is more influential of the mood a song induces than is that song's expression time.

SPACE (INVOLVEMENT FACTORS)

The two involvement factors discussed here – performer-to-microphone distance and the the ambience of the recording site – were described in chapter 10. The three-stage dynamic sound plane, with its categories of "immediate," "support," and "background," is a central consideration (see Table 11.9).

Testing for Spacial Factors in the Vocals
and/or Instrumentals

In testing for spacial factors in the voices and/or instrumentation, programmers auditioning music need simply to decide which aural elements are immediate,

Table 11.9
Three-Stage Dynamic Sound Plane

(Listener)	Immediate	Support	Background	(Site ambience)

which are in support, and which are in the background. As pointed out earlier, some voices and instruments shift position during a song. If the shift seems crucial, probably that voice or instrument should be listed in both its old and new positions. Otherwise, it can just be listed under the position where the majority of its time is spent.

Testing for Spacial Factors in the Recording Site's Ambience

Similarly, the music audition process needs to assess the recording site's apparent ambience, using a simple three-part scale: words like "dry" or "dead" are used for spaces with no or very low reverberation, whereas "live" or "reverberant" can be used for spaces with relatively long sound reflections. "Moderate" can be used for spaces in between the two extremes. (Actual *echo*–the discrete *repetition* of whole syllables–is not acoustic ambience; it is a special effect, and does not deserve to be counted as "live" or "reverberant.")

FORCE (ACCEPTANCE FACTORS)

The factors to be tested under the force heading are presentational style (timbre), instrumentation, and lyrics, all of which were discussed in chapter 10. There, in considering presentational style and instrumentation, the timbre, number, and density of voices or instruments were explored.

Intensity Matrices for Timbre, Number, and Density of Voices or Instruments

Three simple "intensity" checklists can be completed by programmers auditioning music for radio airplay. These checklists track vocal and instrumental force factors. They are "timbre intensity," "number intensity," and "density intensity." A checkmark in the appropriate columns is all that is required (see Table 11.10). In each case shown in Table 11.10, the record listener decides which of the three left-hand attributes best describes the sound he or she is hearing (say, "harsh/gritty" for timbre), and then selects a gentle, moderate, or powerful intensity level to describe that attribute's presentational force (for example, "powerful" for a metal-type rock song).

Table 11.10
Intensity Checklists for Timbre, Number, and Density of Voices or Instruments

		Intensity		
	Descriptor	*Gentle*	*Moderate*	*Powerful*
Timbre of voices or instruments	Harsh/Gritty			
	Moderate/Medium			
	Soft/Smooth			
Number of voices or instruments	Many			
	Moderate/Medium			
	Few			
Density of voices or instruments	Dense			
	Moderate/Medium			
	Sparse			

Lyrics

Chapter 10 also introduced research about the emotions evoked by song lyrics, and showed similarities between Clynes' expression times and frequency modulations, and Joel Davitz's findings about rate and inflection of speech. It was clear from that comparison that instrumental expression and vocal expression had a similar list of emotions, similar rates or expression times, and similar inflections.

Here, we need to consider the lyrics themselves. We do so using a matrix that considers reality/fantasy imagery along one axis, with levels of narrative action meanings along the other. What Kenneth Burke[3] referred to as "jingle" (the pleasure from just the sound of the words) is here labeled as "sound," and it is a separate single-column checkoff.

The empty matrix of Table 11.11 invites the reader to place single lines of lyrics on its grid. For instance, the opening line from the Steve Winwood hit "While You See a Chance" is "Stand up in a clear blue morning." It would be listed on the vertical axis (narrative action) at the "personal" level. Because it works on the horizontal axis of reality/fantasy imagery in every category, it would be listed once under "actual," once under "wishes," and again under "dreams." Such multiple appearances are not errors or flaws.

The *inability* to be confined to a single cell indicates a lyric that has the advantage of working on several verbal levels. Such a lyric, in turn, should translate into appeal

---

[3]See Burke, K. (1967). *The philosophy of literary form* (pp. 5–6, 36–37). Baton Rouge, LA: Louisiana State University Press.

Table 11.11
Narrative Action and Reality/Fantasy Imagery

	Actual	*Wishes*	*Dreams*
Abstraction			
Dictionary			
Personal			
Sound			

across several different demographics. It also means that the song has at least a greater *lyrical* complexity than some. As shown in the portion of this chapter on complexity, that could help prevent early burnout for this song.

There is no intention of minimizing the importance of the sound of words by confining "jingle" to its own area and renaming it "sound." The fun of saying and hearing certain sounds plays an important part in the appeal of the Crystals' oldie "Da Doo Ron Ron"

Clearly, "Da Doo Ron Ron" does not have the lyrical complexity and breadth of narrative action and symbolic meaning that "While You See a Chance" does. Fully half (15) of the (30) lines analyzed would fall into the actual (realistic)/dictionary (ordinary definitions) category. Strong narrative action, symbolism and richness of meaning are at a minimum. Only four lines move away from the literal language: two that use the metaphorical "my heart stood still" as a better way of saying "I was impressed" and two that dream of "making him mine." But the song succeeds anyway, on the strength of the 11 repetitions of "Da Doo Ron Ron Ron, Da Doo Ron Ron." It is such fun to say and sing that however pedestrian the other lyrics are, it does not matter.

The point is, not every song's lyrics need to rise to a level of epic action, symbolism, and imagery, nor to the wit of an Ira Gershwin. Phrases that are just fun to say will always be an important part of pop lyrics.

One other way to look at lyrics is in terms of the way they describe arousal, fantasy, and satiation. (Refer back to Milkman and Sunderwirth in chapter 4.) If these are indeed the main psychological states most people crave to be in, then we should expect to find lyrics that help the listener "hook into" one, two, or all three of them. Table 11.12 lists the three terms, each followed by a list of synonyms from a thesaurus.

A person auditioning music for radio airplay would not necessarily expect to hear any of the listed words verbatim; instead, he or she would probably hear a word or phrase whose emotional content suggest one of the three terms or their synonyms. Whichever of the three terms winds up with the most phrases connected to it would then be the one tagged to the song: arousal-oriented, fantasy-oriented, or satiation-

Table 11.12
Lyrics Descriptive of Arousal/Fantasy/Satiation

Arousal	Fantasy	Satiation
stimulate	unusual	relaxation
excite	uncommon	satisfaction
inflame	unfamiliar	full
energize	incredible	plenty
animate	rare	redundance
invigorate	imaginary	saturation
active	visionary	abundance
potent	utopian	lavish
	ideal	affluent
	legendary	profusion
	fabulous	
	illusory	
	extravagant	
	dreamlike	

oriented. These are important in identifying potential target listeners, and they are also influential later in determing the ordering of the songs for airplay.

SPECIAL CONSIDERATIONS

The same tests that have been recommended so far in this chapter should also be applied to the "special cases" listed here, but with the following additional guidelines also considered.

Recurrents

As alluded to in earlier chapters, there is very little agreement about what constitutes a "recurrent" song, and not much science to prove that the category should get the exposure that it does. The category of recurrents may have been invented for a very unscientific reason: because music directors did not know what to do with songs that were no longer hits, but that were not yet oldies, either. They were physically present in the music library–shouldn't they be played, like everything else there?

Radio and Records surveyed a panel of CHR programmers about their practices in airing recurrents. The lead-in to the article stated:

no records have the potential for more familiarity and popularity than recurrents, even though powers are the hottest of your currents. That's the up side of recurrents. The down side: recurrents also have the potential to bore listeners and make them punch out, especially if the record in question has been played too much.[4]

[4]Denver, J. (1988, June 10). The real deal on recurrents. *Radio & Records,* p. 40.

The article reported the programmers agreed that a recurrent had to be a former power song but not a novelty, and be familiar but not be burned out. From that point on, the panelists disagreed. One programmer tended to move a power song into the recurrent category when 12- to 17-year-olds stopped calling for it and adults *started* calling for it. (This person apparently chose to ignore the strong research that shows how remarkably different callers are from the typical listener.) He had 26 titles in his recurrent category, played two of them an hour, and left them in that rotation for 4 weeks before moving them to a "new gold" category.

Another programmer had two categories of recurrents – one with 13 titles that were the most recent records off the chart and that were played three to four times a day, and a second category with 40 titles that extended back about 18 months. This person said he tried to get maximum benefit from recurrents without sacrificing familiarity by resting the currents for *a week or so* before putting them in the recurrent category. (He apparently believes that a week of not airing a song is actually enough time for the majority audience of casual listeners to notice that the song is missing from the playlist.) Probably this person relies on recurrents so heavily because of his stated beliefs that recurrents are the records that keep the passive listeners tuned in while the station plays newer music appealing to active listeners.

A third programmer had 15 titles in a primary recurrent rotation and played them twice an hour for about 5 weeks. He also had about 60 titles in a secondary recurrent rotation that recycled about every 30 hours and that extended back to 9 months to a year old.

Yet another CHR programmer on *Radio & Records'* panel defined recurrents as "hit records up to a year-and-a-half old."[5] On the other hand, a PD at a Virginia Adult Contemporary station said his recurrents could be from 2 to 3 years old.[6] And in a speech to the Alaska Broadcasters convention, veteran programmer Rick Sklar said that most of today's music will appear for about 6 weeks on the hit list, spend 6 months in a recurrent category, then be around for another 3 years or so in a minimal rotation.[7]

This bewildering variety of approaches to airing recurrents in part reflects the differences in audience targeting among various formats, competitive strategies in different markets, and divergent methods of tracking music popularity. But in my view, the *age* of a record is largely irrelevant to airplay decisions. As was stated earlier, measures of familiarity and continued popularity are not as important as *reliability:* that the song still generates nearly the same emotional reaction in the listener as it originally did. Given this way of thinking, powers, currents, recurrents, and oldies can theoretically all have equal weight – and can share rotation with new music and album cuts.

---

[5]Ibid., p. 40.

[6]Kinosian, M. (1988, June 24). Testing for the right oldies. *Radio & Records,* p. 46.

[7]Sklar, R. (1987, September 11). Surviving the age of 'disposable' music. *Radio & Records,* p. 56.

A heavily played song that has very recently dropped off the charts could be burned out to the point of being "toast." It has lost its emotional *reliability*. It is especially important to avoid exposing such a recurrent to the high-risk groups in the station's audience. For a hit-music station, that group is the heavy listener (typically younger), for whom the original hit would have become very familiar, or might even have burned out. Playing the song again soon after it drops off the charts is a big risk with the heavy listening groups. It is less of a risk with older, occasional listeners, who would not have heard it so often originally.

As pointed out in chapter 8, performers go through popularity cycles that are very much like product cycles. Again, especially with a younger audience, unsure of its values, there can be a great fickleness about *who* is cool and who is not, quite apart from the continuing value of the music. It might not be a singer's *music* that is death as a recurrent; it might be the singer. Sometimes the best music testing will try to discover attitudes about the *performers*.

Oldies

One reason why there is great latitude in the age-range of what constitutes a recurrent song at various stations is because there is also not much agreement on when a former hit becomes an oldie.

With undergraduate researchers Jim Ridenour and Mark Kahler, Bill Adams and I have carried out a preliminary study of the terms listeners use to describe noncurrent popular music. The participants in the old music survey were the same persons who completed the Clynes music moods terms survey reported earlier in this chapter, so the same demographic profile and notes apply. The old music survey asked respondents to develop their own definitions for the terms *oldie, classic, gold* and *supergold,* and *recurrent,* and then to apply their definitions in categorizing recorded excerpts from several dozen old songs. We asked the respondents to briefly tell us how they thought the four terms used for old music by radio stations differed from each other, especially on the basis of the age difference in the music, expressed in months and/or years. We were able to categorize the results by age group, but a summary of the general findings is most useful here.

Oldie. This was generally described as music from the 1950s and 1960s, although more than a few people thought this term applied to the 1970s as well. There also seemed to be a consensus that this term generically fit all the music in this time period, regardless of whether or not it was a hit. The respondents' definitions corresponded well with definitions that were given to us by a small sample of program directors and music directors in large and small midwestern markets who were interviewed for this project. The consensus of the PDs and MDs was that an oldie was any single pop music (Top 40) hit from the mid-1950s to about the mid-1970s.

Classic. Survey respondents most often described classics as music from the late 1960s and early 1970s. This term seemed to have a little wider range than the rest. Part of the explanation for this may be found in one person's comment that the age of the song was not as important as its impact. For that matter, a song released 2 years ago could be a classic if it fit the typical criteria mentioned by respondents: "tireless," "then & now inspiring," "a song that everybody knows." The interviewed PDs and MDs emphasized that a classic song was an *album-oriented* rock hit, including singles released off of an album – but it had to be based on an album. Some of the PDs and MDs said that classic rock songs began in the mid-1960s and continue to be made today. Our survey respondents were not as clear on a beginning time, nor did they emphasize that classic songs had to be album-based. Radio people are probably much more aware than they need to be that some classic songs achieved number one status on AOR charts without ever reaching the top 20 on the Top 40 charts. This differentiation did not seem to matter to our survey respondents.

Gold and Supergold. Fewer survey respondents described these two terms by placing them within a certain time period. According to them, a Gold song could be as old as an oldie, but had to be a hit, at least in the Top 40. If Gold was described as good, Supergold was great. Gold was usually a Top 10–40 hit that sold 1 million or more copies, and Supergold was almost always listed as a multimillion selling number 1 hit. Also, there were a few people who defined each of the terms strictly by age. To them, Gold was old, and Supergold was very old. The MDs and PDs we interviewed, on the other hand, defined the two terms more on the basis of sales than on age or "goodness." Some programmers continue to define gold as any song that has sold over half a million records, while supergold is applied more to artists (those who have had a string of gold hits) than to the songs themselves.

Recurrent. We gave a general definition of this term in the second paragraph of our survey description. We said that "some stations have a category called 'recurrent' which is for music that is in-between being a current hit and being classified as older music." Nonetheless, more than a few survey respondents seemed to confuse it with the term *remake*. We also had a surprising number of respondents who chose to reword the definition we had given them, when in fact we just wanted them to tell us the time span in which a song was classified as a recurrent. In general, respondents said it was either a fading hit, or something brought back 3 months to 10 years later. This wide divergence of opinion coincides with the same disparities among music programmers reported earlier. One interesting discovery made while compiling this section was that the older the age group, the narrower the margin they assigned the term recurrent, and the newer a song could be before it was called an oldie.

While the youngest age group (12–17) seemed to be the most vague on what each of these terms meant, the most telling information they gave us was in what time period each of the terms fell. Except for the term *recurrent,* they all seemed to think that "old music" was something that was popular before they were actively listening to pop music. None of them described old music as something that was popular in the 1980s, when the survey was done. Most of this group probably received little to no exposure to pop music, or have no real memory of it, until they were just starting school. Because this young group has only been exposed to pop music for about 10 years, their concept of old music is very limited. This also explains some of the answers they gave us, such as "classic" being described by one student as being "20 to 40 years old."

Our next oldest age group, the 18- to 22-year-olds, were more precise in their definitions of the terms and in what time period they fell. They still seemed to feel that an oldie was something that was popular in their parent's time, but also included the 1970s, during which time they were already listening. This group, along with the 23- to 34-age group, gave some of the most complete definitions for gold and supergold. Again, we can attribute this to the fact that they have been exposed to these terms more than the other two groups. Unlike the term *classic,* these terms seem to have more to do with a song's chart placement and number of records sold, rather than its lasting impact.

The research just reported points up some of the differences between audience members and radio people in the meaning of terms used to describe old music. Especially as the population ages, these terms are likely to change fairly dramatically, even if the terminology employed by the industry remained static, which it probably will not.

Music and Memory

Another approach to defining old music is to explore the relationship of memory to music. Jonathan Winson, in a chapter on "Memory, Perception and Emotion," in his book *Brain and Psyche,* detailed cases of psychosurgery in which memory capabilities were altered. Winson summarized as follows:

> Apparently a slow neural process occurs in the human brain over a period of approximately three years, by which recent events become stabilized as long-term memories. The hippocampus appears to be central to the process, for unless the structure is present and functioning during the three-year period, memories cannot be recalled at a later time. . . . However, once three years have passed, memories are stored in a form that no longer requires the hippocampus for recall . . .[8]

What this summary of recent memory research appears to say is that in the human brain, *long*-term memory begins at roughly 3 years. *Short*-term memory, then, covers

---

[8]Winson, J. (1985). *Brain and psyche* (pp. 15–16). Garden City, NY: Anchor Press/Doubleday.

anything that happened a second ago up to 3 years ago. It makes sense, therefore, to define old music as being at least 3 years old, for most audiences.

For teenagers, especially because they have been alive such a relatively short while, 3 years seems like a very long time. If teens are the station's target, old music should probably be considerably younger than that.

For nonteen-targeted stations, anything more than 3 years old would be classified as old. But even if teens are not the target of the station, it is useful to think of the teenage years as perhaps the most emotionally fertile for creating later adult nostalgia, because it is a time when youngsters are having their first adult experiences, and their first experiences as independent personalities. Targeting oldies to the desired adult listener's teenage years thus makes good sense.

Predicting Burnout

Songs with simple choruses, or several back-to-back repetitions of a typical chorus can be trouble. Some listeners can hear a record just once, and because the chorus is either very simple or is repeated often, they can sing the chorus verbatim by the time the record is over. The chorus, then, is going to burn out first, long before the verses do. That fact should cause the music programmer to either lower that song's level of exposure, or have it spend less time in a heavy rotation. The Guns 'N' Roses song "Paradise City" (which made it to the top on MTV) is an example of a song with a very limited radio life for the reasons just given.

It is possible to try to predict burnout based on a number of the song attributes studied in this chapter.[9] We can look at each characteristic according to the amount of *effort* that it takes us to understand or appreciate it. Score a 1 for the easiest/least effort; score a 10 for the hardest to understand/most effort.

First, look at the rhythm. If the rhythm is extremely regular, and is maintained throughout (as in a disco tune), we might give it just a 1. If the rhythm is 5/4 time as in Dave Brubeck's classic "Take Five," it deserves a 10.

Then consider the melody, both in the chorus and the verses. The 1988 hit by Toto, "Pamela," is an example of a song deserving high marks in both areas for its melodic novelty. Does the song modulate into another key?

Go on to analyze the lyrics of the chorus and the verses for the amount of effort needed to understand them. Compare "While You See a Chance" (high marks) and "Da Doo Ron Ron" (low marks). How many different verses are there?

Finally, consider the complexity of the overall presentation, as we did in chapter 10 with the Righteous Brothers' "You've Lost That Lovin' Feelin'," which would get a high score. How many recognizably different instruments and voices are there?

Add all the scores together and you get a complexity score. Divide the score by

---

[9]This scheme was suggested in an article by Simanaitis, D. (1986, July). Beauty is the button just to the right of square root. *Road & Track,* pp. 174–175.

the number of times the song will be exposed to its target audience and you get the song's burnout index for that audience on your station. The higher the score, the longer the song should take to burn out.

MOST – An Afterword

What is proposed here is far more music testing than most stations care to do, or would be able to do with limited staff. But these tests for song selection are offered because they are important to consider in making airplay decisions, often at least as important as a song's popularity. It may not seem practical to worry about all these details. But the more competitive the radio market, the more music selection and presentation comes down to getting the details right.

MAJOR POINTS

1. The mood-oriented selection testing system (MOST) seeks to answer the question "Which songs do we play?" without resorting to mere popularity measures for an answer.

2. The seven emotions Clynes has isolated have expression times quantifiable in seconds. These are not the same as beats per minute – they are more related to phrasing.

3. Clynes' terms also seem related to an expectation about scale: major, minor, or blues. Reverence seems linked to the major scale, anger to the minor scale. Grief and hate seem linked to minor or blues scales; love and joy seem linked to major or blues scales. Sex seems linked to all three.

4. Open-ended music testing has revealed songs that seem to elicit no reportable emotion among listeners. Therefore, caution must be used in classifying music employing only expression times and scales as measures.

5. Among the spacial factors to be looked at in a song are the positioning of voices or instruments in immediate, support, and background distances, and the ambience of the recording site.

6. Among the force (acceptance factors) to be considered are the timbre, number, and density of voices or instruments as compared to their intensity.

7. Lyrics can be considered on the bases of symbolic and narrative action, and dramatic and realistic images. A matrix for displaying action/imagery/meanings will reveal certain songs whose lyrics refuse to be contained in a single cell, but that instead work on several levels. This should translate into lyric appeal across several demographic categories. However, lyrics that are simply fun to say are important in pop music, too.

8. Lyrics can also be analyzed using synonyms for the three behavior states: arousal, fantasy, and satiation. Whichever of the three terms has the most phrases associated with it would then alert the programmer to the potential target listeners for that lyric.

9. Recurrents are a category that probably exists (a) because every other song in the music library is being played, either as a hit or an oldie, so excluding these songs seems odd, and (b) because there is little agreement in the radio industry about when a former hit becomes an oldie.

10. Evidence suggests that the human brain processes events for up to 3 years as short-term memory; after about 3 years, events are stored in long-term memory. Oldies might thus be defined as being at least 3 years old, for most audiences. (Teenage listeners would probably expect a shorter waiting period.)

11. It is especially important not to overexpose recurrents to the "high risk" heavy listening groups in the audience, who might already be burned-out on the song.

12. Recurrents and oldies sufer from audience fickleness about the popularity of the *performer,* quite apart from the value of the music.

13. Some simple choruses burn out before the verses do. The music programmer should either lower the song's level of exposure, or cause it to spend less time in a heavy rotation.

14. Burnout on other factors can be predicted based on the effort the listener must exert to appreciate or understand such elements as rhythm, melody, lyrics, and overall presentation. Each of these factors is given a complexity score (1–10). Adding all complexity scores together and dividing by the number of times the song will be exposed to its target audience yields the song's burnout index.

CHAPTER 12

Factors in MEMO–
Mood-Evoking Music Order

What, in fact, is "rationality" but the desire for an accurate chart for naming what is going on?

–Kenneth Burke[1]

This chapter offers several charts for naming what could be going on in a music presentation system. What could be going on is the evocation of moods, and that is why the thrust of this chapter is the demonstration of mood-evoking music order systems (MEMO). The systems are built around the characteristics of general audiences and individual listeners that we have already explored (see Tables 10.4. 10.5 and 10.6 on p. 163).

In regard to Time (communal and personal rhythm) factors, these are the questions a programmer should ask when putting together the music order for his or her station: (a) What seasonal and cultural rhythms (such as holidays, celebrations, etc., should be factored in? (b) What circadian body rhythms are my audience reacting to, and (c) what needs caused by the predominating lifestyles in my community need to be considered?

Relative to space (involvement) factors, the programmer needs to consider (a) the structure and appeals of a music order presentation system, and (b) how they will impact on the listening place and listening situation.

The force (acceptance) factors to be studied revolve around the arousal/ fantasy/satiation drives that propel audience behavior.

Having made all these considerations, what we do next is to structure a music presentation system that takes them into account. Figure 12.1 shows again Aristotelian dramatic structure, first introduced in chapter 4. Note the curve illustrating the

---

[1]Burke, K. (1967). *The philosophy of literary form* (pp. 113–114). Baton Rouge, LA: Louisiana State University Press.

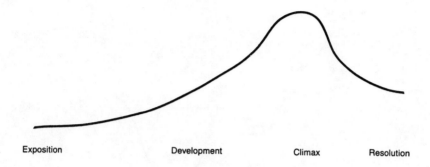

| Exposition | Development | Climax | Resolution |

FIG. 12.1   Aristotelian structure expressed as a curve.

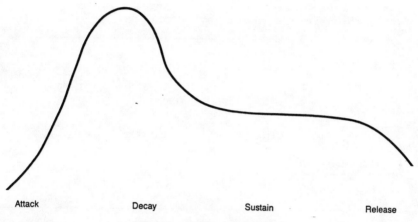

| Attack | Decay | Sustain | Release |

FIG. 12.2.   ADSR sound envelope.

rising and falling action of exposition, development, climax, and resolution. Figure 12.2 illustrates, once more, the ADSR sound envelope of "attack-decay-sustain-release." Note how the attack has a rapid rise time and a brief decay, then a long sustain until the release.

Figure 12.3 again takes a look at the opponent-process arousal/satiation behavior curve offered by Milkman and Sunderwirth, this time with added interpretations. Notice how the curve starts to repeat itself on the far right-hand edge, which corresponds to its beginning at the far left. You have already discovered that the curve looks a lot like Aristotle and ADSR.

Next (in Fig. 12.4), we take the arousal/satiation behavior modes and express them as a continuum, alongside of which we place Clynes' emotion categories and their expression times.

The continuum can also be extended, in effect starting at the end, repeating the behavior term *satiation*. Then the Clynes' terms are interpolated to follow the rise and fall of arousal and satiation (see Fig. 12.5).

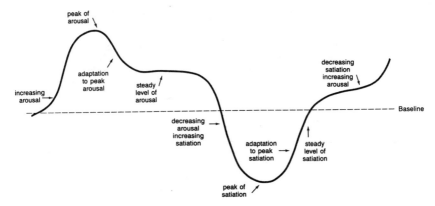

FIG. 12.3. Opponent-process arousal/satiation behavior curve (after Solomon, in Milkman and Sunderwirth) with elaboration by the present author.[2]

BEHAVIOR:						
AROUSAL					SATIATION	
EMOTION:						
Anger	Joy	Hate	Sex	Love	Grief	Reverence
EXPRESSION TIME:						
0.7 sec	1.1 sec	1.6 sec	2.0 sec.	5.2 sec.	9.0 sec.	9.8 sec

FIG. 12.4. Arousal/satiation behavior modes expressed as an extended continuum, with Clynes' expression times

BEHAVIOR:												
Satiation					Arousal						Satiation	
EMOTION:												
Rev.	Grief	Love	Sex	Hate	Joy	Anger	Joy	Hate	Sex	Love	Grief	Rev.
EXPRESSION TIME:												
9.8	9.0	5.2	2.0	1.6	1.1	0.7	1.1	1.6	2.0	5.2	9.0	9.8

FIG. 12.5. Arousal/satiation behavior modes expressed as an extended continuum, with Clynes' expression times

[2]Milkman, H.B., & Sunderwirth, S.G. (1987). *Craving for ecstasy: The consciousness and chemistry of escape* (p. 106). Lexington, MA: Lexington Books.

COMPOSITE MOOD CURVE

Finally, all the previous graphs and curves can be combined into a composite mood curve (CMC; see Fig. 12.6) to show how Aristotelian dramatic structure, the ADSR sound envelope, the arousal-satiation behavior curve, and Clynes' expression times and categories can all coincide. Figure 12.6 is *not* a formula for a "hot clock." It is merely a way of showing the commonality among previous curves. For it to work as a music order presentation system, various refinements and caveats (given later) need to be observed.

What the composite mood curve shows is nine cells, the ninth repeating the first as the curve starts over.

ADSR Sound Envelope

The ADSR sound envelope terms are the first text line under the cell number. In sound, an attack is virtually instantaneous, and the decay begins immediately, but this does not leave any time at the peak (how like life!), so the ADSR terms break at the peaks. Also note that the time of release coincides with a new attack.

Arousal/Satiation Behavior Modes

The second text line gives an interpretation of the behavior modes corresponding to arousal and satiation. Notice that I have decreed that decreasing arousal and increasing satiation happen simultaneously in Cell 5, just as do their opposites(decreasing satiation and increasing arousal) in Cell 9. Notice, too, that all of the curve in Cells 5, 6, 7, and 8 are very close to being a reversed, upside-down version of the arousal curve, as if satiation were almost the flip-side of arousal.

Aristotelian Dramatic Structure

The third text line lists the familiar Aristotelian dramatic structure terms. In case it seems odd that "development" in Cell 5 should describe a *downward*-pointing curve, remember that depths of emotion can be developed just as well as heights.

Pitch-Related Feelings

At both the extreme upper left and the extreme upper right of the chart, the words "pitch-related feelings" appear, heading a column of words labeling those feelings. You may want to re-read the research by Hevner, reported in chapter 9, which found people tending to describe high-pitched music as playful and happy, low-pitched music as serious and sad (although tempo was the single most important factor in determining the mood). Also cited there was the research by Thayer et al., which found that reactions to music on a "pleasantness" continuum (which ranged from happiness at one extreme to sadness at the other) were most affected by the pitch (while "activation" was most affected by tempo). In regard to lyrics, chapter 10 reported research that found that the pitch of expressions of happiness was higher

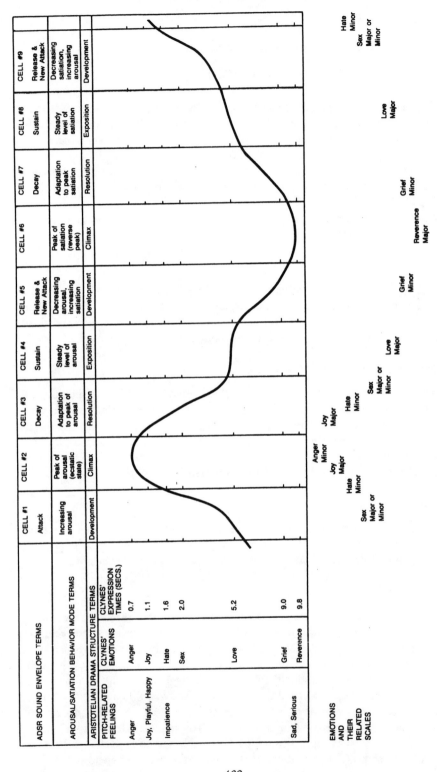

FIG. 12.6. Composite mood curve.

than the pitch of either neutral or sad expressions. And the work of Joel Davitz in relating pitch to vocal expression found the feelings of "anger" and "joy" related to a high pitch, the feeling of "affection" linked to a low pitch. As a consequence of all these findings about pitch, the pitch-related feelings terms have been placed in either a high or low position, reflecting their relationship to a high or low pitch. Recall that pitch applies both to instrumental music and to music with lyrics.

Clynes' Emotions and Their Expression Times

Next in from the extreme left and right sides of the composite mood curve are columns listing Clynes' emotions and their expression times in seconds. The longest (slowest) times (corresponding to reverence) are at the bottom; the shortest (fastest) times (corresponding to anger) are at the top. The approximate expression time of each emotion is shown by a point on the curve. For clarity, the emotions are listed again, in order from left to right, at the bottom of the chart, along with the scale (major or minor) that has been related to them.

The Clynes categories and expression times are the the single element shown from the time/space/force triumvirate because expression times (tempo, rhythms, etc.) have been shown to be the single most influential factor in determining the emotion evoked by music. Space factors (such as mike-to-performer distance and the ambience of the recording site), and force factors (such as the timbre of voices or instruments, and the number and density of the voices or instruments), are more important in determining *continuation*—that is, what song should be played next—than in evoking a mood. We take up the question of continuation shortly.

Emotions and Their Related Scales

Twelve emotions are listed across the bottom of the figure (14 if you count the repeats in Cell 9). Just as the curve is a theoretical model, so is that list of song moods. For instance, suppose the station made the simple rule that only songs in the major scale would be played. Immediately, songs with expression times corresponding to hate, anger, grief, and some sex would drop off the air. The resulting curve would not reach quite so high as when anger was the mood projected for the peak, although it would still drop as deeply into reverence. But the big change would be in the length of time spent at any one expression time level. In fact, with most changes in the curve, that is the major consequence—not so much a change in height or depth, but a difference in how long any one emotion is sustained.

Using the CMC to Target Specific Demographics

Of course, most stations target a particular segment of the audience. Doing so virtually forces a change in the time spent in various parts of the curve. For example, in the fantasies survey cited in chapter 4 ("Fantasies and Daydreams"), men were shown to be more *arousal*-oriented, especially in terms of participation in physical activities, whereas women were found to be more interested in the satisfaction (*satiation*) of social acceptance. Keep that in mind when considering the old saw that (especially younger) men like faster, harder music, whereas women like slower, softer music. If we now link a higher desired expression time to male *arousal* needs, and a lower desired expression time to female *satiation* needs, then it appears that controlling the amount of the sound hour spent at a given expression time would operate not only to evoke the mood, but would also differentiate by sex. Thus, a station that lengthens the time spent in the arousal part of the CMC by playing more short expression time songs will tend to get more men; a station that lengthens the time spent in the *satiation* part of the curve by playing more long expression time songs will tend to get more women.

Now, suppose the target audience is young men, who we will define as mid/late teens and early 20s. Maybe the reason some young men like to listen to hour upon hour of high BPM music is not just about expressing "anger" in the mood sense. Maybe it is a way of saying by association with the music that they have the youthful potency to sustain and extend the moments of climax.

Imagine now that the target is men in their late 20s and early 30s. In this age range, when men become less anger-oriented, and as the hormone-driven need to prove virility slacks a little, we would expect to find the time men desire to remain at "orgasmic" beat intensity also declining. For these men, the time spent at the peak BPM should be shorter (the peaks more pointed). Women in their 30s are no less interested in sex than before, but a more mature understanding of love is probable. For both sexes, desired expression times simply lengthen out (slow down) with increasing age.

In general, playing more music having short expression times would lengthen the amount of the curve spent in the region of joy and anger. This would increase the appeal of the music for those listeners seeking enhancement of an aroused state. Similarly, playing more music having long expression times would lengthen the amount of time the curve remained in the region of grief and reverence. This would increase the appeal of the music for those listeners seeking enhancement of a satiated state.

Playing more music while lingering at one extreme high or low part of the curve is a way of serving the "music mood stability seeker" whom we met earlier. On the other hand, moving along the curve fairly rapidly is a way of pleasing the "music mood novelty seeker." These assertions are consonant with the findings of Washburn and Dickinson over 50 years ago, that music which was either much more exciting than usual or much more relaxing and soothing than usual was appreciated more than music that straddled the middle ground. Straddling the middle of the curve (in a vertical sense) would lead to listener indifference. And recall that Schoen and Gatewood found that listeners to exhilarating music wanted more of the same, whereas listeners to sad, depressing music wanted a change, although even some passive listeners preferred to continue to listen to passive music. Listeners to music that was neither exhilarating nor sad were again found to be indifferent about what they heard next.

Using the CMC to Optimize Daypart Impact

The material in chapter 4 on circadian rhythms can be applied to make changes in the curve that would have the effect of fitting the music more closely to some average listener's lifestyle. This can be accomplished by dropping some mood categories entirely, or by presenting desired mood categories for longer periods. When some categories are left out, there will be a more abrupt jump from one mood to another, if no other elements are introduced as buffers. This is okay, because the CMC is not intended to imitate a "dance mix"—it is *not* supposed to be all at one BPM level. The more nonmusical (talk) elements in an hour, the less nuance there should be in dramatic structure. For example, between 7–8 a.m., when there is usually heavy information/talk, each of the four parts of dramatic structure should probably be represented only once before the cycle repeats. In slack times (as at night), the cycles can be much longer and can emphasize any of the structural elements.

A day might go like this: Mornings are a "fresh start." It tends to be the most optimistic time of day for many people—"Today, anything is possible." Morning programming could enhance that emotion by emphasizing the positive emotions: joy, sex, love, and reverence. But because morning radio listeners have always seemed to gravitate to stations that play music which acts like a percolator or battery jumper cables, the music should get you going. In the morning daypart, then, faster tempi should predominate. Thus, more time would be spent with joy and sex, less with love and reverence.

In mid- and late-morning, and early-afternoon dayparts, the programmer might add grief, and slow and soften the overall sound by reducing the ratio of joy songs. The net effect will be an increase in the sex, love, grief, and reverence moods.

In mid-afternoon, the programmer might add to the joy category, and in afternoon drive, he or she might increase (or begin to play) the hate category.

In early evening, more joy songs might be added. By mid-evening, when teens predominate as listeners, the programmer might delete reverence and add songs in the anger category. In late evenings, still more anger songs might be played.

CONTINUATION

What song should be played next? That is the question that a continuation scheme seeks to answer. We have explored the pros and cons of continuing the present mood versus moving on to the next area of the curve. Clearly, how much of any one mood to offer at a given time is heavily dependent on the target audience.

But what about the other methods of "growth," the other ways of moving forward? If mood is related most of all to (expression) time, what about space and force factors? And what about that slipperiest of all musical factors, melody?

Recall from chapter 10 LaRue's four basic options for continuation. They were summarized this way:

Recurrence – an immediate repetition, or one that happens after an intervening change.

Development – a continuation closely related by melody. (Development is not usually done in radio since melodies are not tracked. "Key" is the closest radio music programmers get.)

Response – a continuation unrelated melodically. (Rhythmic response continuation is common in radio music formats, but probably need still more emphasis.)

Contrast – a complete change, usually following (and confirming) a heavy articulation by cadences and rests. (In the case of a radio sound hour, the cadences and rests could be something as obvious as a commercial set, or as subtle as an ID jingle which begins with one key or rhythm and ends with another.)

Recurrence

First, don't confuse the continuation term *recurrence* with the music-library term *recurrents*.) Recurrence would not mean a literal repetition of the song, but rather repetition of at least one of its time, space, or force factors. For example, the programmer – using recordings tagged with information generated by the MOST system – would be able to select a song with the same kinds of voices and instruments in the "immediate" space. And/or, the programmer could repeat the same general recording site ambience, matching "dry" with "dry," and so on. Among the force factors, an example of one that could be repeated is "timbre intensity," wherein the soft, smooth vocal of the previous song is offered again.

Development

LaRue said development is a continuation closely related by melody. Because the incredible variety of melodies makes them just about impossible to track, the best we can hope for is matching the key: for example, C minor to C minor. Matching *scales* (major with major, minor with minor) is a given *within* a certain mood. Changing scales probably also generates a change in mood (except possibly with sex).

Response

Response, according to La Rue, is a continuation that is unrelated melodically, so this is the place where we would expect to find "developmental" (not wholesale) changes. Responses should grow logically and organically out of what came before. This is the place where radio music programming can work most profitably to improve. Much of the time, what is heard instead of response is contrast—LaRue's fourth continuation option—in which there is a complete change. But those complete changes are usually unmotivated. They do not necessarily occur only at natural breaks in the program flow, where LaRue said they would confirm cadences or rests (which were earlier analogized to stop sets). Many times, contrast is employed as continuation when response is what should occur.

Examples of response in terms of space would include a move of a voice or an instrument that was in the "immediate" aural position to a "support" position, or a change from a "dry" ambience to a slightly livelier one.

Examples of response in terms of force might include a change from a sparse density of instrumentation to a more moderate one, or from just a few voices to a moderate number of voices.

Lyrics

Only the last two of these continuation options could also be adapted to lyrics. You would not want to air a literal recurrence, and development is related to melody, not words. That leaves response and contrast as areas of possible lyric continuation.

Response lyrically might mean a move from a song whose lyrics are mostly dictionary-based to one with more abstractions, or from one heavy on wishes to be followed by one more reflective of actual events. Or, if the lyrics were tracked for their arousal/fantasy/satiation components, it might be possible to construct a sound hour in which the lyrical responses also follow the CMC in terms of the Milkman and Sunderwirth behaviors.

The CMC could also be a model for varying lyrical complexity, with more demanding lyrics at one point of the curve, less demanding ones at another.

Finally, lyrics can simply correspond to the moods on the CMC. As already stated about lyrics, they often mean what they seem to mean. If the lyric seems to be about love, maybe the simplest thing to do is to air it at the "love" part of the curve, assuming that other factors will correspond as well.

POPULARITY

This presentation would be incomplete if we did not discuss popularity as part of the composite mood curve. Popularity gets too much emphasis at most stations, but it would be naive to think song popularity is just going to go away and hide.

If hit songs are to be put into the typical sort of "heavy" rotation, then the following caution should be kept in mind: the most dangerous time for adult tuneout – because of music repetition – is when the listener hears a *second* song for the second time. The listener will accept a repeat of one song in a mix of other music not heard during that listening period. But when he or she hears a *second* song that was played before (the second song heard for the second time), the listener is cued that the music rotation has indeed started over. At that point, many adults will tune away, because your station is obviously playing something they have already heard. And for adults, that can be almost as bad as telling them something they already know.

Popularity probably should not be superimposed on the curve in a literal way: by playing the big hits only at the peaks. The problem with using that approach would be that there is an awful lot of the curve which is not at a peak.

Instead of laying popularity rankings over the curve, perhaps "reliability" would be a better factor to consider. (See chapter 8 for a discussion of how "reliability" extends the concept of familiarity.) "Reliability" would cover hits, oldies, newcomers, and (if you must) recurrents. Only one of those four music categories is literally "popular" – the hits. Tracking the degree of reliability would turn things around somewhat: it could be argued that many oldies are actually more familiar and reliable than some top ten hits. On a reliability curve, then, oldies might appear at the peaks, newcomers in the troughs, and hits in the places in between.

Finally, there is no reason why popularity needs to fit the Curve at all. Popularity is an arbitrary, constantly changing factor. The stabler components of the composite mood curve are interrelated so that they produce a logical continuation from one element to the next. A station could have a good air sound using the composite mood curve and do so with very little thought to popularity. Indeed, one of the most appealing attributes of the composite mood curve is that *any music type is theoretically possible*. In practice, selecting music from (or adjacent to) the natural clusters in the four quadrants shown in chapter 5 makes the most sense. But in both cases, the importance of instrumentation and force factors in determining acceptability and placement should not be overlooked.

USING THE CMC FOR OTHER ELEMENTS

In designing sound hours (or perhaps 90-minute hours in circadian time), the programmer might also want to consider elements beyond the tunes. For instance, what is the expression time of spoken material in a stop set? Is it as slow as grief or reverence? If so, could spoken stop sets substitute for grief and reverence songs? Or suppose music beds are prominent in the station's productions. Then the music bed of a stop set element can be measured for *its* expression time, and the stop set element could then fit into the curve at the appropriate point. In following this practice, a programmer might even decide that stop set elements need not be played by any particular clock or cluster. Instead, they could be inserted wherever/whenever the expression time of the spot's music bed fits the CMC. If this were done, stop sets would no longer exist as unrelated clusters, but would instead be inserted where they match the surrounding mood. Then, where there is a gap between expression time levels in the music (as in the morning drive example, where neither anger nor grief were played), stop set elements could fit *between* the two levels, acting as a sort of buffer.

MAJOR POINTS

1. A mood-evoking music order system (MEMO) seeks to answer the question "In what order do we play the songs we've selected?" It does so by building on the programmer's knowledge of seasonal, cultural, and circadian rhythms, of program appeals, the likely listening place and situation, and the listener's drives for arousal, satiation, and fantasy.

2. The ADSR sound envelope is a microtime version of the Aristotelian dramatic structure curve, except it has been flipped left to right. Both of these are congruent with the arousal/satiation opponent-process behavior curve.

3. The arousal/satiation opponent process can be expressed as an extended continuum, with Clynes' emotions and their expression times related.

4. All the previous graphs and curves can be combined in a composite mood curve (CMC). The CMC is not a formula for a "hot clock," but a way of demonstrating commonality among elements that generate mood.

5. Changes in the CMC in the vertical direction (those that affect the height of peaks and the depth of troughs—and thus the relative moods) are often not as influential overall as changes in the horizontal direction (which affect the total time spent at any given expression time level.) Varying the duration at any given expression time level may allow a station to target particular audience segments by such factors as age and sex, or the desire for arousal or satiation.

6. Lengthening the time spent playing music at any point on the curve—but especially at the peaks and the troughs—helps to serve the music mood stability seeker, while moving along the curve rapidly pleases the music mood novelty seeker.

7. The CMC can be adapted to circadian and lifestyle rhythms to optimize daypart impact.

8. The question of which song to play next can also be answered apart from the song's mood characteristics. Among the "recurrence" (repetition) factors are its time, space, and force elements. "Development" factors relate to melody, or in this case, merely to the matching of scales. "Response" factors include shifts in spacial positioning, or in the density or number of voices and instruments.

9. The CMC can be used to program lyrics in a progression that allows "response" on the basis of changes in the ratio of real to abstract terms, or from wishes to actual events. Lyrics can also be tracked for arousal/satiation/fantasy components, or simply for changes in their complexity.

10. The CMC could be used to chart familiarity ranking, with oldies played at the peaks, newcomers at the troughs, and current tunes in the places between.

11. The CMC can also be used for non-music material, such as the spoken material in a stop set. Stop sets could even be broken apart, with individual spots being played where the announcing and/or the music bed matches the appropriate expression time on the CMC.

CHAPTER 13

Toward MERIT

SHOULD RADIO LEAD OR FOLLOW SOCIETY?

The question of whether mass media lead society or follow society has been debated for decades, so it is not useful to guess which is "true." But this book concludes with the outline of a radio format that tries to both follow society, and to lead it.

The arguments in the music programming section for a music presentation system based on moods is largely built on concepts that are reflective of the audience's needs, desires, and drives, so MOST and MEMO are schemes that "follow" the patterns society already has. On the other hand, offering music that is chosen to match or evoke a mood is an attempt to "lead" a radio audience into new listening territory, perhaps away from dependence on the hits. An audience that is actually more in control of radio programming would be closer to "leading" society.

More than 30 years ago, the Top 40 pioneers took a step away from autocracy toward democracy by deciding to play the music that the public – rather than the station owner and the announcers – wanted to hear. But over the years, the system of selecting music for radio airplay has become very industry-oriented, with only faint reference today to the desires of the great majority of the potential listening public. MOST and MEMO are music selection and presentation concepts that could allow radio to break out of that self-referential cycle, to play songs that satisfy the needs of listeners whose musical desires have nothing to do with keeping up with the hits.

But what if the audience had a still greater role in determining the programming, and through that leadership by the public, the radio station took on an enhanced leadership role in society? At that point, the question of who leads and who follows becomes moot, as radio and society become symbiotically interactive. Imagine a radio station that is continuously, intentionally interactive with its audience.

A GLIMPSE OF WHAT MERIT MIGHT BE:
MOOD-EVOKING RESPONDENT-INTERACTIVE-TRACKING

Begin With News

Perhaps the place to begin is with your news – something this book has passed over until now. Why (beside sponsorship) are newscasts always a pre-determined length? Your audience knows that some days there are not 5 minutes of crucial items, and that your newscaster is padding to make it sound as if there were. Other days, there are 10 minutes of important events that get butchered into two-sentence stories to get them all in. You would not play truly unimportant music just to fill a time slot, and you would not play just the middle 30 seconds of each song. Why do that with the news? Let the length vary by importance.

Beyond that, why schedule newscasts at all (except perhaps in the morning)? If the items are really *news,* they probably should not wait for a whole hour before they are said. Truly newsworthy news can be done like drop-ins.

Jingles and Liners

Next, consider your jingles and your liners. Even the most limited hot rotation music playlist has more than 10 or so titles, but many stations play just 3 or 4 shotgun jingles over and over and over. You think you are doing it for logo consistency. The public thinks you are doing it because you are too cheap to buy more. Are you? Shouldn't a variety of jingles and liners be part of the entertainment too? What would it be like if every month a different person or group in your audience played and voiced a few ID jingles to be dropped-in very occasionally, just as a way of keeping things fresh, local, and inconsistent?

Commercials and PSAs

What about spots? Are you ready to turn down a buy that has just one version of a national ad in heavy saturation? Are you set up to write and produce multiple versions of a local campaign that will run for more than a few days?

Then there are PSAs. Perhaps your station just quits airing public service material whose content is corporate and distant factgiving (downward flow), and instead begins to conceive of public service as an input-gathering opportunity that processes what people say. The station says "We're listening to you." But it begins with a view of humanity that says, "We don't believe people are as narrow as traditional formats have made you appear. You can appreciate more things than you think you do." And that is the hope for the station that sincerely wants to be many things to a substantial number of people, without being a hodgepodge. It is the way it can succeed in the face of a plethora of stations that provide formats for the "tunable personalities," one at time, just by hitting a button. Radio needs input from the listeners that will in fact shape what they get from their radio station. Today, we have talk shows where the host says "Tell me how you're feeling." Fine, but only a minority of people ever bother to call in – the actives. The passives never get heard from.

Commentlines and Clotheslines

Now let's expand our focus from 30-second PSAs to longer form public affairs shows. Your station may have tried "public affairs programming" with your audience in the past, and might have found it unsatisfactory. Public affairs program-ming means either a talk show with a host, guest, and call-ins, or the typical procedure of announcing a daily topic for audience discussion, accessed via a phone call to an automatic telephone call recorder, with a selection of the calls played later on the air. Your experience might have been disappointing. You may have found that your audience was better equipped to talk about getting their wash clean than in expressing opinions on "controversial issues of public importance." By casting your everyday listeners in the role of advocates and knowledgeable persons (which they know they are not), you narrow the prospective speakers on your air to only a few (perhaps the same few) "loudmouths" out of the thousands who actually listen.

But maybe the reason you only get a few calls on a talk show is because everybody knows that your talk show is probably not going to change anything. What if the talk show *did* change things?

It is not necessary to assume that your audience is suffering from depression to consider using the three Cs that cure it: control, commitment, and challenge. They work this way: start *behaving,* and then feelings (positive ones) will follow. In other words, you come to feel as you behave. What would your station's community be like if your listeners felt they had control, commitment, and challenge?

Ownership and Feedback

Public TV stations, and some public radio stations, have had to develop a sense of ownership because they depend on it for their financing. But which commercial radio stations have tried to build a similar sense of proprietorship? Which commer-cial stations have tried to develop a format which reflects the community mind on a continuously interactive basis? Is there a community mind? Is there a way to discern a pattern within the noise? The question here is can a radio station be not just a community mirror, not just a socializing force, but a means by which people can help to *determine* their future, instead of being just a bubble in a tide of huge uncontrollable social movements? Some stations have developed advisory boards and "frequent listener clubs" to generate feedback on programming ideas.

What is being proposed here is nothing less than an entire paradigm shift. The paradigm shift needs to be, "You don't have to change the dial. Please don't change the dial. We want you stay on the dial where you are with us and we will provide other ways for you to talk back to us. We're making everyone in the whole radio station alert for feedback – everyone." And from the calls and letters you get, the station pulls out keywords, to track the community mood. Radio stations are natural information processors, because they are reporting the news. But they do not use that information to help shape the format of the station. If they really did that, the logs could not be prepared 6 days ahead.

Toward MERIT

MERIT would be a mood-evoking respondent-interactive tracking format. It would use MOST to select the music, and MEMO would be used to present it, but the presentation order would not be based wholly on pre-conceived mood patterns; instead, it would mix in the moods reflected in the station's pulse-taking of the community.

Think of the way stations and networks suspend their formats–even forego commercials–in times of crisis. Until the crisis passes, the whole presentation is centered on the community's needs, with members of that community (or their surrogates on the station/network staff) talking to and for each other. What MERIT suggests is that audiences should be catered to in less traumatic times too.

MERIT comes down to this concept: that radio people are–whether we know it or not–involved in a dialogue. It is just that for a very long time, radio has not had to be very good at keeping up the listening part of the dialogue, because it was doing most of the talking and the audience was doing plenty of listening. For radio to continue to succeed, there will have to be more listening to the listeners: at the level of their mood needs on a general, theoretical basis at the least; at the level of the community's psycho-social needs for dialogue with itself at the best. A station programmed under the MERIT concept would be the last one in the market to drill away with a single cut of a boring commercial or promo line, because doing so would be a tacit admission that the station was not really in the dialogue business– that its communication is one-way and the listener-be-damned.

One definition of religion is that it is a human attempt to make meaning out of the chaos of life. If radio is an information processor (in all its content, not just the news), then it is religious. For it to be a religion I can practice, radio must program music better than I can do it myself. Radio must be more of a companion to me than all but my best friends and lover. Radio must know where I am in life and be a step ahead of me, helping to push the underbrush out of my way. Radio must lead me to challenges, and show me how to go about winning. Radio must avoid a format which reminds me of how probabilistic, indistinct and chaotic life is, but should instead stress novelty, possibility, and a reason to keep on listening and trying. Radio needs to be a religion I can practice, because this world needs my aspiration. But I need a model.

MAJOR POINTS

1. A radio station that is continuously, intentionally interactive with its audience is the ideal: A mood-evoking respondent-interactive-tracking station (MERIT).

2. Public TV and radio stations have been forced to develop a sense of listener "ownership" because they depend on that sense of loyalty for funding. Commercial stations could take some cues.

3. The MERIT station would want its talk shows to change things. Its role would be not just a community mirror, not just a socializing force, but a means by which people could help determine their future. But for any of this to happen, the station must be much more active in gathering feedback, by being out in–and an integral part of–the community.

4. The MERIT station would present music (and other program elements) in ways that would reflect the station's community pulse-taking.

5. The MERIT station would see itself as being involved in a true dialogue, and would thus do much more listening to its listeners.

6. The MERIT station would help to make meaning out of the chaos of life, by being a model.

Reprinted by permission: Tribune Media Services.

Index